YOU CAN HANDLE THEM ALL

A Discipline Model For Handling Over One Hundred Different Misbehaviors At School And At Home

by
Robert L. DeBruyn
and
Jack L. Larson

The MASTER Teacher, Inc.
Publisher
Manhattan, Kansas
U.S.A.

The MASTER Teacher, Inc.
Publisher
Leadership Lane • P.O. Box 1207
Manhattan, Kansas 66505-1207
www.masterteacher.com

Library of Congress Catalog Card Number: 83-62445
ISBN: 0-914607-04-9

Printed in the United States of America

TABLE OF CONTENTS

Introduction 7
Student Types 13

The Agitator 14
The Alibier 17
The Angel 19
The Angry 21
The Animal 24
The Apathetic 26
The Apple Polisher 28
The Arrogant 30
The Attention Demander 33
The Authority Pusher 36
The Blabbermouth 39
The Blurter 41
The Bully 44
The Cheater 48
The Chiseler 51
The Class Clown 54
The Clique 57
The Complainer 59
The Con Artist 63
The Crier (Who Claims Foul) 66
The Crier (Who Sheds Tears) 69
The Defier 71
The Destroyer 74
The Disorganized 77
The Disrespectful 80
The Disrupter 83
The Distracter 86
The Do-Nothing 88
The Dreamer 90
The Exaggerator 93
The Excuse/Alibi Maker 95
The Exploder 98
The Failer 101

The Fighter 104
The Follower 108
The Forgetter 111
The Foulmouth 114
The Fun Seeker 116
The Goer 118
The Goldbrick 121
The Gossip 123
The Greedy 126
The Griper 128
The Habitual Absentee 130
The Hater 134
The Hider 138
The Hyperactive 140
"I Can't" 143
"I Don't Care" 145
"I Won't Do It" 148
The "Idiot" Syndrome 150
The Immature 152
The Indifferent 155
The Influencer 158
The Intellectual Show-Off 161
The Interrupter 163
The Irresponsible 165
The Know-It-All 167
The Last Worder 170
The Late Arriver 173
The Lazy 176
The Lewd 179
The Liar 181
The Loner 184
The Loudmouth 186
The Lover 188
The Manipulator 190
The Name Caller 192
The Negative Group 194
The Noisemaker 198
The Noncompleter with Grand Plans 201
The Nonparticipator 204
"Not My Fault" 208
The Objector 211
The Overly Aggressive 213
The Pest 217
The Petty Rules Breaker 220
The Pouter 223
The Procrastinator 225
The Questioner 227
The Rabble Rouser 229
The Rebel 232
The Repeater 235

The Rude 238
Satisfied with Second Place 240
The Scrapper 242
The Selfish 244
The Shadow 246
The Show-Off 248
The Shy 251
The Sidetracker 254
The Skipper 256
The Sleeper 258
The Smart Aleck 260
The Smartmouth 262
The Sneak 265
The Snob 267
The Snoop 269
The Snotty 271
The Spoiled Darling 274
The Stewer 277
The Swearer 280
The Talker 283
Talks Back 286
The Tardy 289
The Tattletale 291
The Teaser 294
The Test Challenger 297
The Thief 299
The Tramp 302
The Traveler 305
The Troublemaker 307
The Truant 310
The Underachiever 312
The Unprepared 315
The Vindictive 317
The Whiner 319

INTRODUCTION

The purpose of this book is to provide you with a resource for handling student misbehavior. It presents a complete step-by-step approach to changing inappropriate student behavior to appropriate behavior. It takes the guesswork out of your treatment of discipline problems by offering specific techniques for dealing with various misbehaviors. And it provides a guarantee for the professional handling of student behaviors.

Often, our handling of discipline problems is a reaction to the student's behavior, with little or no thought to whether our reaction is good for the student, other students, or the learning situation in the classroom. Our language concerning discipline problems is often jargon that is not really understood by all teachers, administrators, counselors, or parents. Likewise, we often attempt to handle problem behavior alone. In many cases, our handling of discipline problems may not be considered professionally responsible by colleagues, administrators, or parents.

There are three variables in every discipline situation: the teacher, the problem student, and the rest of the students in the class. The only variable a teacher can control is himself or herself. If the teacher is out of control, the situation is out of control. The discipline model contained in this book will help you understand how to handle discipline concerns effectively, keep yourself in control of the situation, and teach students self-discipline.

The discipline model offers a complete step-by-step guide to many options for handling 117 student behaviors. The model is designed to enable you, your colleagues, counselors, administrators, and the rest of the school team to work together for a mutually satisfying solution to student problems. It will give you assurance that everyone is working from the same firm foundation toward the solution of discipline problems.

Using The Model

Before you can begin trying to change a student behavior, you simply must properly identify that behavior. The identification must be specific — for example, the talker, the cheater, or the bully. Therefore, the first step is identifying the behavior and its characteristics.

I. BEHAVIOR: Specific attitudes and actions of this child at home and/or at school. Study the specific student characteristics listed in this section. Does the student exhibit the characteristics listed?

7

It may be helpful to check the "behavior" section of some of the other related types of behavior listed in the "see also" section at the end of each behavior type.

Pinpointing the student's observed or expressed behavior is vital because it identifies the exact characteristics of the behavior. It helps you avoid generalizing and helps you zero in on the behavior you want to change. It also makes it easier to describe the specific problem behavior to the student, to colleagues, and to parents.

II. EFFECTS: How the behavior affects teachers, classmates, and parents in the school learning environment and the home family situation. Understanding the effects of the behavior is another vital part of your preparation to deal with that behavior. It is important to be able to point out how the behavior actually affects the teacher, classmates, and/or the learning environment in the classroom. Failure to correctly identify the effects of the specific misbehavior will rob you of the vision necessary to see the adjustments you will have to make in order to get the student to change or adjust the behavior. In the school, there are three distinct areas that any misbehavior may affect in addition to the student himself or herself: the teacher, other students, and the learning environment. It's possible that the behavior affects all these areas. To suggest any solution, without first identifying which areas the behavior is affecting, is useless. If you first take the time to observe the effects of the behavior in question, you'll find it much easier to pursue workable solutions designed to bring about positive and constructive change.

It should be noted that often a student behavior affects only the teacher. Yet, if the student's behavior prevents the teacher from teaching, then some changes in the behavior are necessary. However, recognizing that the behavior affects only the teacher prevents such negative teacher action as making a student feel guilty by saying he or she is bothering the rest of the class.

III. ACTION: Identifying causes of misbehavior; pinpointing student needs being revealed; and employing specific methods, procedures, and techniques at school and at home for getting the child to modify or change his or her behavior. In this section, consideration is given to the primary cause of the misbehavior, primary and secondary needs being revealed, and specific suggestions for handling the misbehavior.

Primary Cause of Misbehavior. The good student is good for a reason. Likewise, the student demonstrating inappropriate behavior is misbehaving for a reason. The fact is that all behavior has purpose. This is the primary reason we can't lump all discipline problems under one label and treat them the same. It won't work. The bully does not have the same motivation for misbehavior as the class clown. The late arriver is different from the student who talks back to a teacher.

In maintaining a professional approach to changing unacceptable behavior to acceptable behavior, we must never forget that the *first* step to a solution lies in discovering the purpose of the misbehavior. We cannot treat any misbehavior effectively *until* we know the reasons for it.

To say that there are only four reasons for misbehavior would be untrue. However, the vast majority of misbehavior arises from four causes: lack of attention, lack of power, revenge, and lack of self-confidence. If we could learn to handle misbehavior resulting from these four needs, the vast majority of our classroom discipline problems would be resolved. For this reason, these four receive special attention in the discipline model. Briefly explained they are:

• **Attention:** Most students gain attention in school through normal channels. However, for some students, misbehavior is the only source of attention. Most commonly, these students are the ones who speak out without permission, arrive late for class, or make strange noises which force class and teacher attention. Some students will even tell us all the bad things they have done. They are all misbehaving in an attempt to gain attention.

• **Power:** The need for power also causes misbehavior. This need is expressed by open dissent and refusal to follow rules. Remember, these students usually *feel defeated* if they do as they are told. Most commonly, we know these students as the defiant ones, the rule breakers, and the bullies. They truly feel that *lack of power* lies behind all their woes, and that more power would be the answer to all their problems. If they had more power, they believe, they would be telling teachers what to do rather than vice versa.

• **Revenge:** Some students find their places by being hated. *Failure has made them give up trying for attention and power.* Unfortunately, they find personal satisfaction in being mean, vicious, and violent. They will seek revenge against teachers and classmates in any way they can. They are the students who write on desks, beat up classmates, threaten younger students, break windows, and write on restroom walls. The reason for their misbehavior is revenge.

- **Self-Confidence:** Lack of self-confidence is also a cause of misbehavior. Students who lack self-confidence honestly *expect* failure. They do not feel they have the ability to function in the classroom — but may feel completely adequate outside school. They frustrate us as teachers because they are often capable of handling their studies successfully. We are angered because we feel their behavior is a cop-out. It is — except they really *think* they can't win in school. These students use inability — real or assumed — to escape participation. When they are supposed to be studying, they play and talk to others. Then they make excuses like "I couldn't do it" or "I'm dumb." Their misbehavior is the result of a lack of self-confidence.

Primary Needs Being Revealed. Because it's absolutely necessary to determine why a student is misbehaving as the first step in changing behavior, the technique section considers the primary needs being revealed by the misbehaving student. Thus, observing students' behavior in relation to their efforts to meet primary needs becomes an important step in correcting discipline problems. The primary needs are physiological and unlearned. No matter what our age, we seek continually to meet our primary needs. Therefore, when we as educators attempt to change the behavior of a student, one of our first considerations must be an examination of primary needs *not* being met. These needs must be filled before the student can turn his or her attention to anything else. The primary needs are:

- **Hunger:** The need for food — or poor eating habits — can cause students to be restless or even hostile in the classroom. Students on diets, or those who have stopped eating for any of a wide variety of reasons, will have difficulty concentrating in their classes. Some students may not have enough money to purchase lunches, and others lose their lunch money or use it to buy other things. All these possibilities may lead to behavior problems in the classroom.

- **Thirst:** Excessive thirst may be the result of a medical problem. This possibility should be discussed with parents.

- **Sex:** The evidence of this primary need exists throughout a school, often as a healthy interest in the opposite sex. However, personal adjustment problems and misbehavior may result from a student's difficulty in establishing a boy-girl relationship, the loss of a boyfriend or girlfriend, or the break-up of parents. Likewise, an unwanted pregnancy or the desire to get married can be disturbing and painful. Or a student may have a sincere infatuation with the teacher or another adult. This is an important need of all people, and it should be examined carefully when a student's behavior is being evaluated.

- **Air:** Schools have the highest density of people per square foot of any place in a community, and when kids must work close to each other in small, unventilated classrooms, some of them are likely to misbehave. The air need may also be related to a medical problem, especially for students with asthma. Likewise, various psychological problems, such as claustrophobia, may contribute to behavior problems in the classroom. Some students may be smokers, and they may become restless and irritable in the classroom because of their need to smoke.

- **Rest:** The primary need for rest is revealed often through misbehavior. There are many external forces that prevent students from getting enough rest, such as parents fighting late at night. Likewise, a student may have a job or may be working to complete homework very late each night. Parents working split shifts may affect a student's sleeping habits. A student may be suffering from insomnia, or perhaps he or she just didn't sleep last night. Use of certain drugs may also contribute to a lack of sleep or abnormal drowsiness.

- **Escape from Pain:** Of all the primary needs, this may be the most important one to examine when attempting to discover the reason for misbehavior. People will go to great extremes to escape pain. In fact, they usually don't consider the consequences of their behavior when acting badly to escape pain. They are so intent on escaping the pain, they don't consider how their behavior will be received or how it will affect others.

Drug abuse, cults, suicides, drinking, mental illness, and other social problems are, in large part, responses to pain arising from a variety of causes. We watch the drunk attempting to walk down the street and we remark, "He (or she) is feeling no pain." One need only observe the T.V. commercials to note all the means offered to escape pain.

A student may feel very "dumb" in social studies, for example, and this may cause him or her a great deal of pain. The student's choice of misbehavior may well be a means of covering the pain of not achieving. For instance, the student may be able to prevent others from finding out he or she is "dumb" in social studies by disrupting the class.

Students, like everyone else, experience a great deal of physical or mental pain. The pain may result from the loss of a parent through death or divorce, or from poor health, financial problems, difficulty in relationships with family or friends, or failure in school. Any failure perceived by a student may be so painful that the student's reaction to it may be the major contributor to misbehavior in the school or classroom. It should be remembered that the student may know the behavior is wrong. But he or she may still pursue the behavior in an attempt to reduce the pain. The reduction of pain becomes a primary motivator — and nothing anybody says seems to make a difference. Many discipline problems can be traced back to the primary need to escape pain.

• **Elimination of Waste:** The use — and lack of use — of restrooms causes many problems in school. It's important to understand that some students need to go to the restroom at other than scheduled times. Some students may be shy or afraid to use the restrooms. There may be a medical problem that prevents a student from controlling himself or herself.

Secondary Needs Being Revealed. The secondary motives are psychological and learned. It is through the fulfillment of these needs that people reach for their goals and improve their self-concepts. The secondary needs are intensely felt by highly motivated people, and the opportunity to satisfy these needs is very important to them. The secondary needs are a strong motivating force in all our lives — yet they are immaterial *until* the primary needs have been met. Students will make every effort to meet secondary needs in a positive manner in the classroom and school if possible. However, failure to succeed in a positive effort to meet these needs will cause many to resort to negative efforts to meet their needs.

To help children adjust their behavior, the teacher or parent must appeal to those needs held in high esteem by each child. Rather than fight those needs, we need to meet them. Too often, we think these needs are abnormal. They are not. Remember, each of these needs is within *all* humans. Only the intensity of the need varies from child to child — and from adult to adult. A student's effort to fill a particular need may be the reason behind *appropriate* and *inappropriate* behavior. If we fight fulfillment of a need, we can cause a student to fight us — automatically.

The secondary needs are:

•**Gregariousness:** This is a student's need to associate with a group. This motive is evidenced by students who have a strong desire for inclusion in the "inner circle" or cliques in the school. This need, if unmet, also causes students to be very upset if they are left out of a party, not chosen for a committee, not asked for input on activities, or if decisions are imposed on them with no explanations.

• **Aggression:** Students need to assert themselves. Teachers must allow students to fulfill this need; otherwise, teachers may find themselves being forced into confrontations for no particular reason. Inclusion in certain decisions, involvement in planning activities, and responsibility for choosing certain courses of action in activities are good teaching techniques which can be employed to meet this need.

Many students feel they have *no* say in anything. For them, it is a terrible and helpless feeling. It doesn't mean the teacher has to do what they suggest. What it does mean is that the teacher must *listen* to them. The aggression need can often be met by just listening to and considering the student's point of view.

• **Affiliation:** Developing, maintaining, and strengthening associations with others is a strong human need. Some children have a very strong need to be close to each other, but often they also have an intense desire to be close to the teacher. They need someone in whom they can confide and trust. It makes them feel very secure and special, and they'll do anything to have such an affiliation — with teachers, with classmates, and in school activities — or with a gang outside school.

As teachers, we must be aware of the drive to ward off loneliness and find a "special person." Some teachers who see this student behavior may classify these kids as pests. But such behavior is usually a cry of "I need an adult friend."

• **Inquisitiveness:** People need to know what is going on. The longer pupils are in school, the more evident this need becomes. For some, it's a driving force. This need has been expressed more forcefully in recent years because students want to have more control over their lives. Sometimes, we think students are being nosy, and we brush them off. That is a mistake. Students are motivated by the need to know. It is a motivation that enhances positive behavior and learning. Young people also have a drive to know how we feel about them — as people and as students. This is one reason there is a need for continuous communication with students. Our communication must tell students of our concern for them personally and for their academic progress. Equally important, our communication should reveal the "whys" behind what we are doing and the decisions we have made. Fulfilling the need to know can enhance positive behavior. The scholar *always* has a strong inquisitive need. Certainly, one could not be a scientist without a strong drive in this regard.

• **Achievement:** All people have a need to succeed. They also have a need to be recognized for their success. The truth is that a great deal of misbehavior results because some kids can't win in school — and the only way they can get any recognition is through failure. As teachers, we must be aware that success without recognition weakens motivation. Helping kids win and recognizing their achievements are the two most important things we do. Remember, *any improvement,* no matter how small, is a positive, constructive achievement. Likewise, whenever students make an effort and that effort is not recognized, they soon become aware that they can receive the same reward for doing nothing. Failure offers nothing and, for most students, doesn't even provide motivation to change their behavior. Most students, however, are motivated by recognition of their achievements.

• **Power:** This need may be directed positively or negatively. And for some students it is an extremely strong need. Teachers should recognize that students need to know that they count. This is a form of power. Teachers need to make students feel significant. Remember, students who feel that others believe they are insignificant, or that no one cares whether or not they are in school, may soon become behavior problems.

The teacher must grant power, whenever possible, to students. Never forget, titles can be important tools in filling the power need. Hall monitor, teacher assistant, class officer, captain, best citizen, chairman, etc., are titles that provide a power base that can be very important to some students. Those students who cannot find a power base in the classroom or school may attempt to find it outside school in gangs, jobs, etc. Likewise, when giving assignments to students, make sure they have the authority and responsibility that go with the task. A sense of ownership is power. And students feel a sense of ownership when they are involved in shared decision making in all areas of classroom and school activities.

• **Status:** Everybody wants to be "somebody." For some, this need is a driving force in their lives. Therefore, any dehumanizing effort or action by a teacher is a mistake. If we are to meet this need, we should never do anything that detracts from the uniqueness of the individual. The recognition of the strengths of all individuals within the class helps all children meet their status need.

• **Autonomy:** The need for autonomy is the need to be one's own boss, to be independent, and to have some control over one's own life. Gaining an education is supposed to help all of us meet this need to some degree. Schools are highly structured, but they still must be sensitive to opportunities to fulfill, whenever possible, the need all students have for autonomy. The school or classroom that provides these opportunities will decrease the inappropriate behavior of some students.

Methods, Procedures, and Techniques. The remainder of this section suggests possible approaches to helping the student adjust his/her behavior. It is now your responsibility to select the methods, procedures, or techniques that best fit the student you are working with. For instance, you may select one or two suggestions to implement as your first attempt to work with the problem student. Later, you may consider other suggested ideas for working with the student. If problems persist, seek help from colleagues, and add to the list of suggestions. Your professional responsibility remains: Be open to all possible solutions.

IV. MISTAKES: Common misjudgments and errors in managing the child which may perpetuate or intensify the problem. Often our solution to misbehavior in the classroom is to react to the behavior personally rather than approach the problem professionally. This section points out possible teacher reactions which may compound or perpetuate the problem. Its purpose is to help teachers avoid mistakes commonly made in dealing with certain types of behavior. These errors are destructive to the teacher, the student, and the rest of the class.

The model, *You Can Handle Them All,* is designed to be used either by the individual classroom teacher or by the staff as a group. If the model is used with a group, the individual teacher experiencing the problem should have completed two steps prior to meeting with the group: identifying the behavior and its characteristics, and determining the effects of the behavior on others. Then, colleagues can study this information before they begin brainstorming additional techniques or methods. During the brainstorming session, no judgments should be made about whether solutions are right or wrong. Rather, each solution should be accepted. Later, the teacher with the problem student may decide which solution would be best to implement with this particular student.

It is not always possible for one teacher to deal with all the behavior problems encountered in the classroom. The discipline model allows any teacher to identify the behavior, describe it, and report its effects to colleagues without being unprofessional. At no time should the student be mentioned by name. Thus, colleagues' suggestions can be both objective and professional.

The model is a plan to handle all discipline problems. This book is a resource for 117 types of behaviors in the classroom. There is a plan for each type. It certainly does not include every possible behavior or every possible technique. It does, however, supply quick, effective information to facilitate gaining a positive behavior change in the classroom. *You Can Handle Them All* is a proven approach that works.

STUDENT TYPES

THE AGITATOR

I. BEHAVIOR: Specific attitudes and actions of this child at home and/or at school.

1. Tries to cause trouble — and appears delighted with it.
2. Gets others to do or say what he/she would not do or say.
3. Uproots old controversies, cries "unjust," incites hostilities, and causes as much trouble as he/she can.
4. Tries to appear to be an innocent bystander in any trouble he/she causes.
5. May act upset, stir others to rebelliousness, then walk away from the group when the disturbance is about to take place.
6. Usually gets other students in trouble more often than he/she gets in trouble. More often than not, does not get *openly* and *publicly* involved — but operates from the sidelines.
7. At home, hits, pushes, and trips siblings when out of sight of parents — then says the brother or sister "started it" if problems result.
8. Starts rumors to create turmoil.
9. Plays other people against one another, including teacher against teacher, parent against parent, students against classmates.
10. Often provokes physical confrontations between other people.
11. Consistently immature and irresponsible.
12. Tattletale.
13. Seeks the attention of others.
14. Appears to operate without loyalties, even to those regarded as friends.

II. EFFECTS: How behavior affects teachers, classmates, and parents in the school learning environment and the home family situation.

1. Others are influenced to do or say what the agitator would not do or say him/herself.
2. Learning experience in the classroom is seriously disrupted by the agitator's activities because students and teacher alike are distracted from the work or discussion at hand.
3. Social experience of students in the halls, cafeteria, etc., becomes negative.
4. At times, others are led to admire the agitator's sly and manipulative behavior. Therefore, he/she is a hero to some.
5. Teacher can easily start to feel threatened and as if he/she were losing control of the class.
6. Classmates can begin to feel as if they might be able to get away with similar behavior.
7. Class may be in a continual or almost continual uproar regarding some issue.
8. Teacher influence and credibility may be reduced.
9. Teacher may lose self-control.
10. Teacher may feel inadequate. As a result, he/she can become tense and transmit this tension to the agitator and other students.

III. ACTION: • **Identify causes of misbehavior.**
  • **Pinpoint student needs being revealed.**

- **Employ specific methods, procedures, and techniques at school and at home for getting the child to modify or change his/her behavior.**

1. Primary cause of misbehavior:

   ◗ Power: The need for power is expressed by creating situations that demonstrate this student's ability to be in control.

2. Primary needs being revealed:

   ◗ Hunger, Thirst, Rest: The lack of food and rest may be a form of abuse and should be investigated.

   ◗ Sex: Because of past experiences, this person may find it very difficult to establish any positive relationships.

   ◗ Escape from Pain: This student protects him/herself by the use of power to cover his/her pain.

3. Secondary needs being revealed:

   ◗ Aggression: This student has a need to control.

   ◗ Inquisitiveness: This student may have a strong need to know what's going on. He/she wants to know the *why* behind what we're doing and what's going on.

   ◗ Power, Status: This student may be trying to achieve through agitation.

4. Remember that the agitator's biggest fear is exposure; basically he/she is a pretender as well as a coward. The agitator cannot accept the full and open responsibility of a leadership position, but needs others to fulfill his/her needs.

5. Identify the agitator through these two behaviors: First, he/she is always present — but appears to be an innocent bystander — in trouble situations. Second, he/she is never personally involved in any dispute, if it can be avoided. Whenever you observe an ever-present innocent bystander, look for his/her position of leadership in group situations.

6. Indicate tactfully and professionally, in a private conference, that the disguise has been revealed. This will curtail his/her activities almost immediately.

7. Be careful not to make a total accusation — for he/she can easily deny involvement.

8. Seriously, but gently, tell the student that you suspect what he/she is doing. You may add that you have the professional obligation to discuss this deceitful behavior with parents, his/her other teachers, and administrators.

9. Regardless of the student's response, fear will be his/her emotion. Treat this fear kindly.

10. Listen carefully, then show concern. When you operate in a professional manner in this regard the agitator will make every effort to improve and to make sure that you know he/she is trying. Therefore, confront ... in a caring way ... always.

11. When you confront, use the "*What* Is More Important Than *Why*" technique. Don't ask why the student did something. The student may not even know he/she is agitating. Regardless, "why" is not the immediate issue. You can talk about "why" later. Ask what he/she did, and what he/she is going to do about it. You may even skip asking what the student did — and tell him/her. However, you must ask what he/she is going to do about it.

12. Recognize and acknowledge his/her efforts to improve. Otherwise, the agitating may begin again.

13. Be specific about what kind of behavior you expect. Don't generalize.

14. Be sure the agitator knows that you are not going to forget his/her past actions. Tell the student you want to support positive behavior, and that any time there is even the slightest

indication that he/she is beginning to agitate again you will confront him/her about it and stop it immediately.

15. Assign special duties to the agitator — such as passing out papers, erasing boards, etc. This helps to meet the need for attention and power.

16. Use group and peer pressure in sincere and straightforward ways to help motivate this student to change his/her behavior. This is easily done by making the agitator the appointed leader. Remember, he/she wants influence, but not responsibility. Yet, responsibility is what will change the behavior.

17. Set up a contract with the student. Make specific agreements about what should be done, when and where it should be done, and how it should be done.

18. Try to remain objective and emotionally neutral.

19. Remember, the student who resists authority knows where the power is, yet has chosen a course which he/she knows offers severe consequences. It's almost a form of suicide for the student. Look at such resistance for what it really is — a cry for help. It says everything from "I don't understand" to "I don't know what to do but fight."

20. Rather than fearing such occurrences or regarding them as horrendous episodes, look upon them as opportunities to help a student work through a problem that can only cause trouble for a lifetime. Begin by showing a willingness to listen and talk privately.

21. Fully understand that behind every student rejection is an overwhelming feeling of failure or frustration. That's why teaching rather than forcing is the best course to take. Any other road leads toward a destructive kind of confrontation and puts a teacher on the same level as the distressed student. Hopefully, this is not the road we would choose to take just to prove our power.

IV. MISTAKES: Common misjudgments and errors in managing the child which may perpetuate or intensify the problem.

1. Openly and publicly accusing certain students of being agitators.

2. Failing to see the real fear of being discovered that underlies the agitator's behavior.

3. Believing the agitator's actions are directed personally toward us and, therefore, reacting personally toward the agitator and his/her behavior.

4. Getting into an argument, causing division among the class.

5. Issuing punishments to the group, causing strong student reactions.

6. Jumping to the conclusion that the agitator is responsible for a current situation, based on past history.

7. Overreacting to all incidents of criticism and calling them agitation.

8. Making threats to stop the behavior and backing ourselves into a corner.

9. Feeling that "I must have the last word if I am to be the winner."

10. Becoming involved in a power play.

11. Openly confronting the student in class. This action can only cause serious difficulty for all. And our concern about losing respect may readily become a reality.

12. Accusing a student too harshly and/or in the presence of class members.

13. Playing detective, and acting unfairly when we aren't able to pinpoint the culprit.

14. Attacking the followers rather than confronting the agitator.

SEE ALSO: • The Angry • The Bully • The Defier • The Influencer
• The Overly Aggressive

THE ALIBIER

I. BEHAVIOR: Specific attitudes and actions of this child at home and/or at school.

1. Doesn't fulfill responsibilities.
2. Always offers an excuse regarding why he/she didn't do something.
3. Feels that the fault lies with someone else.
4. Often presents highly creative excuses; can offer a spontaneous excuse which may even seem very probable.
5. Tries to get support from friends, other students, and parents.
6. Tends to feel he/she is treated unfairly by adults at school and at home.
7. Approaches every task as a certain failure before making any attempt.
8. Usually finds faults in teachers and parents quickly.
9. May fall behind in class work.

II. EFFECTS: How behavior affects teachers, classmates, and parents in the school learning environment and the home family situation.

1. Teacher is worn down.
2. Teacher may begin to dislike student personally, may treat alibis as a character defect and start to think of alibier as a liar.
3. Time is wasted listening to alibis; hence, teaching and learning time is lost.
4. Classmates may feel a sense of unfairness and inequity in the classroom if teacher accepts an alibi they know is untrue.
5. Classmates may try offering alibis too.
6. Classmates and teacher may turn against the alibier totally.

III. ACTION:
- **Identify causes of misbehavior.**
- **Pinpoint student needs being revealed.**
- **Employ specific methods, procedures, and techniques at school and at home for getting the child to modify or change his/her behavior.**

1. Primary cause of misbehavior:
   - Self-Confidence: This student has such a lack of self-esteem that he/she is afraid to attempt anything.
2. Primary needs being revealed:
   - Escape from Pain: This student has experienced a lot of failure, and has adjusted by alibiing; he/she may be very successful with the behavior.
   - Sex: He/she has experienced a lot of failure with adult and peer interactions.
3. Secondary needs being revealed:
   - Gregariousness, Affiliation: This student needs to belong to a group and/or have a close friend.
   - Achievement: He/she needs to experience various levels of success.

▶ Status: Finding a sense of worth without alibiing may change his/her behavior.

4. Spend time outside class trying to solve this problem — privately. Go to a neutral ground where the environment will be comfortable and pressure-free to talk more openly about the behavior.

5. When you talk to the student, get to the root of the problem. Don't move around the problem or call it by another name. Rather, talk specifically about the problem of offering alibis, and share instances when the problem has occurred. The student must be very clear about what you are feeling and what you are talking about.

6. When he/she gives an excuse, set a deadline for completion of the task. Don't let the student walk away "free." To change the behavior you must make the excuse more difficult than the performance he/she failed to complete.

7. Try to make the student evaluate the habit, and see what's really happening.

8. Make the consequences for offering alibis consistent for all students, regardless of the alibi.

9. Let the student know that his/her behavior is human. We all make mistakes, but we also must always accept the consequences of our mistakes rather than think an excuse should relieve us of responsibility.

10. Remember, personal problems at home and with peers are often the reason behind alibi behavior.

11. Prepare a plan (contract) with this student and allow opportunity for the plan to succeed. Let the student know your expectations and make it clear that repeated alibis will not be accepted.

12. Inform parents if behavior continues — especially if the student makes no effort to adjust the behavior.

IV. MISTAKES: Common misjudgments and errors in managing the child which may perpetuate or intensify the problem.

1. Considering this student an out-and-out liar and personally disliking him/her.

2. Always accepting the excuse of the alibier.

3. Refusing to listen to any excuses.

4. Refusing to accept any excuses.

5. Trying to deal with an alibi and the student who offers it during class time.

6. Criticizing the excuse offered by a student in front of the class.

7. Setting up unrealistic goals in an attempt to alter the behavior of the alibier.

8. Lowering expectations for him/her.

SEE ALSO: • The Crier (Who Claims Foul) • The Excuse/Alibi Maker • "I Can't"
• "Not My Fault"

THE ANGEL

I. BEHAVIOR: Specific attitudes and actions of this child at home and/or at school.

1. Plays a game of being perfect with adults. Displays attitudes and actions at home and/or school which project him/her as perfect when, indeed, he/she is not.
2. Tells people exactly what they want to hear.
3. Perfect in the presence of authority. Not so perfect when authority is not present.
4. Often reprimands classmates in the presence of others.
5. Defensive and hurt when confronted.
6. Pushes rules, but denies having broken any — ever.
7. Always alludes to innocence — in thought and deed.
8. In some situations, acts naive if confronted.
9. Goes to great lengths to show how "goody-goody" he/she is.
10. Likes seeing classmates "nailed to the wall."

II. EFFECTS: How behavior affects teachers, classmates, and parents in the school learning environment and the home family situation.

1. Classmates dislike him/her.
2. Others often think this student is the teacher's "pet." And the student may be a favorite because he/she "butters us up."
3. Teacher may try to "catch" student at misdeed, only to get long lists of denials which further annoy teacher.
4. Teacher and classmates may find him/her a depressive and disgusting person.
5. Teacher often has feelings of distrust toward this student — and may be unwilling to interact positively with him/her at other times.
6. Teacher loses caring attitude toward student.
7. Classmates think of the angel as a phony, and don't appreciate his/her desire to impress or please.

III. ACTION:
- **Identify causes of misbehavior.**
- **Pinpoint student needs being revealed.**
- **Employ specific methods, procedures, and techniques at school and at home for getting the child to modify or change his/her behavior.**

1. Primary cause of misbehavior:
   ◗ Power: This student sees playing the angel as a form of power — power over teachers, parents, and especially other students. The more he/she can get away with fooling an adult, the more powerful he/she feels. The student sees getting peers in trouble with adults as a way of using power over them.
2. Primary need being revealed:
   ◗ Sex: The primary need of relationships should be investigated. It's possible that this student has had a break-up in the home. It may be that this role has been modeled by

someone at home and he/she is applying the same model in establishing relationships at school.

3. Secondary needs being revealed:

   ▶ Affiliation: This student needs a friend whom he/she can relate to but not control.

   ▶ Achievement: As this student achieves on his/her own merits, he/she will feel a reduced need to impress and control people.

   ▶ Status: Achievement will increase the feeling of worth and the feeling that he/she is somebody.

   ▶ Autonomy: The feeling that the student can be his/her own person without manipulating people can be enhanced by achievement and a feeling of worth.

4. Give this student positive and acceptable ways to get attention.

5. Give him/her significant things to do. This is a vital strategic action.

6. Let the student know that it's not necessary to grovel or "stand on one's head" for approval. The student needs acceptance for "just being." Remember, this student has been taught that he/she must do something "fantastic" to find acceptance. This is the "Cinderella Syndrome." It's a very common feeling among children.

7. Counsel the student about "being oneself" and being "authentic." Remind the student that he/she is good in front of the teacher — and misbehaves when the teacher isn't around. This is because he/she is trying in one place to be "perfect" for teacher approval and, in the other, to be "bad" for peer approval. And the student is losing in both situations.

8. Talk about "fun" things rather than "achievement" topics. This will help him/her relax.

9. Laugh *with* the student about mistakes. Make it clear you don't think his/her mistakes will cause the sky to fall.

10. Take off undue pressure — and explain why.

11. Always talk to parents. Tell them you feel that pressure for acceptance is causing the behavior. Such children often have "professional parents" who "live through their children."

IV. MISTAKES: Common misjudgments and errors in managing the child which may perpetuate or intensify the problem.

1. Always watching and waiting to criticize.

2. Resenting the angel and dealing with him/her in anger or disgust.

3. Disliking this student.

4. Failing to help him/her make friends.

5. Increasing his/her fear of disapproval.

6. Never choosing this student.

7. Ignoring him/her.

8. Failing to talk to parents.

9. Failing to develop a plan with other teachers to help the student change the behavior.

10. Becoming frustrated with this student's attempts to play games, and finally rejecting him/her completely.

11. Exploiting him/her by rewarding the behavior.

SEE ALSO: • The Apple Polisher   • The Spoiled Darling

THE ANGRY

I. BEHAVIOR: Specific attitudes and actions of this child at home and/or at school.

1. Mad all the time — at him/herself, others, or both.

2. Degree of the anger varies, but it is frequent even if not intense.

3. Strikes out verbally and physically at others, including teachers, classmates, and parents. Hostile even toward authority figures he/she doesn't know.

4. May yell out or throw objects.

5. Manifests an attitude of being mad at the world. Has a chip on his/her shoulder.

6. Usually defensive regarding reason for anger. In his/her mind the anger is justified. Will even say, "Who wouldn't be angry?"

7. If his/her reason is not accepted, will become offensive toward the person who does not agree with his/her stance.

8. Has very little self-control. Often loses control of him/herself when angry.

9. May appear to be overindulged by adults and peers alike.

10. At home, may throw tantrums.

11. Almost always blames others for what has caused his/her anger.

12. Often, rather than say "I'm sorry," threatens to get angrier "the next time."

II. EFFECTS: How behavior affects teachers, classmates, and parents in the school learning environment and the home family situation.

1. Crisis is created everywhere — in halls, gyms, cafeterias, classrooms, etc.

2. Resulting turmoil and conflict require someone to intervene continuously.

3. Other people — even teachers — are frightened. And the student often gets his/her way by becoming angry.

4. Classmates and teacher are put on the defensive.

5. Classmates and teacher want to avoid or exclude the angry student whenever possible.

6. People who don't even know the student, but have "heard about" him/her, adopt a fearful attitude.

7. Other students tend to turn into "angry" students as well. At home, parents are likely to get mad too.

8. Some students have a tendency to tease the angry student just to see the anger. Likewise, brothers and sisters will provoke the behavior.

III. ACTION:
- **Identify causes of misbehavior.**
- **Pinpoint student needs being revealed.**
- **Employ specific methods, procedures, and techniques at school and at home for getting the child to modify or change his/her behavior.**

1. Primary cause of misbehavior:

   ▶ Self-Confidence: The student uses anger to hide feelings of low self-esteem from him/herself and from others.

2. Primary needs being revealed:

   ▶ Escape from Pain: Because of his/her feelings of low self-esteem, the student becomes angry to cover the pain of failure.

3. Secondary needs being revealed:

   ▶ Aggression: This student needs to be able to act out frustrations positively — to be in control of him/herself.

   ▶ Affiliation: The student needs an adult or peer with whom he/she can establish a strong relationship.

   ▶ Power: Attempts should be made to give this person responsibility as long as he/she can maintain self-control. The student might be placed in a leadership role or role of responsibility and be rewarded when he/she handles it without becoming angry.

4. Keep your cool and your calm. Deal with this behavior professionally and never react personally.

5. Don't threaten. If you do, the student will get angrier and may even say, "I don't care what you do."

6. Don't put the student down. If you do, he/she will get sarcastic.

7. Try the "Feeling Sorry" technique. If you tell this student that you feel sorry for him/her because he/she is always mad, and ask what you can do to help, you may see a new stance immediately. First, few people ever feel sorry for this student. Second, he/she doesn't want you to because it makes him/her feel inferior. Remember, this student likes to believe that he/she has self-control. Therefore, appeal to this need after you've used this technique.

8. Avoid any situations which would provoke outbursts. The best time to talk is when he/she isn't mad or upset. A close look will reveal that this student is *exceptionally* calm, kind, gentle, and rational when he/she isn't angry. Point out this fact — and appeal to the student at these times.

9. Counsel in regard to his/her lack of self-control. Tell the student, "It's not bad to get mad. But what you do with your anger is what's good or bad." Never attack the emotion as "bad" or "wrong" or you'll never be able to talk to the student.

10. Develop a plan to help the student control his/her anger. Often, something as simple as a prearranged signal for the student to excuse him/herself, go get a drink, or go to the restroom can curtail the behavior immediately. However, your prearrangement should include a time limit of five to ten minutes.

11. Never reward the behavior. Always tell the child, "The response to your anger is likely to be more anger."

12. Never forget, this student needs a calm, adult friend. Usually this is one of the voids in his/her life.

13. Never return the anger; doing so will only justify the behavior.

14. Look the student in the eye, listen, and wait until he/she has finished. In fact, ask if he/she is finished before you begin speaking. If possible, don't interrupt. Rather, let the student "run out of gas."

15. Speak slowly and quietly. It helps him/her calm down. In fact, the student may be embarrassed by the outburst.

16. Use the "Minor Point" technique. Get the student to dissolve the anger over a minor point. Say, "Do you want to talk to Jimmy about this or do you want me to do it?" or "Do you want to go with me to the principal's office?"

17. At home, you can say, "I love you, but I don't necessarily like what you do."

18. Talk to the student about liking him/herself and what he/she does.

19. In the beginning, avoid long talks. Rather, use the "Seed Planting" technique. Mention an idea briefly, in passing. Say, for example, "I don't know; it hurts to be angry all the time," or "When I'm angry, I'm the only one who's hurt." Then say nothing more about it.

20. If it's necessary, isolate the student in some way so that the tendency to become angry will be greatly reduced. In the process, tell him/her *exactly* what you are doing and why.

21. Tell the student in specific terms the kinds of things that need to be done in order to make his/her behavior acceptable.

22. Be prepared for slow improvement in the student's behavior. It will not change overnight. If you expect the student to go from one end of the spectrum to the other, you won't help him/her change.

23. Remember, there will be *no* problem solving until the emotion of anger is eliminated — on both sides of the desk. You must deal with the emotions before the problem solving begins. Therefore, say to the child, "I'll lay it down if you will."

24. Do not fail to recognize your referral responsibilities. Be prepared to recognize signs of abnormality which indicate psychological problems requiring outside help. Your responsibility in such a case is to make a referral, and then to take instructions from the professional who is trained to help such students.

IV. MISTAKES: Common misjudgments and errors in managing the child which may perpetuate or intensify the problem.

1. Returning anger.

2. Avoiding the student.

3. Thinking this child deserves what he/she gets.

4. Making the child feel guilty for getting angry.

5. Thinking this student is the favored child at home.

6. At home, one parent blaming the other for a child's anger.

7. Blaming the student unjustly, without enough factual evidence to confront him/her professionally.

8. Handling angry students inconsistently.

9. Allowing anger in reaction to the child's anger to distract both teacher and parents from the real problem.

10. Assuming more responsibility for the situation than we really should and, therefore, not placing the full responsibility with the angry student — where it really belongs.

11. Treating this student very tenderly because we wish to avoid making him/her angry.

SEE ALSO: • The Bully • The Defier • The Exploder • The Fighter
• The Overly Aggressive

THE ANIMAL

I. BEHAVIOR: **Specific attitudes and actions of this child at home and/or at school.**

1. Tries to gratify all sensual desires — immediately and crudely.
2. Talks when he/she feels like talking.
3. Interrupts.
4. Loud and obnoxious.
5. Eats in class. Table manners are poor. May even take food from others.
6. Demonstrates overly sexual behavior in public. Touches opposite sex. Hugs, kisses, walks arm in arm with companion.
7. Seems oblivious to the values of others.
8. Often behaves worse if someone is watching.
9. Won't accept correction quickly.
10. Criticizes or pokes fun at classmates who are not like him/her.
11. Shows lack of interest in academic or extra-class school activities.

II. EFFECTS: **How behavior affects teachers, classmates, and parents in the school learning environment and the home family situation.**

1. Other students are distracted.
2. Tattling increases.
3. Teacher is intimidated, frustrated, and infuriated.
4. Students who must sit next to him/her in class or cafeteria are dismayed, shocked, or disgusted.
5. Other students may imitate him/her.
6. Teacher is forced to dislike him/her.
7. The student he/she is "pawing" often becomes an additional problem.
8. Teacher is in a constant emotional state.

III. ACTION:
- **Identify causes of misbehavior.**
- **Pinpoint student needs being revealed.**
- **Employ specific methods, procedures, and techniques at school and at home for getting the child to modify or change his/her behavior.**

1. Primary causes of misbehavior.
   - Attention: This student gets attention through inappropriate behavior, which he/she could not get through appropriate behavior.
   - Revenge: This student delights in causing adults and, many times, students to completely lose control of themselves. He/she has been rejected many times and is now striking out in his/her own way.
2. Primary needs being revealed:
   - Sex: This student may have a need for a relationship with the opposite sex and, when the opportunity presents itself, may not know how to handle it.

24

▶ Escape from Pain: This kind of behavior may well be a way to escape the pain of feeling inadequate in relationships, manners, and other expected social behaviors.

It should be noted that the effort to meet these primary needs may prevent this person from making any effort in the classroom; thus it is difficult to determine his/her academic potential.

3. Secondary needs being revealed:

   ▶ Aggression: This person needs to be recognized for something other than his/her present behavior.

   ▶ Achievement: This student needs to do well in accomplishing assigned tasks.

4. Counsel individually — and never in the presence of the animal's companion if he/she has one. This strategic action is paramount.

5. Use the "Group Approach." Talk to counselors, administrators, and other teachers, and then meet as a group with the student. Make it clear that the student can do as he/she likes — but not at school — and that if the behavior persists he/she will be removed. This approach is vital. Otherwise, the student may do anything from avoiding the teacher to making fun of his/her counseling efforts.

6. Next, call in the companion privately and relay the same message.

7. Call parents of both students immediately following the conference. If the parents prefer, they may come to school separately.

8. With both student and parents, use the following rationale:

   • You, as a teacher, do not want to be responsible for such behavior while children are in your care.

   • You have a responsibility to teach these students acceptable public behavior.

   • You have a responsibility to other children to maintain standards of good conduct.

   • These kids can do what they like in their own homes or off school grounds, but not in school.

9. Counsel student separately, of course, regarding eating habits, talking, etc. However, keep in mind that this student does not know acceptable behavior. He/she must be taught.

IV. MISTAKES: Common misjudgments and errors in managing the child which may perpetuate or intensify the problem.

1. Treating him/her as a misfit.

2. Asking the student why he/she does these things. "Why" is not the issue and only opens up the matter for debate. *What* the student is doing is the issue.

3. Being sarcastic.

4. Ignoring — hoping the problem will go away.

5. Showing disdain for the student rather than the behavior.

6. Believing he/she is not coachable.

7. Crossing this student off as not having any potential to achieve in the classroom.

SEE ALSO: • The Authority Pusher • The Defier • The Hater • The Lewd

THE APATHETIC

I. BEHAVIOR: **Specific attitudes and actions of this child at home and/or at school.**

1. Doesn't pay attention in class.
2. Doesn't do assignments and, therefore, has poor grades.
3. Will not enter into any class discussions, or discussions regarding anything.
4. Has a poor sense of self.
5. Immature and easily distracted to relatively unimportant matters.
6. Has a short attention span.
7. Frequently absent, tardy, or both.
8. Isolates him/herself socially.
9. Generally has a sloppy personal appearance and negative attitude.
10. Displays "I don't care" attitude in everything that he/she does.
11. In many ways, seems emotionally dead.
12. Tends to be slow in physical movements — even in leaving class.
13. Doesn't have a lot of friends.
14. Personal history is not marked by success.
15. May watch TV excessively, or spend time driving or riding in cars.

II. EFFECTS: **How behavior affects teachers, classmates, and parents in the school learning environment and the home family situation.**

1. Other marginal students are influenced to become apathetic as well.
2. Importance of academic work and the school itself is diminished.
3. Teacher becomes frustrated easily and frequently with his/her lack of success in trying to motivate this student.
4. Class morale is often lowered.
5. Other students often become disturbed and can't concentrate themselves.
6. Teacher often devotes too much time to the apathetic student, and ends up losing control of the class.
7. Continued prodding during class time is necessary.
8. Necessity of make-up work, extended deadlines, and varied standards is increased.
9. Teacher may ignore student's existence if he/she is not a troublemaker.

III. ACTION: • **Identify causes of misbehavior.**
  • **Pinpoint student needs being revealed.**
  • **Employ specific methods, procedures, and techniques at school and at home for getting the child to modify or change his/her behavior.**

1. Primary cause of misbehavior:

   ▶ Self-Confidence: Due to a feeling that he/she has little worth, this student feels rejected.

2. Primary needs being revealed:

   ◗ Escape from Pain: The apathetic person is feeling a lot of pain and chooses to be apathetic as a means of insulating him/herself from others who might possibly cause him/her pain.

3. Secondary needs being revealed:

   ◗ Affiliation: This student needs to develop a close friendship with an adult or peer.

   ◗ Gregariousness: This student needs to belong to a group of some kind. Such a membership increases motivation.

   ◗ Status: He/she needs to improve self-esteem and develop a sense of being a worthwhile person, important to someone.

4. Provide the student with short-term tasks for which goals are clearly seen and clearly achievable. This strategic action is an absolute.

5. Ask for his/her opinions during class and after class.

6. Give concrete rewards for *any* altered behavior.

7. Find a "payoff" for the apathetic student which will turn him/her on to learning in the school. It may be an extra-class activity.

8. Remember, involvement is a key. Therefore, involve the student in the learning process by creating a sense of ownership. It must be *the student's room, teacher, and class,* before he/she will become involved. Never forget, this student doesn't believe anything belongs to him/her.

9. Attempt to make materials more relevant and available to the student.

10. Accept the fact that not everything that happens in the classroom or in the school is going to be of interest to everyone, and that some students who are *not* really apathetic may be labeled thus erroneously.

11. Contact parents immediately when you begin to observe this problem. Don't wait until the student is so far behind in his/her work that this, rather than the apathetic behavior, becomes the primary problem.

12. Seek input from the counselor or from other teachers who have had this student in their classes.

13. At every opportunity, express your concern and your desire for this student to succeed. Until you can give the student a *win,* he/she will remain apathetic.

14. Therefore, consider adjusting your standards to reach this student. This action is a primary consideration in changing the behavior. Too, you may have to forget make-up work.

IV. MISTAKES: Common misjudgments and errors in managing the child which may perpetuate or intensify the problem.

1. Failing to *create* opportunities for this student to succeed.

2. Ignoring the student altogether, or assuming he/she doesn't want to learn.

3. Failing to check to see that the student is completing assignments on a daily basis.

4. Requiring less from this student than we do from other students.

5. Failing to make a sincere effort to really get to know the student personally.

6. Confronting the student in front of the class.

7. Assuming that the student is physically well and ready to learn.

SEE ALSO:　• "I Can't"　• "I Don't Care"　• The Noncompleter with Grand Plans

THE APPLE POLISHER

I. BEHAVIOR: **Specific attitudes and actions of this child at home and/or at school.**

1. Makes calculated moves to achieve his/her own self-serving ends.
2. Manipulates by giving praise to gain a personal advantage.
3. Tells us how right, good, and wonderful we are.
4. Volunteers to help.
5. Tries to anticipate our requests.
6. Volunteers, before we ask for volunteers, with the answer he/she thinks we'll like.
7. Usually puts his/her relationship with teacher ahead of relationships with peers.
8. May be a tattletale as well as an apple polisher.

II. EFFECTS: **How behavior affects teachers, classmates, and parents in the school learning environment and the home family situation.**

1. Teacher may be grateful for praise and accept it, and therefore may even promote the behavior.
2. Teacher may be completely turned off by student and his/her actions, and may therefore reject student.
3. Teacher may feel a void of security and trust.
4. Teacher may grant special favors or concessions — or not give an inch.
5. Peers usually don't like or trust this student.
6. Some other students may imitate such behavior if they see it working for this student.

III. ACTION:
- **Identify causes of misbehavior.**
- **Pinpoint student needs being revealed.**
- **Employ specific methods, procedures, and techniques at school and at home for getting the child to modify or change his/her behavior.**

1. Primary cause of misbehavior:
   - Attention: Apple polishing is a form of attention getting. It is dishonest behavior. We do not want to teach students to use dishonest behavior to gain attention from others.

2. Primary needs being revealed:
   - Sex: This student may have such poor relationships in the home and with peers that he/she will do almost anything to establish a relationship with the teacher.
   - Escape from Pain: School may be a very painful experience, and to avoid failure the student attempts to establish a successful relationship with the teacher.

3. Secondary needs being revealed:
   - Achievement: This student must be able to achieve in the classroom. By doing so he/she will meet other secondary needs.
   - Gregariousness: Achievement will mean acceptance by various groups.
   - Aggression: Acceptance in a group will give the student an opportunity to assert by having a voice in the group's decision.

▶ Status: Self-confidence will be enhanced and the need for attention reduced with achievement.

4. Counsel this child privately for teaching purposes. In the process, try to discover the needs of the apple polisher. This strategic action must be included in your approach.

5. Remember, all behavior has purpose. Once you discover the reason for the behavior, your course of action will be made clearer. However, if you fight the student's needs, he/she will continue apple polishing to get acceptance.

6. Remember that the reason behind his/her manipulating is to gain advantage and acceptance. This student fears rejection, may be starved for love, and finds no acceptance for "just being." Rather, he/she feels it's necessary to be patronizing or to do something fantastic to gain approval.

7. Make sure your words and actions accurately reflect your real feelings toward the student and his/her behavior. Express concern about the student, but not about his/her behavior. Say, "Relax. Be yourself." Above all, do not reject.

8. Talk about the student's ability to give. Praise him/her for not being a taker. Say that the desire to please is nice — to a point. Then talk about the need for honesty and sincerity. Explain that, while others have problems of "not being nice to people," this student is so "nice" that his/her sincerity is questioned.

9. Remember, this student is the product of adults who have required achievement before acceptance could be expected. If you accept him/her without making such requirements, you'll find that he/she can change the behavior. Don't reject the student for being honest and sincere, or he/she may "test" you and resort to old ways.

IV. MISTAKES: Common misjudgments and errors in managing the child which may perpetuate or intensify the problem.

1. Using this student and thus perpetuating the behavior.

2. Thinking he/she is weak.

3. Avoiding the student or rejecting his/her attempts to apple polish.

4. Turning classmates against him/her.

5. Believing he/she is lying or being deceitful.

6. Failing to include the student.

7. Making him/her polish apples to get strokes.

8. Trusting the student completely, believing this child only behaves this way with us because he/she likes us.

9. Using excessive flattery as a technique to motivate and control students. Students soon realize that such praise is insincere and teacher-centered rather than student-centered, and will regard the teacher as weak, as well as phony. Praise should be used extensively in the classroom, but it must be a sincere, friendly recognition of students and their achievement.

SEE ALSO: • The Angel   • The Spoiled Darling   • The Tattletale

THE ARROGANT

I. BEHAVIOR: **Specific attitudes and actions of this child at home and/or at school.**

1. Generally very bright.
2. Has an inflated ego.
3. May excel in one area, such as athletics, and be arrogant as a result.
4. Often ill-mannered and disrespectful of classmates, teachers, and parents.
5. Probably behaves equally badly at home.
6. Often questions the purpose of teacher decisions, requests, and/or assignments.
7. Will speak out and say things like "This is dumb," or indicate that others don't measure up in some way.
8. Always seems to be asking, "Why?" in a belittling manner.
9. Often fails to complete routine assignments or comply with basic rules and regulations.
10. Questions teacher's knowledge and authority, and will often present facts and ideas in the hope of contradicting the teacher or showing that the teacher's knowledge, performance, or thinking is inadequate.
11. Does not appear to like other people.
12. Acts superior. However, the key to this behavior is that the student makes him/herself look superior by making others look inferior.

II. EFFECTS: **How behavior affects teachers, classmates, and parents in the school learning environment and the home family situation.**

1. Others suffer from the arrogant student's ridicule; they feel uncomfortable at best, inferior at worst.
2. Feelings of exclusiveness rather than inclusiveness result from the behavior.
3. Teacher's credibility with other students is often hindered.
4. Decision making becomes more difficult.
5. Classroom discussions and study may be disrupted.
6. Others become angry.
7. Unfortunately, others may hope the worst will happen to this student. They may like to see him/her fail or have problems.

III. ACTION:
- **Identify causes of misbehavior.**
- **Pinpoint student needs being revealed.**
- **Employ specific methods, procedures, and techniques at school and at home for getting the child to modify or change his/her behavior.**

1. Primary cause of misbehavior:
   ▶ Attention: This student has a strong need to be recognized by peers and adults.
2. Primary needs being revealed:
   ▶ Sex: The student may be experiencing family problems or other difficulties with people interactions.

♦ Escape from Pain: The struggle to relate to people may be very painful.

3. Secondary needs being revealed:

♦ Status: Every attempt should be made to assist this student to develop a positive self-concept.

♦ Power: This student needs to learn that he/she counts, by being recognized for what he/she does or is. It's important that this be done in order to create a positive form of power.

4. Never surrender to your gut reaction to "level." It won't work.

5. Try the "Seed Planting" technique. Seed planting is responding to the student's words or actions with one sentence of objective truth, and stopping there. You can say such things as "Do you really think that is true?" "Are you sure?" "Do you think that's really that good an idea?" or "Your success doesn't seem to be making you happy." Seed planting serves several purposes. First, it makes the child think. Second, you can use it publicly without belittling or putting him/her down in any way. Third, it gets the student *ready* for in-depth conversations and counseling. And getting the student ready for counseling is half the task insofar as changing the behavior is concerned. Fourth, it makes the student think that you're pretty smart and may be worth talking to and listening to.

6. Confer with the student privately. More than one such discussion will be necessary.

7. Use the in-depth approach in all discussions. The student must be engaged in a meaningful and in-depth discussion regarding whatever he/she is being arrogant about. This takes time — and a willing attitude about giving of your time. Serious conferences change fake arrogance into real knowledge and hold the student accountable instead of allowing him/her to continue acting superior.

8. Appeal to the student's ego. If the student sees that you recognize any special ability, he/she will think you are smart, and may even believe you're the only one wise enough to see his/her potential. Then you can do some meaningful teaching. For instance, tell the student that his/her initial and surface thinking is very good, but that he/she is missing some points — including seeing and respecting the skills of others.

9. Help the student capitalize on his/her intellectual abilities by giving challenging assignments, extra reading, class reports, essays, and other opportunities to expand knowledge — and to show it. Remember, this child is trying to be somebody.

10. Do not fight or "put down" the arrogant student. Rather, realize that this student needs to be taught how to act to get what he/she wants: status, power, and autonomy. To get the student to listen, talk about being sharp, mature, responsible — and show how behaviors other than these work against him/her.

11. In a private conference, discuss precise behavior that is unacceptable, making sure the student understands the problem.

12. Create an atmosphere of acceptance of the student and the specific knowledge or attitudes he/she can bring to the class. It's often in a denial of these strengths that the problem is accented.

13. Give the student an opportunity to express knowledge and abilities through special projects. He/she needs additional responsibilities and may be bored.

14. In private sessions, always challenge the student to *prove* his/her ability to handle the special gifts he/she claims. You might tell the student, "Talk is cheap."

15. Talk to him/her about potential. Explain that true potential is a gift that helps one bring others into his/her orbit — not push them away. In the process, remind the student that unused potential means nothing and that achievement, not potential, is the real issue.

16. Use the "Narrative" technique. Here, you can relate stories of people who had great abilities and potential, but failed because they couldn't get along with people. Also, relate that 85% of

all people who lose or leave jobs do so because of people problems, not inability to do their work.

17. Be very careful not to show any arrogance of your own, no matter how mad you get. If you do, you only prove to the student that the biggest ego is the winner.

IV. MISTAKES: Common misjudgments and errors in managing the child which may perpetuate or intensify the problem.

1. Becoming defensive, emotional, and irrationally angry at the arrogant student. This makes the teacher act in inferior ways and, therefore, confirms the belief of the arrogant child.

2. Overdisciplining, or pushing the consequences of behavior out of proportion to the act itself.

3. Verbally putting down the student in class or in front of other adults.

4. Grading this student harder than others. We may tend to do this if the student is arrogant about his/her intelligence or academic ability.

5. Letting the student "hang" him/herself.

6. Taking the behavior of this student personally and, therefore, not reacting professionally.

7. Trying to handle all relationships publicly rather than privately. This is one of the biggest mistakes.

8. Failing to contact parents. Remember, they are probably experiencing the same behavior at home.

SEE ALSO: • The Disrespectful   • The Intellectual Show-Off   • The Know-It-All
• The Smart Aleck   • The Smartmouth

THE ATTENTION DEMANDER

I. BEHAVIOR: Specific attitudes and actions of this child at home and/or at school.

1. Usually loud.
2. Responds negatively to authority.
3. Tries to force his/her way into peer groups.
4. Frequently late to class.
5. Late in getting materials ready and assignments turned in.
6. Frequently out of his/her seat.
7. Picks on other students.
8. Usually asks unnecessary questions.
9. Often tries to be nonconformist in order to gain attention.
10. Says the wrong thing at the wrong time.
11. Often wears unusual or attention-getting clothing.
12. May use profanity or crude language.

II. EFFECTS: How behavior affects teachers, classmates, and parents in the school learning environment and the home family situation.

1. Teacher is forced to give additional time to this student.
2. Concentration of teacher and class is often broken.
3. Teacher is antagonized.
4. Teacher often loses track of what he/she is trying to say in class presentations.
5. Peers may react by excluding the attention demander from student groups.
6. Classmates may begin putting the attention demander down or avoiding him/her at every opportunity.

III. ACTION: • Identify causes of misbehavior.
• Pinpoint student needs being revealed.
• Employ specific methods, procedures, and techniques at school and at home for getting the child to modify or change his/her behavior.

1. Primary cause of misbehavior:
   ▶ Attention: This student is doing everything possible to let the teacher, parents, and peers know he/she exists.
2. Primary needs being revealed:
   ▶ Sex: This student may be attempting to "prove" him/herself to others by getting attention.
   ▶ Escape from Pain: Inability in social relationships and academic performance may cause this student to demonstrate such behavior.
3. Secondary needs being revealed:
   ▶ Gregariousness: This student needs to belong to some group.

- Achievement: The various attempts to gain attention point to a need to gain success in something.

- Status: The attention demander is shouting, verbally and nonverbally, "I am somebody."

4. Create a visibility or leadership role for this student.

5. Give him/her additional responsibilities.

6. Take time for an individual student conference to discover the real problems and insecurities that the student may feel.

7. Bolster the student's confidence at every opportunity — in a quiet way. You must find a constructive way for the attention demander to meet his/her need for attention. Above all, attention cannot be denied, or he/she will go to extremes to get it.

8. Seek help from psychologists and counselors as well as parents to reinforce changes in this behavior, not only at school but at home.

9. Be consistent in the way you handle situations with all attention demanders.

10. Be kind, polite, and *firm* at all times.

11. Model the behavior you want. Speak softly and quietly.

12. Reinforce appropriate questions when the attention demander asks them. This will help the attention demander and other students to realize which questions are constructive and relevant.

13. Don't cause the student unnecessary embarrassment when he/she asks to go to a counselor, nurse, or the restroom. Asking publicly, "What for?" or "Is it necessary?" — even in a gentle way — can be very embarrassing and even traumatic for some students because their need can be urgent.

14. Watch for improvement. Then, relate how pleased you are with the improvement in behavior.

15. Make weekly checks to ensure you are recognizing all students, even if it's just with "Good morning." Use the class roster and make a check next to the name of each student with whom you have interacted; you may find you go a whole week without talking to some students. Correcting this situation may prevent misbehavior.

16. Be constantly aware of the times you give attention to the attention demander. Be aware of this student's strong need for attention and provide it for positive actions — not just for disruptions.

17. Never exclude this student.

18. Never make the student anxious, or the behavior will become worse.

IV. MISTAKES: Common misjudgments and errors in managing the child which may perpetuate or intensify the problem.

1. Assuming that the attention demander doesn't have the skills to do the job, when he/she really does.

2. Ignoring the behavior.

3. Failing to listen carefully to what the student is saying.

4. Making hasty and inconsistent judgments about this student.

5. Trying to anticipate the kinds of situations that will cause the student to get what he/she needs by misbehaving.

6. Assuming that you can generalize and understand this student and the real motivations for his/her behavior.

7. Failing to comprehend the importance of his/her message.

8. Trying to keep him/her from getting any attention.

SEE ALSO: • The Blurter   • The Late Arriver   • The Procrastinator

THE AUTHORITY PUSHER

I. BEHAVIOR: **Specific attitudes and actions of this child at home and/or at school.**

1. Dislikes rules.

2. Sees no need to have anyone tell him/her what to do or how to do it.

3. Tests or questions teacher authority.

4. Usually tends to make every issue a public one.

5. Will argue openly against any request from the person in authority. Does so in a superior and/or attacking way.

6. Challenges all incidents, big and small, with equal intensity.

7. Causes turmoil in the classroom over the most minor issues.

8. Will base his/her whole case on the teacher's reaction to his/her upset rather than on the issue at hand.

9. May act belligerent but, unlike the defier, will bend. Keeps "pushing" with any technique that works, but will change the technique — and usually stop when he/she gets into real trouble.

10. Talks a better game than he/she plays — especially if given responsibility. However, with proper teaching, can become an outstanding leader.

II. EFFECTS: **How behavior affects teachers, classmates, and parents in the school learning environment and the home family situation.**

1. Establishing rules and procedures becomes difficult.

2. Decision making is hampered.

3. A great deal of time is required to correct nonproblem situations.

4. Other students, and even the teacher, may be involved in verbal confrontations.

5. Teacher is upset, and classmates are distracted.

6. Teacher may become confused — if not actually angry.

7. Other students may be influenced to demonstrate the same behavior.

8. Teacher may feel inadequate and insecure.

9. Teacher gets tired of the "game playing."

III. ACTION: • **Identify causes of misbehavior.**
• **Pinpoint student needs being revealed.**
• **Employ specific methods, procedures, and techniques at school and at home for getting the child to modify or change his/her behavior.**

1. Primary cause of misbehavior:

   ◗ Power: Disregard for rules is a way of seeking power.

2. Primary needs being revealed:

   ◗ Sex: This student may have had some poor experiences with adult authority, and sees his/her behavior as a means of gaining control over adults. He/she may experience such problems only with adults of the same sex — or only with those of the opposite sex. At home, this child may dominate one parent.

3. Secondary needs being revealed:

   ◆ Aggression: This student needs to participate in leadership roles or to be directed in responsible behavior.

   ◆ Inquisitiveness: The teacher can explain rules to the satisfaction of this student.

   ◆ Power: This student needs to express authority in positive ways — maybe by being in charge of enforcing some rules.

   ◆ Status: This student must know that the teacher regards him/her as "somebody."

4. Use the "Caution-Warning" technique. Immediately say, "I know you're upset or you wouldn't have said that — but let's not say that any more." This simple statement can prevent a discipline situation from developing. In addition, this teacher action lets the student know that you are aware of the situation — and gives him/her a second chance to respond in appropriate ways. If the student keeps pushing, which is less likely, he/she is aware of having erred twice — and is doubly responsible for the action. If he/she doesn't realize this double mistake, you can use it as your beginning in a private conference. In the meantime, teacher control and dignity can be maintained.

5. Always handle the student professionally rather than reacting in personal ways to his/her behavior. Reacting personally only worsens an already negative situation.

6. Always hear the student out — privately. Do not provide an audience. Recognize the student's need for attention and recognition. Without attention from you, he/she will seek it from any source.

7. Don't feel compelled to give immediate answers. Rather, promise to give an answer as soon as possible.

8. Tell the student yes or no, and why, and do so in a respectful and considerate way — always. Never make him/her look foolish. Explain why your decision is best for the learning situation in the classroom.

9. Remind the student of his/her choice to do it your way or as he/she wishes. Emphasize that he/she must be prepared to face the consequences of interfering with teaching and learning. Say, "If you're man (or woman) enough to push, be man (or woman) enough to accept any possible consequences of your pushing."

10. Confer with the student privately; this is a must. Conferences keep the issues from taking valuable classroom time and forcing teachers to discuss things publicly that they don't want to.

11. If, after a conference, the authority pusher doesn't follow rules, meet with parents and administrators to reinforce your decision. Remember, others can support any decision if it's in the best interest of the student and the class.

12. Let the student know that you have a responsibility to teach the class and that you intend to fulfill that responsibility.

13. Finally, realize that exclusion will make this child behave worse. For best results, you must find a way to include the student, give him/her responsibility, and hold him/her accountable for that responsibility. Remember, this is the kind of attention he/she is seeking.

IV. MISTAKES: Common misjudgments and errors in managing the child which may perpetuate or intensify the problem.

1. Losing control and turning this student into a serious discipline problem.

2. Getting angry.

3. Trying to pass him/her off.

4. Making threats that can't be enforced.

5. Arguing publicly with this student.

6. Reacting as if dealing with the student were a test of power, and going into an "I win — you lose" situation.

7. Being firm one day, and letting him/her "get away with murder" the next.

8. Acting as if we're "tired of messing with" this student. Remember, in our world, important people do not get ignored. And this child is misbehaving because he/she needs to feel important.

9. Asking administrators to punish him/her severely.

SEE ALSO: • The Bully   • The Hater   • The Influencer   • The Know-It-All
• The Overly Aggressive

THE BLABBERMOUTH

I. BEHAVIOR: **Specific attitudes and actions of this child at home and/or at school.**

1. Has a compulsive and uncontrollable need to talk about someone or something.
2. "Tells tales" and is a known source of gossip.
3. Spreads rumors and drops innuendos.
4. Will talk to anybody, anytime, about anything he/she knows and considers significant.
5. Wants and needs only a listener.
6. Would reveal the life secrets of a best friend to any stranger who would provide a listening ear.
7. Has a social problem caused by a distorted self-concept.
8. Seeks attention by telling secrets.
9. Experiences fear, anxiety, and rejection, which lead to the offensive behavior.
10. Doesn't care what he/she talks about, as long as he/she can talk to someone. Will even run him/herself down.

II. EFFECTS: **How behavior affects teachers, classmates, and parents in the school learning environment and the home family situation.**

1. Both peers and teachers dislike this student, and for good reason.
2. Neither teachers nor students really trust the blabbermouth.
3. Classmates only "use" this student as a source of information — or to spread information.
4. Other students may react physically toward this student, and fights may result.
5. Classmates are worried by the information this student holds.
6. The climate of trust in the classroom deteriorates.

III. ACTION:
- **Identify causes of misbehavior.**
- **Pinpoint student needs being revealed.**
- **Employ specific methods, procedures, and techniques at school and at home for getting the child to modify or change his/her behavior.**

1. Primary causes of misbehavior.
   - Attention: This negative behavior is a cry for attention.
   - Self-Confidence: Because of fear of not being accepted for him/herself, this student resorts to tall tales.
2. Primary need being revealed:
   - Escape from Pain: To escape the pain of being a nobody, this person covers his/her pain by being a somebody who is able to gain the ears of others by blabbing.
3. Secondary needs being revealed:
   - Affiliation: A close adult friend can really help change this student's behavior.
   - Status: The more value this person places on him/herself, the less he/she will need to continue the negative behavior.

4. Provide a listening ear first — and take a counseling stand second. This is the key to understanding and helping this student.

5. Don't scold or reprimand for violating a confidence; this is a waste of time. Because the student *can't* hold information secret he/she feels justified in "only telling John or Mary."

6. Realize that the blabbermouth needs attention — and needs it more than anyone can imagine. You must understand this fact before you can even begin to help him/her. If a teacher doesn't help this student, nobody will. Certainly classmates won't.

7. Be aware that the only way this student can establish a friendship — even momentarily — is by telling someone all he/she knows. And never forget — *experience* has proven to the student that this is true. In addition, the problem is perpetuated because he/she must continually search for more information to tell someone. Remember this fact — and respond accordingly. It must be a part of your strategic action.

8. Use empathy, sympathy, and corrective counseling. These can easily help the blabbermouth.

9. Deal privately — in an open and caring way — with the cause of the problem.

10. See that, in addition to counseling, this student gets attention for positive behavior. Then he/she will stop the habit for a very good reason. The blabbermouth hates it as much as others do.

11. Keep in mind that your efforts must be long term. The relationship you are developing is the one the student wants most.

IV. MISTAKES: Common misjudgments and errors in managing the child which may perpetuate or intensify the problem.

1. Ignoring this student. This approach never works, and makes the behavior worse.

2. Putting him/her down.

3. Calling this student untrustworthy. Remember, he/she is "telling" to get the trust of someone.

4. Believing he/she is malicious.

SEE ALSO: • The Blurter • The Gossip • The Talker

THE BLURTER

I. BEHAVIOR: Specific attitudes and actions of this child at home and/or at school.

1. Speaks out automatically — without permission; acts compulsively. Behavior appears over-anxious.

2. Answers when others are called upon. Interrupts when others are talking.

3. Speaks out before teacher finishes speaking.

4. Makes comments during conversation which are irrelevant to the topic at hand.

5. Seeks attention.

6. Oblivious to the needs of others.

7. Seems to lack a sense of fair play.

8. Often slow to complete tasks. However, is quick to promise and seems to have good intentions. Regardless, a lack of follow-through is common.

9. Different from the talker; while the talker talks all the time, this student simply blurts out his/her thoughts spontaneously for the world to hear.

II. EFFECTS: How behavior affects teachers, classmates, and parents in the school learning environment and the home family situation.

1. Class is disrupted and interrupted.

2. Teacher must concentrate more on this student than on the class.

3. Teachers, and some students, are irritated by the behavior.

4. Bad example is set. Others must show consideration, wait their turn, and operate in agreement with class etiquette. Those who are tempted to create disturbances, or who want class deviated for the moment, may follow the lead of the blurter.

5. Teacher is unnerved.

6. Teacher may doubt his/her capability in handling the situation.

7. Continuity of lesson is deviated and teaching plan can be ruined.

8. Time is wasted.

9. Teacher is continually trying to recapture interest in the topic at hand.

10. Enforcing rules becomes more difficult.

11. Teacher feels other students will behave similarly.

III. ACTION:
- **Identify causes of misbehavior.**
- **Pinpoint student needs being revealed.**
- **Employ specific methods, procedures, and techniques at school and at home for getting the child to modify or change his/her behavior.**

1. Primary cause of misbehavior:

   ◗ Attention: This is more a social problem than a discipline problem. It may become a discipline problem if treated as such.

2. Primary need being revealed:

♦ Sex: This student may be attempting to establish a relationship with the opposite sex and using this behavior to attract attention.

3. Secondary needs being revealed:

♦ Affiliation: A close friend may be a strong influence for the reduction of negative behavior.

♦ Status: This student is trying to be somebody who is noticed, to enhance his/her position among peers and/or adults.

4. Accept one important fact: This student is more disturbing to the teacher than to classmates. With this acceptance, a teacher is more likely to respond in a professional way. Without it, a teacher may create a total disturbance in the classroom.

5. Remember, behavior of the blurter is either overanxious or attention-seeking.

6. Don't show the class your anxiety by blurting back; if you do, you give this student the attention he/she wants, as well as the opportunity to be disruptive and continue the exchange. Responding with silence — especially without appearing sarcastic and vindictive — will often sober students more quickly than anything else. Too, saying something like "I'd like to continue this conversation privately after class — so I'll see you then" may also prove effective.

7. Acknowledge the student — whenever this behavior occurs — with eye contact or hand movements, but *no* verbal comment.

8. Give the student opportunities to participate at a planned time. Tell him/her before class the question you will ask.

9. Use the student's name *before* you ask a question, and tell him/her this is what you are going to do to help solve the problem.

10. Above all, be patient. It may take the student time to control his/her anxiousness. However, with teacher concern, caring, and attention, you can count on one important factor: This student will try.

11. Speak softly and calmly, and never reprimand him/her in the presence of other students.

12. Stand close to this student during class discussions.

13. When you talk to the blurter privately, tell him/her *all* the techniques you plan to employ. Be patient because it may take a long time to begin to control his/her anxiousness, which is the source of the blurting.

14. Be sure to tell this student why his/her blurting isn't really appropriate behavior in the classroom. Share specific instances.

15. Talk to the blurter about the difference between assertion and aggression.

16. Call on this student for responses when he/she is quiet and not trying to blurt out.

17. Praise other children for being good listeners. Praise the blurter as well, when he/she is a good listener.

18. Give extra attention in positive ways when the blurter is not being disruptive — rather than allowing him/her to be recognized only negatively.

19. Develop a relationship. This student has few, if any, meaningful relationships with adults.

20. Occasionally, ignore blurting. But tell the student that you are going to do so.

IV. MISTAKES: Common misjudgments and errors in managing the child which may perpetuate or intensify the problem.

1. Blurting back a quick retort, such as "Shut up" or "I'm going to tape your mouth." We model the behavior we are criticizing with such actions.

2. Becoming unnecessarily loud when calmness would be more effective.

3. Thinking that the entire class is disturbed and annoyed by the behavior.

4. Anticipating that all other students will begin to exhibit this behavior.

5. Creating rules for an entire class as a preventive measure.

6. Making an issue out of each interruption.

7. Ignoring the interruption completely, then treating the student as though he/she were not part of the class.

8. "Putting down" or reprimanding this student in full view of classmates.

9. Showing frustration and revealing anxiety.

10. Believing our teaching plan is ruined.

11. Ignoring valuable contributions or spontaneity.

12. Failing to see the blurter's appropriate involvement in class.

13. Losing patience.

14. Removing child from group.

SEE ALSO: • The Blabbermouth • The Gossip • The Talker

THE BULLY

I. BEHAVIOR: Specific attitudes and actions of this child at home and/or at school.

1. Pushes people around, verbally and physically.
2. Threatens others continually.
3. Has a bad temper — and often a bad mouth. Brags loudly and often about his/her strength.
4. Extremely negative. Also has a very poor self-concept. As a result, becomes aggressive with other people at the first hint of trouble. A close look will reveal that this student always thinks others are trying to "put down" or take advantage of him/her.
5. Talks back. Usually very public in announcing what he/she plans to do.
6. Often has learning problems.
7. Uses physical aggression but, generally, only outside the classroom. In the classroom, makes verbal threats about what he/she will do after leaving the classroom.
8. If articulate, may be verbally aggressive.
9. Degrades others and humiliates others in public view.
10. Generally either a loner with few friends, or a gang leader. Those who join gangs identify with the bully in order to intimidate others. Regardless, the bully usually has a genuine reputation for being a fighter.
11. Responds to all interaction negatively and physically.
12. Looks for trouble.
13. Parents may promote fighting.

II. EFFECTS: How behavior affects teachers, classmates, and parents in the school learning environment and the home family situation.

1. Many students are frightened.
2. Some think it's funny when they experience the immature behavior of a bully.
3. A climate of fear exists in the classroom.
4. Rights of others are restrained.
5. Confrontations take place.
6. A bad example is set. Others see problems being dealt with by violence.
7. School time is wasted.
8. Many students wish they had the nerve to act the very same way because power gives them a great deal of attention.
9. Students who are being bullied are threatened. They're apt to become highly emotional and upset — and may be afraid to come to school.
10. Physically weak students may follow the bully for protection — from this bully or from other bullies.
11. A bullying experience in class immediately stops the learning process. Lectures and discussions are interrupted — and perhaps attention is lost.
12. Teacher may be affected personally because of a feeling that he/she has lost power in the eyes of the rest of the class.

13. A negative atmosphere is created.

14. Occasionally, teacher may be afraid of a bully.

III. ACTION: • **Identify causes of misbehavior.**
• **Pinpoint student needs being revealed.**
• **Employ specific methods, procedures, and techniques at school and at home for getting the child to modify or change his/her behavior.**

1. Primary causes of misbehavior:

   ◗ Attention: This student is an attention seeker and enjoys the attention he/she gets from peers and adults.

   ◗ Power: This student demonstrates power by his/her ability to physically hurt others. Being physical gives him/her a feeling of being in control.

   ◗ Self-Confidence: The bully usually knows that hurting is wrong, but being physically strong makes him/her somebody — it improves a poor self-concept.

2. Primary needs being revealed:

   ◗ Sex: This student can establish a relationship only by being the strongest. This could well be the lesson that is being taught at home.

   ◗ Escape from Pain: This person's life could be so negative, and he/she could be so afraid of what is going to happen next, that he/she adopts bully behavior for protection from others.

3. Secondary needs being revealed:

   ◗ Gregariousness: This student needs to belong to a group, but he/she is unacceptable; thus the student becomes the leader of his/her own group.

   ◗ Power: Because of an inability to function socially, the bully exerts power by physical force. He/she may get beaten up at home, and may win approval at home by being tough at school.

   ◗ Autonomy: Physical power makes this student feel independent, in charge of his/her life.

4. Use the "Delay" technique. If the bully threatens to "get someone" after class, hold him/her after class. Don't let the bully leave — or he/she may have to carry through to keep peer respect. Say, "You made a threat. Now you've had time to think. If you carry through, that's premeditated." Then explain what this means: If the student chooses to go ahead, he/she must be prepared to face the full consequences, whatever they may be. However, don't tell the student what the specific consequences will be.

5. Don't assume this student is tough. The bully may in fact be weak, and may be using his/her antics to cover up insecurity. Likewise, a student who is loud is not necessarily an extrovert.

6. Establish a one-to-one relationship with the bully. This student needs — and always lacks — such a relationship with a strong and successful adult model.

7. Be gentle rather than tough. The bully can handle toughness — it's his/her forte. However, the bully can't fight gentleness, and this is what he/she really wants.

8. Take the student off the hook. The bully usually accepts bigger responsibilities well, and will do as you say. To take the student off the hook, you could encourage him/her to say to others, "Miss Jones won't let me fight."

9. Keep in mind that kids who fight an authority figure do so only to compensate for a flaw in their own characters which they themselves may or may not recognize. Therefore, you must help the student make the identification.

10. Make it safe for the bully to be vulnerable to others. Otherwise, he/she will keep bullying because that behavior keeps others away and shields areas of insecurity.

11. Openly address the problem of his/her insecurity; it is the main issue. Give this student big responsibilities — and rechannel his/her energies constructively.

12. Praise him/her for appropriate behavior continually. And when you do, call the new behavior "strong."

13. Design activities which will bring out his/her leadership and assertion strengths in a positive way. However, be sure to make success or failure "safe" when you do.

14. Show the student that you care about, respect, and trust him/her. This type of student tends to be extremely loyal.

15. Discuss the problem with parents. However, make sure the student attends any private conference. If you don't, a credibility gap may develop between you and the student.

16. Let the student help decide any consequences should he/she falter.

17. Let the student know that you like him/her, but that you dislike the behavior.

18. Don't put the student in a position in which he/she must "prove" him/herself, or the bully behavior may recur.

19. Let the student know that bullying can't be tolerated — no matter what you think of him/her. The bully must be aware of your respect for people. Therefore, make sure *you* don't do anything which could be considered "bullying," or abusing power.

20. Athletics are a good outlet for this behavior. Talk to your physical education colleagues and coaches.

21. Have him/her sit near or work with the opposite sex.

22. Never forget the motivational force of pride. However, remember that true pride has one source: solid personal achievement coupled with the respect for others that grows out of self-respect. To instill pride in a student, a teacher must give him/her personal success and meaningful accomplishments. If not, lack of self-respect, degradation, and even shame make pride a difficult achievement for some students, especially the bully.

IV. MISTAKES: Common misjudgments and errors in managing the child which may perpetuate or intensify the problem.

1. Teachers or parents saying, "People won't like you when you act that way." This is exactly what the bully wants because it gives him/her the desired attention. We fail to recognize that this child will pay any price for attention.

2. Publicly putting down a bully — or publicly showing pride or pleasure in his/her physical victories.

3. Prejudging a child a bully in every situation because of past behavior.

4. Treating the bully inconsistently.

5. Reacting personally and making threats in an attempt to change behavior.

6. Trying to bribe the bully.

7. Attacking the individual and not the behavior.

8. Failing to dig out the bully's true underlying motives.

9. Failing to reinforce positive behavior of the bully.

10. Believing all bullies are extroverts. A loud outer facade can be deceptive, and teachers and parents alike can often feel that every bully is an extrovert. Yet, the opposite is often true.

11. Overlooking his/her potential.

12. Excluding the bully.

13. Protecting others, but never protecting the bully.

14. Getting into a value argument with parents over whether fighting is "right" or "wrong."

15. Putting hands on students in any situation, whether professional guidance or discipline. Of course, every teacher must know the rules concerning corporal punishment. However, even holding, pulling, and touching can lead to trouble. One violation can ruin an otherwise good career.

16. Failing to treat both sides of the trouble. We all know that trouble has two sides. For instance, we know it usually takes two students to get into a fight. Yet, we are often likely to handle the more aggressive of the two rather than deal with both. Even if another student's wisecracks caused the confrontation, the one who struck the physical blow is likely to receive most of our attention and reprimand.

SEE ALSO: • The Angry   • The Defier   • The Fighter   • The Overly Aggressive

THE CHEATER

I. BEHAVIOR: **Specific attitudes and actions of this child at home and/or at school.**

1. Copies other students' work during class.

2. Turns in another's homework.

3. May even form partnerships with others in the room for test days.

4. As a general rule, denies all guilt if suspected or caught cheating.

5. Concentrates on cheating rather than working. Spends time, therefore, finding out how to cheat rather than how to study.

II. EFFECTS: **How behavior affects teachers, classmates, and parents in the school learning environment and the home family situation.**

1. Teacher must "play detective" rather than be a learning partner.

2. If others are involved, two problems are created.

3. Classmates are aware of his/her practice and are displeased by it.

4. Teacher is frustrated because he/she is aware of the activity, but unable to catch the student cheating.

5. Teacher becomes angry.

6. Teacher is disturbed when he/she doesn't know how to handle a cheating situation.

7. Other students' confidence in the teaching-testing system is destroyed.

8. Obviously, if the cheater is successful, other students will be encouraged to cheat as well.

III. ACTION:
- **Identify causes of misbehavior.**
- **Pinpoint student needs being revealed.**
- **Employ specific methods, procedures, and techniques at school and at home for getting the child to modify or change his/her behavior.**

1. Primary cause of misbehavior:
   ▶ Self-Confidence: This student wants to be successful in school, but does not believe he/she is capable of achieving without cheating.

2. Primary needs being revealed:
   ▶ Hunger, Thirst, Rest: This student may not be eating or getting enough rest because of his/her fear of failure.
   ▶ Escape from Pain: Rather than fear parents, teacher, and peers, the student will cheat to escape the pain of failure.

3. Secondary needs being revealed:
   ▶ Aggression: This student needs to assert him/herself and be responsible for his/her academic performance.
   ▶ Achievement: This student has a strong need to be successful. Remember, the cheater does care, and wants to be successful — that's why he/she cheats.

4. Remember, the root of the problem lies in the fact that this student is aware of what is expected, but fears that he/she cannot meet those expectations. This may make the student

resort to cheating in order to succeed. Punishment for cheating may or may not help the student. It may only force him/her to be a more careful cheater in the future.

5. If you are uncertain, but suspect that a particular student has cheated, question him/her tactfully — but don't be afraid to question.

6. Exercise the utmost tact and diplomacy in handling this student. First, decide whether you want to punish the student or change the behavior. Before you say or do one thing, know what you want — because you probably won't accomplish both. Changing the behavior is the wiser choice.

7. Approach the student and, when necessary, the parents, in a private, quiet, and professional manner rather than an accusing one. If you do so, you are much more likely to help the student solve his/her problem.

8. Use the "Worried-Concerned" approach. Reveal doubt, as well as disappointment in the apparent behavior, but never anger or condemnation, especially when talking with parents.

9. When you present facts to students, parents, and administrators, present the facts as you saw them — not as absolutes. As you do, reveal a professional concern for the student or students involved.

10. Don't point out the obvious. Both student and parents will more readily and openly accept the situation if they are allowed to share your suspicions rather than accept your condemnations. If you start condemning, others may start denying.

11. Remember that your purpose is to prevent a severe character defect from developing rather than to punish the violator of an honor code.

12. At the height of your anger, upset, or disappointment, ask yourself: "Have I ever cheated?" This will help your perspective because most of us have cheated in some way. Also, remember that the reason for cheating is to be successful.

13. Never use the word "cheat." Say instead, in private at a later time, "John, I don't think you're being completely honest on this test."

14. Discuss, with the class, situations students may have to face, and ask them what they think would be good solutions. Some possible situations might include: "What would you do if you saw a classmate taking someone's money?" or "What would you do if someone asked you to help him or her cheat on a test?" Such discussions help these students learn values and build healthy relationships in the process.

IV. MISTAKES: Common misjudgments and errors in managing the child which may perpetuate or intensify the problem.

1. Reacting to cheating before carefully thinking through effects on student and rest of class.

2. Grabbing paper, tearing it up, and throwing it away before talking to the student.

3. Making statements such as "You know you're cheating and so do I," or "You've been cheating all year."

4. Compounding the problem by destroying the teacher-student-parent relationship that we need in order to help the child solve his/her problem.

5. Mishandling situations or reacting to the cheater — rather than to the cheating — and allowing cheating to become the only issue for student and parent concern.

6. Failing to take into account that more than one student may be involved in the act.

7. Ignoring the problem so we will not have to face it.

8. Accusing student openly and in a final way.

9. Using one student against another or urging classmates or friends to reveal details of the misbehavior when we suspect a student of cheating. This teacher practice only breeds resentment between students in the class and causes disrespect for the teacher.

10. Failing to take into account that other students are observing our reaction to the cheating situation.

SEE ALSO: • The Liar   • The Thief

THE CHISELER

I. BEHAVIOR: **Specific attitudes and actions of this child at home and/or at school.**

1. Seeks "more" — regardless of what it is. If the class is given a "special day," asks for two. If the class is given five extra minutes, asks for ten. No matter what the teacher response — always makes a plea for more.

2. If teacher concedes and changes an answer on a test question, immediately starts pressuring him/her to change another.

3. Tries to get out of tasks.

4. "Runs over" the inexperienced teacher and exasperates the experienced.

5. Talks to administrators and counselors in an effort to get an additional benefit or a grade raised.

6. Will offer any rationalization to achieve more.

II. EFFECTS: **How behavior affects teachers, classmates, and parents in the school learning environment and the home family situation.**

1. Teacher attitude is threatened. Teacher mood may be reversed. A flexible teacher may become inflexible, and the teacher may feel and express ill feelings toward an entire class.

2. Teacher may become inconsistent.

3. Classmates may get angry because the chiseler gets extra advantages or privileges.

4. Time is wasted.

5. Conflict is created.

6. Teacher must make rules for the entire class. Everybody pays for the chiseler's actions.

III. ACTION: • **Identify causes of misbehavior.**
           • **Pinpoint student needs being revealed.**
           • **Employ specific methods, procedures, and techniques at school and at home for getting the child to modify or change his/her behavior.**

1. Primary causes of misbehavior:

   ▶ Attention: This student always gets attention from everybody by this behavior.

   ▶ Power: The ability to get more is a form of power.

2. Primary needs being revealed:

   ▶ Hunger, Thirst: This behavior may be a carry-over of behavior the student is forced to adopt at home in order to satisfy hunger and thirst.

   ▶ Sex: This student may not understand how to have positive relationships with people.

   ▶ Escape from Pain: It may be that family problems or low potential to achieve in school causes this student much pain.

3. Secondary needs being revealed:

   ▶ Aggression: This student needs to be able to assert in a positive way, such as approaching problems in school and working toward constructive solutions.

> ▶ Inquisitiveness: This could be a very real need for the chiseler as he/she might be the type who needs an explanation for everything.

> ▶ Power: If this student is placed in responsible situations in which he/she has authority and is accountable, he/she may give up the chiseling position.

4. Remember that, unfortunately, greed is this student's number one problem and the reason behind his/her behavior.

5. In addition, be aware that "getting more" can become a game he/she plays with teachers, friends, and parents.

6. Always be fair. However, never give in simply to pacify or get rid of this student.

7. Make the student realize that you have identified his/her behavior. Talk to the student closely and firmly regarding what he/she is doing.

8. In the process, make sure he/she knows you do *not* approve of the chiseling.

9. Explain to the student that people will shy away from him/her forever if he/she doesn't change. Your job is to help change a behavior.

10. Tell the student that you would change the grade in a minute or give in to the request immediately if he/she were right. But the student is wrong and, therefore, you cannot.

11. Remember, once you are sure you have identified a chiseler, don't be afraid to question and expose his/her technique for what it really is. This is basic to getting him/her to change.

12. Tell the student privately, "It's a dangerous game you play."

13. Reveal to the student that others are offended and even angered by his/her tactics. Say, "Others do not regard your tactics as fair — and neither do I."

14. Make it clear that the chiseler cannot chisel you. Then he/she will usually relax and become a reasonable student.

15. The next time a chiseler begins — stop him/her immediately. Don't let the discussion get to the pleading stage. Simply terminate the discussion after you have made a simple, firm, and clear explanation.

16. Direct a "smile of knowing awareness" toward this student when such behavior begins. This will often terminate the pleas more quickly than a defensive argument. A smile lets you avoid harsh words and reveals the lightness you feel toward the request.

17. Approach discipline situations from the "I'm good, you're good" position. This provides a better chance of acceptance, because you're criticizing the behavior, not the student. That's why you can "joke" the chiseler out of his/her stance. If you attack from the position that "I'm good, but you're not," more trouble may lie ahead. Always keep in mind that blanket condemnations rather than criticisms of a specific attitude or behavior can create problems rather than solve them.

18. Remember, the chiseler knows what he/she is doing, and needs to know that you know too.

19. Use the "ego" approach when counseling the chiseler if other approaches fail. If you want action, avoid challenging the excuses students give you. Often, a student cannot admit doing anything wrong when confronted. Therefore, accept the excuse momentarily and go on. In the process, try this technique. Point out the merits and benefits of making the situation right or carrying out a task successfully. Remember, you're dealing with an ego confrontation, so appeal to the ego rather than fight it and you can walk by excuse problems easily.

20. Don't ignore the social setting in which the behavior occurs. A child's behavior is best understood if it is observed in terms of its social setting. Problems do not arise from within a person — they arise from conflicts with others in given situations. Teachers must remember these facts in every discipline situation.

IV. MISTAKES: Common misjudgments and errors in managing the child which may perpetuate or intensify the problem.

1. Getting angry or frustrated and saying things we shouldn't.

2. Arguing; this is always a mistake.

3. Trying to prevent the student from appealing to a "higher authority."

4. Responding to the claim that others allow what he/she is requesting.

5. Making rules for the majority because of fear of the minority. Doing so may make the rest of the class difficult to motivate. Some students will require special handling no matter what a teacher does.

SEE ALSO: • The Greedy • The Selfish

THE CLASS CLOWN

I. BEHAVIOR: Specific attitudes and actions of this child at home and/or at school.

1. Continually disrupts class with wisecracks.
2. Will do or say anything to be in the spotlight.
3. Doesn't know when to stop.
4. Has a smart aleck response for everything that happens.
5. May even enjoy the attention of being reprimanded.
6. Actually quite funny at times. This is a reality a teacher cannot overlook.
7. May be either a very bright or a very poor student.
8. Won't quit until he/she gets attention. Behavior cannot be ignored.
9. May be popular and gregarious.
10. Physically and mentally active.
11. Usually, emotionally immature.
12. Bothers other students — touching, grabbing, etc.
13. Not really a leader; may actually be a loner.
14. Too busy clowning to get work done in class.
15. Very peer conscious.
16. Clowns to cover up for poor performance.
17. May be hyperactive.
18. Tries not to be serious — makes a joke out of everything.
19. Very insecure.
20. Often unprepared; doesn't bring books or supplies to class.

II. EFFECTS: How behavior affects teachers, classmates, and parents in the school learning environment and the home family situation.

1. Attention of teacher and classmates is constantly diverted to the class clown.
2. Teacher is upset by his/her inability to channel this student's energy constructively.
3. Teacher fears other children may begin imitating the class clown.
4. Teacher often becomes upset because this student is not working up to his/her potential.
5. Other students are prevented from concentrating.
6. Class is either entertained or disgusted by the behavior.
7. A real danger can be presented by such behavior in open equipment classes.
8. Often, classmates resent the fact that the teacher is spending so much time with the class clown.
9. Regaining attention is difficult because some kids linger on the class clown's humor.
10. Creating a serious tone in the classroom is difficult.

III. ACTION:
- **Identify causes of misbehavior.**
- **Pinpoint student needs being revealed.**

- **Employ specific methods, procedures, and techniques at school and at home for getting the child to modify or change his/her behavior.**

1. Primary cause of misbehavior:

    ▶ Attention: This student desires attention at any price, and feels clowning is the only way he/she can get it.

2. Primary needs being revealed:

    ▶ Sex: This person desires to establish relationships with people and is very unsure about how to go about it.

    ▶ Escape from Pain: Situations at home or at school may be very painful and this student may be hiding the pain by being the class clown.

3. Secondary needs being revealed:

    ▶ Achievement: Sometimes the student's inability to achieve in the academic world causes him/her to become the class clown.

    ▶ Status: The class clown is saying, "Look, I'm somebody!" He/she seeks a feeling of being worthwhile. Some of these students have high self-esteem and just like to entertain.

4. Remember, this student may not like the role of class clown.

5. Help the student find a way out of this behavior, knowing he/she will pay any price for attention.

6. Don't ignore this student. His/her personality and needs will not allow it.

7. Enjoy the humor briefly with the class. Remember, the class clown is often funny. The humor is not the major problem — knowing when to quit is always a problem. Therefore, signal by hand movement, rather than words, that "enough is enough."

8. Fulfill the class clown's need for attention at times other than when he/she is "cutting up."

9. In private conference, use the "Time and Place" strategy. Say, "Humor is a good thing. Yet, you may forfeit respect if you always allow yourself to be laughed at."

10. Respond with silence. In a powerful way, this response gets the student to settle down, because he/she knows that each added word is getting him/her in more trouble. When the student stops, however, don't say one word. Rather, go on with the lesson. If you say anything, the student will start up again.

11. With the class, use the "Mature Class" technique. Explain that a teacher would like to be able to have fun with the class. However, a teacher can do this only if the class is mature enough to sense the right time and place for humor. Ask students if they know what a mature class is. It's one that knows when to work and when to have fun, one that can stop having fun and get back to work when the teacher so requests.

12. Don't attempt to handle this student with anger, rejection, or sarcasm, and don't try to outwit this student. Such attempts will fail.

13. Isolate the class clown from his/her audience — but don't forget this student's need for attention.

14. After his/her next clowning episode, laugh with the class. The second time it happens, wait until the incident is over and then explain to the class that humor is a good thing in the classroom, at the right time and place.

15. Following the talk to the class, give the same talk privately to the class clown. In your conference with him/her, emphasize the concepts of *maturity* and *respect*. Tell the student you resent people laughing at him/her and it troubles you that he/she is helping them laugh.

Tell the student you are going to help him/her handle humor in a mature manner so he/she can make it a personal asset, rather than a handicap.

16. Be prepared to provide the patience and help he/she will need. Your efforts should begin to pay behavior dividends almost immediately.

17. At appropriate times and places, give this student a chance to "perform."

18. When humor interrupts your class, try combating it with more humor. When the class becomes unruly because of "something funny" that the class clown says or does, a problem exists only if the teacher cannot regain interest. The best way to do this is to join in the laughter for a few moments, relax, and then urge the class back to the lesson at hand. The majority will quickly obey. For the others, silence and a serious look in the necessary direction should bring order. If it becomes necessary to discipline a few, the rest of the class is aware of your fairness as well as the need for your action.

IV. MISTAKES: Common misjudgments and errors in managing the child which may perpetuate or intensify the problem.

1. Overreacting to the class clown both in personal conferences and in the classroom.

2. Calling the class's attention to the problem.

3. Trying to ignore the problem.

4. Issuing threats that can't really be carried out.

5. Trying to isolate the student physically in order to stop the problem.

6. Feeling that the class clown is operating the way he/she is in order to "bug" the teacher.

7. Failing to see any benefits in the humor of the class clown.

8. Having two standards of expectations and allowances — one for the class clown and one for other students.

9. Failing to realize and acknowledge that his/her humor is not a negative human characteristic. It is a positive one — and can be a constructive factor in the success of an individual.

10. Feeling that the student invariably enjoys being a clown and is making no real effort to change this behavior.

SEE ALSO: • The Con Artist • The Show-Off

THE CLIQUE

I. BEHAVIOR: **Specific attitudes and actions of these students at home and/or at school.**

1. A small group of students who are together continuously.
2. Dominate others by treating them as inferior.
3. Ignore other students.
4. Desire special treatment and privileges.
5. Defend their group unswervingly.
6. Usually argumentative and cause class discord.
7. Show disrespect.
8. Laugh at and make fun of others.
9. Totally exclusive.

II. EFFECTS: **How behavior affects teachers, classmates, and parents in the school learning environment and the home family situation.**

1. Often, teacher and classmates are pulled into a power struggle with clique members.
2. Teacher's time is dominated by these students.
3. Other students are inhibited and made to feel inferior.
4. Arguments that arise can often interrupt class discussion and interaction.
5. Being inclusive in class becomes difficult.
6. Obtaining cooperation becomes difficult when clique needs are not considered.
7. Some students may become fearful.
8. Clique members may always want to work together on classroom assignments or tasks.

III. ACTION:
- **Identify causes of misbehavior.**
- **Pinpoint student needs being revealed.**
- **Employ specific methods, procedures, and techniques at school and at home for getting the child to modify or change his/her behavior.**

1. Primary cause of misbehavior:
   - Power: Each individual in the clique feels more powerful with the group. The student may not have confidence but, within the clique, feels capable of doing almost anything.
2. Primary needs being revealed:
   - Sex: The student may be so insecure about relationships that he/she will do anything to stay in the clique.
   - Escape from Pain: The feeling of not being able to make it alone is very painful, thus the importance of belonging to a clique.
3. Secondary needs being revealed:
   - Gregariousness: A need to belong to an "inner circle" is satisfied by belonging to a clique. Through the clique, the person may act out other needs.

◗ Aggression: The student is unable to be assertive alone, but can be as part of a group.

◗ Achievement: The student may well work harder in the classroom in order to remain in the group.

◗ Status: The acceptance of the student by the group gives him/her a feeling of being somebody.

4. Do not try overtly to break up the group.

5. Find out individual needs.

6. Identify the leader of the group — and work with this student.

7. Create study groups that separate members of the clique. Or create a study group made up of clique members. Then members may determine that there are reasons to leave the group.

8. Try to use the leadership ability of clique members constructively in every classroom situation.

9. Motivate the clique leader to better behavior by acknowledging positive behavior when it occurs.

10. Refrain from talking to these students as a group. They will stick together at almost any cost. Talk to individual members of a clique on a one-to-one basis, if their inclusiveness is hurting class performance. It is better, however, to work on the leader.

11. When a problem arises, find out what their real gripe or problem is — and never speculate.

12. Never attack the group. Remember, a constructive positive action to help eliminate and resolve the problem in an up-front and sincere manner is the best approach.

13. Always tell students that you understand and appreciate their close friendship.

14. Tell them that if their behavior interferes with the learning of other students, you'll have to talk to them again — that you'll have to break the group up in the classroom. Tell them that you would rather not do this because you understand that they would rather sit together in class. You never want them to think that you're against the group. But explain to them that you have to deal with what is in the best interest of the class.

15. If the behavior continues, explain that it is not in the best interest of the class to have them sit together and talk during class time. This will help them understand the justness of your decision.

16. If you change seating, always tell each student that it was his/her *behavior* that told you what you had to do. In effect, you did not move the student — the student did.

IV. MISTAKES: Common misjudgments and errors in managing students which may perpetuate or intensify the problem.

1. Mistakenly concluding that all cliques are bad.

2. Creating a situation in which one clique is actually pitted against another.

3. Underestimating the actual power of a clique.

4. Failing to recognize that students need to belong to groups and that it's healthy.

5. Embarrassing them or using sarcasm in the presence of other students. They will simply group against you.

6. Capitulating to group whims.

7. Failing to recognize that these students together are different from the same students as individuals.

SEE ALSO: • The Follower   • The Negative Group

THE COMPLAINER

I. BEHAVIOR: Specific attitudes and actions of this child at home and/or at school.

1. Whines and cries about situations — as well as about what he/she has to do. Acts as if he/she has a persecution complex.

2. Usually lazy.

3. Doesn't have materials or assignments, but always has excuses.

4. Because of lack of self-motivation, uses complaining as a form of rationalization.

5. Repeatedly points out the errors and weaknesses of others in an attempt to get out of doing things and bolster his/her own ego.

6. Seeks attention with comments such as "I never get to go first," or "I don't see why I have to do it; nobody else does."

7. Acts as if he/she is the only one who does anything — but, in reality, does very little except complain.

8. Often seems to be very bored.

9. Argumentative and questioning about decisions, rules, deadlines, etc.

10. Shows irritability the minute an excuse doesn't work.

11. Does just enough to get by as far as class work and assignments are concerned.

12. Generally speaking, has a poor self-concept, and is not held in high esteem by peers.

13. Seeks attention by complaining.

14. May use standard responses, such as "Oh, man," "I never get a break," or "You're on me all the time."

II. EFFECTS: How behavior affects teachers, classmates, and parents in the school learning environment and the home family situation.

1. Classmates and teachers are disrupted during classroom experiences.

2. Teacher fairness is undermined.

3. Class morale is affected.

4. Teacher is irritated and angered.

5. Class time is wasted.

6. Conflict between teacher and parents may arise.

7. If the behavior of the complainer is successful, others are encouraged to imitate the behavior.

8. Many peers feel annoyed at the behavior of the complainer because they see through to the selfishness and deception inherent in his/her complaining.

III. ACTION:
- **Identify causes of misbehavior.**
- **Pinpoint student needs being revealed.**
- **Employ specific methods, procedures, and techniques at school and at home for getting the child to modify or change his/her behavior.**

1. Primary causes of misbehavior:

- ◗ Self-Confidence: This student has a very low feeling of self-worth and sees everybody else as to blame for his/her failure.

- ◗ Attention: This student needs to know that you know he/she exists, and needs to be able to do something that gets attention.

2. Primary needs being revealed:

   - ◗ Sex: Opportunities should be given in which this student may develop relationships.

   - ◗ Escape from Pain: The complainer finds his/her own personal life very painful. And it becomes easier to blame everybody else rather than look into his/her own responsibilities.

3. Secondary needs being revealed:

   - ◗ Affiliation: This student may need a strong positive relationship with a teacher or a fellow student.

   - ◗ Achievement: Academic success can reduce complaining.

   - ◗ Power: The student is struggling for independence, but needs to channel energies in more constructive ways. The teacher might explain that it is OK to complain constructively when a valid complaint exists. Thus the power need will be met and respected.

   - ◗ Autonomy: This student needs to understand that he/she is in control of his/her success or failure as a person.

4. Recognize that student complaints are usually the result of some kind of upset. They are expressed by saying, "This isn't fair," or "I don't think we should have to do this."

5. Don't overlook this one important facet of complaints: Inherent in complaints is interest. Furthermore, complaints usually indicate involvement. That's why if we ignore a complaining student, we may turn interest off.

6. For best results, allow a student to say what is on his/her mind. Complaints require a full explanation.

7. Be personal. It's your best motivational tool. Tell your students that you do care. Use such phrases as "Let me help you," "Could we work on that together?" and "I think you have a good idea." Use personal pronouns, and students will respond in positive ways.

8. If the student is totally or partially right, correct the situation immediately and thank the student for bringing the complaint to your attention. If the student is wrong, explain and give assurance in a caring way.

9. Above all, don't do anything that makes either the student or the complaint appear unimportant.

10. Study the student's background to find out his/her real needs.

11. Remember, this student fears failure, and bolsters his/her ego by complaining to the point that he/she believes the rationalization. Talk to previous teachers to try to gain a comprehensive view of what is bothering the student. Check the student's ability *closely.* The class work may be too difficult for him/her.

12. Don't work on long-term goals. Rather, present more immediate goals through short-term assignments. Even if this student is behind classmates, make-up work will result in his/her giving up almost completely. Helping the student set short-term goals and selecting tasks which he/she can complete will give you the opportunity to reinforce this student's actions with consideration and encouragement.

13. Don't react defensively to complaints. Accept them at face value with a comment such as "That may be a point I should consider." Then, encourage private discussion and counseling by saying, "Could you give me a little time to think about it and then stop by after school to discuss it with me?"

14. Always have a private conference. Tell the student, "I would very much like to talk to you

privately about your various complaints." Counsel in regard to negative and constructive criticism. When counseling, say, "If you're going to criticize, you must have solutions." This helps make the student accountable.

15. When this student offers a complaint, treat him/her as you do other students. Do not be quick to reject the complaint. Rather, try to create a situation in which you can discuss the complaint privately rather than publicly. Then you are in a position to help the student as well as maintain your relationship with other students.

16. During the private conference, always begin the conversation by asking for the student's constructive criticism. Agree with any of the student's legitimate complaints. This is the key to developing a working relationship, and enables you to establish a base for guiding the student toward gaining skill in voicing criticism in a positive, appropriate way. If you reject all criticism, all is lost.

17. During the meeting, don't appear offended or irritated. Listen sincerely. If possible, respond with immediate action. Regardless, be sure the student understands the reasons for the requirements or policy you have established. Students gain perspective from teacher explanations. Usually, there are few complaints a teacher cannot solve with communication.

18. Give this student attention on a daily basis. Such a continuous program of attention is an important part of his/her guidance. Talk specifically to him/her once every day.

19. *Listen* to the student. When you do, he/she will consider you "special" and may "bend your ear" so often that you'll feel the behavior is getting worse rather than better. You'll be surprised at how much you can help this student. He/she is often heard but seldom listened to.

20. Remember, the person who complains still cares. However, if he/she is not helped, the next step is uninvolvement. Never forget, the primary reason for complaining is to get attention. Don't let this need for attention get you down.

21. Discover some ground upon which to compliment this student.

22. Above all, know that this student must have success. This includes academic success as well as help to see the positive aspects of his/her life.

23. Don't encourage complaining. However, students do need to know you have an "open-door" policy. Too, they need to know *how* to voice criticism. Remind the students that you discuss privately the suggestions you may have for them — and that you would appreciate the same consideration.

24. Explain that it's OK to be wrong and make mistakes.

IV. MISTAKES: Common misjudgments and errors in managing the child which may perpetuate or intensify the problem.

1. Becoming thoroughly disgusted and showing our disgust.

2. Failing to deal individually with this student because of time restraints.

3. Ignoring all requests — and calling them complaints.

4. Being sarcastic.

5. Becoming defensive and getting involved in arguments with the student.

6. Giving unequal treatment and unequal responses to this student.

7. Rejecting the validity of all criticism.

8. Siding with other students against the complainer.

9. Using threats and/or negative reinforcements.

10. Failing to seek counsel of parents.

The Complainer

11. Constantly changing our minds to accommodate or get rid of this student.

12. Assuming ownership of the child's problem.

SEE ALSO: • The Alibier • The Crier (Who Claims Foul) • The Excuse/Alibi Maker
• The Griper • The Loudmouth • The Objector • The Questioner
• The Vindictive

THE CON ARTIST

I. BEHAVIOR: **Specific attitudes and actions of this child at home and/or at school.**

1. Usually personable and very likable.
2. Relates to people readily.
3. Often can talk teachers — as well as classmates — into and out of everything.
4. Unfortunately, seems to enjoy and gain satisfaction from his/her manipulative skill.
5. Would rather achieve through conning than through normal channels.
6. Will usually brag about what he/she has done and intends to do.
7. Uses his/her influence to get people to do what they don't want to do — and wouldn't ordinarily do.
8. Conning is seldom positive.
9. Thinks it's OK to deceive others.
10. Usually "looks down" on those he/she deceives — classmates, teachers, or parents.

II. EFFECTS: **How behavior affects teachers, classmates, and parents in the school learning environment and the home family situation.**

1. Many classmates think the con artist is clever.
2. Classmates may encourage the behavior.
3. Others may even try to imitate the con artist, and be upset with teacher when conning efforts are unsuccessful or are met with resistance.
4. Teacher may become irritated after the fact rather than during the behavior.
5. Teacher may receive disrespect as a result of handling the con artist in the wrong way or falling into his/her trap.
6. Teacher may feel helpless in working with this student.
7. Teacher and classmates may be embarrassed by being conned.
8. A climate of distrust exists in the classroom.

III. ACTION:
- **Identify causes of misbehavior.**
- **Pinpoint student needs being revealed.**
- **Employ specific methods, procedures, and techniques at school and at home for getting the child to modify or change his/her behavior.**

1. Primary cause of misbehavior:
   - Power: This person experiences a feeling of victory or power over adults or students by outwitting them.
2. Primary need being revealed:
   - Sex: This student feels that when dealing with people, one always has to win, and conning is as good a technique as any for winning.
3. Secondary needs being revealed:

- ► Power: This student has a strong need for power, and needs assistance to meet that need in the school setting.

- ► Autonomy: Conning people is a way of getting one's own way. Human interaction skills can position a student to feel he/she has control over his/her life.

4. Counsel this student privately.

5. Let the student know you recognize his/her motives. Once the student knows this and has experienced your disapproving stance, he/she will usually stop — after another try or two. However, this student will not abandon the behavior with others unless confronted by them too.

6. Employ the "Using" technique when counseling. To change the behavior, talk to the student about the fact that he/she is "using people." Reveal that it won't be long before only strangers will trust him/her. Likewise, remind the student that such behavior is *not* clever. After all, he/she would *not* experience any success without the trust of others. Therefore, the con artist is successful only when he/she "betrays a trust."

7. Counsel this student seriously about directing his/her leadership abilities and skills to help people rather than exploit them.

8. Talk about fairness. It's a very important word to young people. Remind the student that conning is an example of "unfair" in the worst sense.

9. Explain that you are going to stop the student immediately each time you see him/her conning someone.

10. See the student after class or after school following every incident. Do *not* let the behavior work for the student.

11. Don't attempt to prod or nag this student into behaving properly. More often than not, it won't work. Nagging usually consists of threats, rash statements, exaggerations, teasing, and promises. These teacher actions will not change behavior. Nagging can also ruin a professional teacher personality — and make a teacher unfit for human companionship. Never forget, the student who cons other people needs concrete and logical reasons for changing his/her behavior. He/she *respects* thought, not pleas or threats.

12. Above all, reinforce all healthy behavior — that means praise and acknowledge all success that is not won through conning. If you don't, the student will resume conning to gain attention and self-satisfaction.

13. Remember, there's no quick cure for this problem behavior. It requires intensive counseling because the behavior works so well for the student.

14. Never forget that even when students misbehave, they need to be encouraged, cared for, and forgiven. That is, they do if you want to change a behavior permanently. Remember this fact the next time you need to counsel this student. Then fit your action to the student and to making things better — not worse. If you do, you'll be more effective in getting this student to listen and respond to what you say.

IV. MISTAKES: Common misjudgments and errors in managing the child which may perpetuate or intensify the problem.

1. Letting this student think he/she is cute, smart, or clever.

2. Exposing publicly rather than confronting privately. Public exposure almost always brings problems of another kind.

3. Becoming angry and reacting in a crude and harsh manner after having been taken advantage of by the con artist.

4. Rejecting the child rather than the behavior.

5. Letting the behavior go unattended.

SEE ALSO: • The Class Clown   • The Show-Off

THE CRIER (WHO CLAIMS FOUL)

I. BEHAVIOR: **Specific attitudes and actions of this child at home and/or at school.**

1. Cries immediately — even before anyone can respond to what he/she is crying about.
2. Cries habitually, not occasionally.
3. Cries when faced with mistakes — and even when he/she succeeds.
4. Withdraws from group — withdraws into self.
5. Cries to get his/her own way.
6. Cries when feeling overwhelmed.
7. Cries when faced with authority (teacher).
8. Disturbed by everything, not just a specific issue.
9. Picked on and teased by classmates.
10. May stop immediately when concession is made.

II. EFFECTS: **How behavior affects teachers, classmates, and parents in the school learning environment and the home family situation.**

1. Teacher may feel sorry for student — or angry.
2. Classroom "flow" is disrupted.
3. Teacher questions expectations of student.
4. Other students may be pitted against teacher.
5. Other students reject crybaby.
6. Feeling of fairness in the classroom is difficult to maintain.
7. Teacher may feel that concessions must be explained or defended to other students.
8. Teacher may give in, but feel he/she shouldn't.

III. ACTION:
- **Identify causes of misbehavior.**
- **Pinpoint student needs being revealed.**
- **Employ specific methods, procedures, and techniques at school and at home for getting the child to modify or change his/her behavior.**

1. Primary cause of misbehavior:
   - Self-Confidence: This student uses his/her crying as a protection of self.
2. Primary needs being revealed:
   - Escape from Pain: This student could be experiencing pain in school and at home.
   - Sex: This student has not learned how to relate to people, and continues to use the immature technique of crying.
3. Secondary needs being revealed:
   - Achievement: Achievement must come in the form of improvement in social interactions as well as in academic productivity.

◗ Status: The crier must learn to see him/herself in a role of being able to cope with peers — to feel that he/she has at least a chance of being able to hold his/her own with peers. Once this student is able to accept this role, self-esteem will be enhanced.

4. Don't take this student's bait. Many of these kids actually play the role of underdogs. Everything they do says, "I'm always getting pushed around." Worse, some of them continually send out invitations to get attacked via their "I'm getting picked on" complaints. If you take this bait, you'll never get the student to deal with the two real issues of his/her problem: expecting defeat and not doing much to avoid it.

5. Use the "Lame Duck" technique in counseling this student. Talk to the student calmly and patiently — but directly. Tell the crier you can't accept — or allow him/her to accept — alibis or excuses because of tears. Once he/she knows for sure that you won't accept the lame duck stance, you're better positioned to move to the work at hand rather than the excuse at hand.

6. Try to raise the self-concept of this child so that he/she can be successful. This is one of the more difficult teacher tasks. As we all know well, there's a direct correlation between how children feel about themselves and how well they do in the classroom. Some students seem to have a failure mentality when it comes to what they think they can do academically and with other people. So it is with the crier who claims foul.

7. Always keep in mind that this student feels inadequate. Everything he/she says and does relates, "I'm not good enough." His/her feelings of inadequacy will be reinforced by a teacher's avoidance or impatience.

8. Remember that adults rarely address the feelings of this student in an objective and serious way.

9. Provide the student specific expressions of objective expectations — with explanations. Then offer learning options. Remember, poor students have trouble seeing options — and the crier is often an unsuccessful student.

10. If you want permanent solutions, don't let the crier talk you into settling his/her disputes with other students. Don't get into rivalry games. Rather, use the "Direct Solution" approach. Make these students talk directly to each other and find their own solutions. If you don't, students will compete to get you to agree with them and settle in their favor. Your task is to bring them together and serve as mediator — not to serve as judge and jury.

11. To avoid taking the heat, the crier will try to get classmates in trouble with you. Typically, the student sets up a "let's see you get them" situation. The crier does this for many reasons, including a desire to take the pressure off him/herself. When dealing with these situations, adopt this stance: Get more information, but don't take the bait. Likewise, avoid the tendency to attack or punish the child. Rather, get firm regarding responsibilities to others and him/herself. Then, with caring rather than pressure, make the student fulfill his/her responsibilities.

12. The crier often honestly thinks that classmates are responsible for his/her problems. "See what they made me do" is a common form of such blaming. Don't let this kind of behavior pass, or it will intensify. Rather, counsel immediately. In the process, see that behavior for what it is — a reluctance to accept responsibility. Talk to the student about this fact. Second, remember never to interrupt when the crier is doing class work, or he/she will blame *you* for any failure — and the behavior will be harder to change.

13. When the crier makes one negative accusation after another, stop this student dead in his/her tracks. The student isn't looking for solutions, but is employing overkill — sometimes to divert you completely from the original issue. When such a situation occurs, stop. Avoid explanations until another time. Let the student know that he/she is making you angry. It's an appropriate motivator in this case. Say, "You don't want solutions or you wouldn't be

using such an approach." Finally, tell the student that both of you had better think — and meet tomorrow. You'll find tomorrow will bring a more considerate tone.

14. Encourage the student not to be afraid of you.

15. Keep your emotions under control.

16. Remind the crier often that everyone makes mistakes; don't let the student think others are trying to hurt him/her.

IV. MISTAKES: Common misjudgments and errors in managing the child which may perpetuate or intensify the problem.

1. Reinforcing the crying by calling attention to it.

2. Treating the student without pity.

3. Letting classmates handle the problem.

4. Believing this student is just selfish.

5. Rejecting both the student and the behavior.

SEE ALSO:
- The Alibier • The Disrespectful • The Loudmouth
- "Not My Fault" • The Rabble Rouser

THE CRIER (WHO SHEDS TEARS)

I. BEHAVIOR: Specific attitudes and actions of this child at home and/or at school.

1. Responds to any kind of pressure or conflict with tears. This behavior is different from that of the crier who is always crying foul.
2. Extremely sensitive and often worries that everything will go wrong.
3. Sometimes seems to feel the burden of the world on his/her shoulders.
4. May also think that he/she is "different" and disliked by classmates and teachers.
5. Believes that his/her class work or personality will never be acceptable to teachers.
6. Often teased by classmates.
7. Often a loner.
8. Seems to need a friend.
9. Usually relates easily to caring adults.

II. EFFECTS: How behavior affects teachers, classmates, and parents in the school learning environment and the home family situation.

1. Teacher may not know how to talk to this student — much less how to relate to him/her, and may avoid the student as a result.
2. Teacher may feel so uncomfortable that he/she fears approaching this student.
3. Unfortunately, teacher may punish this behavior, feel it's a sign of immaturity, or treat crying as a discipline problem.

III. ACTION:
- **Identify causes of misbehavior.**
- **Pinpoint student needs being revealed.**
- **Employ specific methods, procedures, and techniques at school and at home for getting the child to modify or change his/her behavior.**

1. Primary cause of misbehavior:
   ▸ Self-Confidence: This student honestly cannot face people, especially if failure in any form is involved.
2. Primary need being revealed:
   ▸ Escape from Pain: This student is easily hurt and reacts with much feeling to the world about him/her.
3. Secondary needs being revealed:
   ▸ Aggression: This student needs to learn to assert him/herself.
   ▸ Status: This student needs to develop an understanding of self and a belief that he/she is OK. The student may come to accept that it's not bad to be a very sensitive person.
4. Be patient. This is the first step in helping this child change or cope with such behavior.
5. Next, remove any negative feelings you hold toward crying. It's not necessarily a bad or abnormal behavior.
6. Talk to this student in positive ways about his/her sensitivity. Tell him/her that sensitivity is a strength — if kept in perspective. Say, "Just as some people hide their feelings, yours are

simply out in the open for all to see. Your friends are lucky — for they know more easily how you feel." This technique allows the student to minimize rather than maximize negative feelings he/she may hold regarding crying.

7. Let the student know that you're on his/her side. Remember, this child thinks others are against him/her because of too many tears.

8. Get involved in his/her goals. This is the best stance you can take to help the child use his/her sensitivity constructively.

9. Always contact parents for insights.

10. Seek the help of former teachers and counselors if deeper emotional problems may exist. Chances are, however, this child is just a very nice, caring, loving, and sensitive person who can't hide his/her sensitivity.

11. Remember, the crier may be a very capable person, but is very emotional in any kind of stressful situation. This emotional makeup may never change, and it will take patience to work with this student.

IV. MISTAKES: Common misjudgments and errors in managing the child which may perpetuate or intensify the problem.

1. Calling this student a crybaby.

2. Trying to shame him/her.

3. Believing he/she is weak.

4. Failing to look at crying as a positive act. This may intensify the problem. Remember, tears are not negatives. In truth, they may be totally positive.

5. Overprotecting this student and failing to deal with the behavior.

6. Failing to understand that this may be an emotional characteristic that will never change.

SEE ALSO: • The Angel   • "I Can't"   • The Immature   • The Spoiled Darling

THE DEFIER

I. BEHAVIOR: Specific attitudes and actions of this child at home and/or at school.

1. Will openly challenge teacher or parents at almost every opportunity.
2. Talks back.
3. Dares punishment.
4. Usually appears unaffected by what teacher says or does — and may even laugh at it.
5. May even refuse to accept punishment.
6. Usually overly critical of teacher's fairness.
7. Quick to claim "injustice" by saying, "Nobody likes me." Thus, extremely conscious and critical of teacher's treatment of him/her.
8. Does not appear to feel very good about him/herself; seems to think he/she is not being treated well by others, including classmates, parents, and teachers.
9. Loses sight of the fact that his/her behavior is actually the reason for what is happening in relationships with other people.
10. Has little self-control.
11. Often highly emotional.
12. Always tries to rationalize or justify what's happening as someone else's fault.
13. Picks fights with classmates — in addition to taunting teachers. Picks fights at home too — over the smallest of incidents, which he/she claims are significant.

II. EFFECTS: How behavior affects teachers, classmates, and parents in the school learning environment and the home family situation.

1. Neither teacher nor classmates know how to respond to or handle this student.
2. Lessons are disrupted.
3. Rules are challenged.
4. Classroom is in turmoil and crises arise daily.
5. Teacher experiences much anguish.
6. Teacher feels uneasy and may even become ineffective.
7. Teacher worries about disciplining other students because he/she hasn't been successful with the defier.
8. If the defier's behavior is allowed to go unchecked, classmates may question teacher fairness when they are reprimanded.
9. Tension becomes an ever-present condition in the classroom.

III. ACTION:
- **Identify causes of misbehavior.**
- **Pinpoint student needs being revealed.**
- **Employ specific methods, procedures, and techniques at school and at home for getting the child to modify or change his/her behavior.**

The Defier

1. Primary cause of misbehavior:
   - ♦ Revenge: This student wants to be disliked. Failure has made him/her give up trying to get attention in an acceptable way.

2. Primary needs being revealed:
   - ♦ Escape from Pain: This student is feeling a lot of pain and his/her behavior demonstrates this pain.
   - ♦ Sex: This person's interactions with people are very negative.

3. Secondary needs being revealed:
   - ♦ Aggression: This person is using assertion as a means of survival. This assertion must be directed toward a more positive involvement in the class.
   - ♦ Achievement: Personal responsibility is a form of achievement for this student.
   - ♦ Power: A form of power must be offered to this student.
   - ♦ Status: Everything must be done to demonstrate the worth of this student. This does not mean you accept his/her behavior, but you do accept the person.
   - ♦ Autonomy: The student has many ways to be in control of his/her life other than defiance.

4. Regardless of the situation, never get into a "yes you will" contest with this student. Silence is a better response.

5. Whatever you do, don't lose your dignity, and never, never raise your voice or argue with the student.

6. Use the "Third-Person" technique. Remember, you are the outlet, not the cause, for this student's defiance — unless you are shouting, arguing, or attempting to handle him/her with sarcasm. Therefore, don't take the defiance personally. Rather, say, "John, what's the matter? That doesn't sound like you," or "What's making you so upset?" By using this approach, even if it doesn't reflect your feelings, you place yourself in the position of a third person who can help rather than affront, and you can maintain both your dignity and your professional position. In addition, you emphatically convey to all students that the defier is the problem, not you. If you don't use this approach, especially in front of other students, you may feel forced into saying or doing something that will only aggravate the situation.

7. If a student says, "I won't do it" or "You can't make me," don't let the student make you believe his/her defiance is directed toward you. Again, become a third-party participant by saying in a questioning or even bewildered way, "What's the matter?" or "That's not like you." This reaction may not agree with your feelings, but it will produce the best results. Follow this response with "What happened to make you so upset?" or "Is there anything I can do to help you?" If the student replies, "Yes, get off my back," don't lose your composure. Rather, continue using the third-person stance and the problem has a chance for a solution rather than a guarantee of an unfortunate scene.

8. The "Delayed Teacher Reaction" also works well. For example, if a student says, "I won't do it" — do not say anything for a moment. Rather, look at him/her in surprise and say, "I don't think I heard you." This response gives the student a chance to retract the statement — to change unacceptable behavior into an apology without teacher reprimand. If your situation with the defier has already deteriorated to the point that you could not use this approach in front of other students, then do it privately. This problem can *never* be handled past this point publicly. Sometimes, you can only try to quiet the student by saying, "Let's not talk about it here. Let's visit later when you can tell me everything that's on your mind."

9. Put this student on your priority list for after school, between classes, or recess-time conversation.

10. Speak to this student in conferences outside the classroom setting. A quiet, private, neutral place is best.

11. Be caring, but honest. Tell the student exactly what it is that is causing problems as far as you are concerned. Be sure you listen to the student as well. In the process, insist upon one rule — that you both be respectful.

12. Alert administrators and counselors to the problem if the behavior persists.

13. Avoid power struggles with this student. They will get you nowhere.

14. Try to convince the student that he/she must produce in order to survive in a meaningful way.

15. Give this student some classroom responsibilities.

16. Create various group activities so the student can have experiences with peers.

17. Always listen to this student. Let him/her talk. Don't interrupt until he/she finishes.

18. Ask if isolation would help. But don't force it on the student prior to talking about it. Such "surprises" will only make him/her more defiant.

19. Make the student a part of any plan to change behavior. If you don't, you'll become the enemy.

20. Above all, reach an agreement with the student on how you will treat each other.

21. Be very specific in relating what behavior is unacceptable.

IV. MISTAKES: Common misjudgments and errors in managing the child which may perpetuate or intensify the problem.

1. Getting involved in "yes you will" contests with these students.

2. Becoming emotionally involved.

3. Losing our professional dignity, raising our voices, or arguing with the defiant student.

4. Feeling we are the cause of the defiance. This is not true unless we shout, argue, or attempt to handle the student with sarcasm in retaliation. These tactics can increase the intensity of the problem.

5. Taking this defiance personally.

6. Dealing with the student in class rather than on a one-to-one basis in private.

7. Trying to get other students on our side.

8. Trying to effect unusually harsh and inappropriate punishments in retaliation.

9. Issuing threats which we are really not even prepared to carry out or capable of carrying out.

10. Trying to appease the defier — or letting the student think we are afraid of him/her.

SEE ALSO: • The Angry • The Animal • The Authority Pusher
• The Disrespectful • The Hater • The Overly Aggressive

THE DESTROYER

I. BEHAVIOR: **Specific attitudes and actions of this child at home and/or at school.**

1. Always exhibits destructive behavior.
2. Repeatedly breaks things.
3. Takes furniture apart.
4. Writes on desks.
5. Tears pages out of books.
6. Pounds on desks, writes in books, dents lockers.
7. Mutilates equipment, mars walls.
8. Destroys materials belonging to other students.
9. Often goes to one of two extremes with his/her own possessions: Doesn't take care of them, or is meticulous about things he/she owns.
10. May not treat people any better than property.

II. EFFECTS: **How behavior affects teachers, classmates, and parents in the school learning environment and the home family situation.**

1. Teacher is irritated, angered, and frightened.
2. Educators and parents alike are confused, baffled, and at a loss to understand why the student acts this way.
3. Some classmates may be amused and delighted — which reinforces the behavior.
4. Resources of the school — which aren't easy to replace — are wasted.
5. Teacher may want to punish — harshly — rather than help.
6. Teacher finds it hard to explain to other teachers and administrators why this kind of behavior is occurring in his/her room.
7. Teacher is frustrated and doesn't know what to do to correct the behavior.
8. Teacher may feel lax and/or incompetent.
9. Others may blame teacher for the behavior — because this child may not behave in such a manner with other teachers.
10. Teacher may dislike — almost hate — this student.
11. Disciplining other students for comparatively "minor" misbehavior becomes more difficult.
12. Confusion and controversy are created regarding who should pay for what and how much.

III. ACTION:
- **Identify causes of misbehavior.**
- **Pinpoint student needs being revealed.**
- **Employ specific methods, procedures, and techniques at school and at home for getting the child to modify or change his/her behavior.**

1. Primary cause of misbehavior:
   ▶ Revenge: This student, in many instances, is acting out of hostility against everyone.

He/she is successful at instilling fear in people and destroying property. This makes up for his/her many other failures in school.

2. Primary need being revealed:

   ▶ Escape from Pain: This student is feeling a great deal of pain and frustration. He/she feels "on the outside" of everybody and everything.

3. Secondary needs being revealed:

   ▶ Achievement: This student needs to be recognized for any positive behavior.

   ▶ Aggression: This student has a strong need to "act out" feelings but in a positive way.

   ▶ Power: The student must be given opportunities to be trusted and must be recognized when a task is well done. Many times the destroyer wants to get caught. Confronting adults makes him/her feel powerful.

   ▶ Autonomy: Trust is a part of being in control of self. If this person feels he/she is trusted, then he/she may begin to make decisions not to destroy.

4. React professionally — and never take an incident personally.

5. Never openly involve the student in a specific situation if you don't have overwhelming proof or witnesses. Rather, privately discuss your concern about "a problem being experienced" with the student as soon as you suspect him/her. Do so gently, in a *very quiet,* concerned, and serious way. A "hard-nosed" approach will only make your immediate and long-term tasks more difficult. If the student is only a suspect, discuss the situation without making any accusations. This strategic action is vital.

6. Always inform your administrator at the time of the incident. Likewise, notify the administrator before any conferences take place. You must never conceal the act from others in authority.

7. Once you have identified a destroyer — or think you have — always talk to parents before talking to the child. Remember, if you are not going to do anything about the destruction, parents may or may not be concerned. If you intend action, however, failing to call parents can have serious results.

8. Never ignore acts of destruction. Make sure destroyers know that you and other staff members are genuine in your concern. They must know that counselors, administrators, and parents have been informed.

9. At first, long lectures about why the student has been destructive accomplish very little. Instead, talk about what is happening. Then, present the student with a definite plan that includes restitution as well as short-term goals and school involvement. As you will note, talks about "why" are necessary — but come later.

10. Touch the hurt. Don't talk around the issue. Rather, talk about the fact that revenge because of failure to get attention and success in healthy ways lies at the core of the problem.

11. Look at both viewpoints. Always let the student tell you what his/her problem is.

12. Find a need and fill it: This student is hurting badly in some way.

13. Help this student find an activity which forces involvement in school. This can be the key to helping him/her turn unacceptable behavior into acceptable behavior. For instance, if the student has "torn up" a restroom, put him/her in charge of the restroom for a month or more.

14. Try to discover possible alternate causes for the behavior; the student may be seeking attention.

15. Once "what has been done" is determined, discuss *"why"* with the student. Once determined, "what has been done" is obvious.

16. Give the student recognition for each positive "thought" or solution. Don't turn off to

anything he/she has to say about the situation. Rather, get the student to *say* what should be done.

17. Allow the student to restore what has been destroyed. This is the most appropriate behavior adjustment and should be prescribed with parents' consent.

18. Arrange for this student to experience a relationship of trust with one member of the faculty. The buddy system works well. Above all, the student must have "someone" and must not be abandoned by all after such incidents. If you can't find the good in this student at this time, you have nothing to build upon.

19. Search for some school activity in which this student would enjoy involvement.

20. Emphasize to this student that his/her behavior, not you, determines what action becomes necessary. This is vitally important. Don't say, "I am going to punish you." Rather, say, "You have told us to do something. Your behavior tells us what we have to do." This strategic action keeps the focus on his/her behavior — not teacher or administrator action.

21. Remember that school is not a friend to this student. Try to make it one.

22. Try to cultivate a sense of pride in his/her school. This can only be done by giving this student a sense of ownership. At this point, most of the problem exists because the student feels that it is not "my" school — but "their" school.

23. Refer the student for professional counseling, if necessary.

24. Remember, to change the behavior, you want to avoid doing anything which would allow this student or his/her parents to get on the *offensive* or *defensive*. The problem is obvious, and the student has been neutralized by being caught. Keep him/her in neutral, and the problem is much, much easier to handle. In fact, you may make a grateful friend who is very willing to listen to you and eager for your help.

IV. MISTAKES: Common misjudgments and errors in managing the child which may perpetuate or intensify the problem.

1. Ignoring the situation.

2. Concealing the problem from colleagues and administrators.

3. Losing composure and revealing frustration and anger publicly.

4. Acting as if the student "did this thing to us" or "against us."

5. Establishing rules that are too strict, too numerous, or not enforceable, in an attempt to stop the behavior.

6. Becoming prejudiced against certain kids or particular classes.

7. Accusing a suspect openly and publicly.

8. Trying to get this student out of our class permanently.

9. Unleashing dislike, disdain, and hate.

10. Believing we can't help or change the behavior.

11. Piling on schoolwork in an attempt to punish.

12. Dwelling on what he/she has done and continuously reminding the student that we will never forget his/her behavior.

13. Having high expectations of his/her academic achievement and failing to understand that personal behavior must be worked through before any effort will be made to accomplish schoolwork.

14. Failing to see this behavior as a cry for help.

SEE ALSO: • The Disorganized   • The Irresponsible

THE DISORGANIZED

I. BEHAVIOR: Specific attitudes and actions of this child at home and/or at school.

1. Disorganized in terms of schoolwork, materials, schedules, desk, locker, and literally his/her entire life.
2. Doesn't have books in class.
3. Can't find papers.
4. Can't remember appointments.
5. May hold a job outside school and give the job higher priority than school.
6. Just doesn't seem to have a motivation for order.
7. Attention span is very short. Thinking is "scattered."
8. Disorganization makes schoolwork and homework much harder than it need be.
9. Easily distracted by anything that goes on in class. Really wants to be distracted because he/she is not prepared for class.
10. Seldom completes an assigned task as instructed.
11. Makes all kinds of excuses which involve others and blame them for his/her disorder.
12. Paradoxically, constantly keeps track of the teacher and class.
13. Takes a long time to get back on track, and then has no time left to do anything really productive.
14. Wastes considerable time and effort.
15. Because of disorganization, is constantly in motion — physically and mentally. And even this motion is disorganized.

II. EFFECTS: How behavior affects teachers, classmates, and parents in the school learning environment and the home family situation.

1. Teacher is constantly irritated because this student just can't get into the swing of things.
2. Classroom commotion results, but not discipline problems per se.
3. Time is wasted.
4. Constant help and concessions are required because of his/her disorganization.
5. During discussions, teacher may be distracted and lose train of thought.
6. Teacher may lose patience and develop a sense of helplessness as far as helping the student get organized is concerned.
7. Learning process is seriously disrupted by this student's disorganization.
8. Teacher's attitude toward the whole class may be affected.
9. Classmates may start to model the behavior of the disorganized student.

III. ACTION:
- **Identify causes of misbehavior.**
- **Pinpoint student needs being revealed.**

> ● **Employ specific methods, procedures, and techniques at school and at home for getting the child to modify or change his/her behavior.**

1. Primary cause of misbehavior:

   ◗ Self-Confidence: Being disorganized covers up this student's feeling of inability to do the work. Being disorganized is his/her crutch for future failures.

2. Primary needs being revealed:

   ◗ Hunger, Thirst, Rest: This student may be disorganized because of his/her need for nutrition and/or rest.

   ◗ Escape from Pain: This student may feel that his/her academic ability is inadequate, and it's much easier to be disorganized.

   ◗ Elimination of Waste: This person may be afraid to ask to go to the restroom because he/she has asked so often. This student never gets around to going during class breaks.

3. Secondary needs being revealed:

   ◗ Achievement: This student needs to achieve in some area, and needs to experience several little successes quickly.

   ◗ Autonomy: This person must develop pride in being in control of him/herself.

4. Help this student organize priorities. This strategic action is a must. He/she cannot get organized alone. Make out a daily or weekly calendar or chart and list clearly and simply for the student everything that has to be done and when.

5. Help the student organize his/her subject matter and materials; help him/her learn where to begin. Outline the specific steps to be taken before beginning an assignment, recommend materials to be used, and then tell the student specifically how to begin the task. Your personal touch with the student will help reduce classroom disruptions when beginning assignments.

6. Show positive reinforcement for any results achieved. Show how disorganization can affect his/her class work and the class work of fellow students.

7. Simplify requirements, steps in completing assignments, etc., for this student.

8. Create a strong one-to-one relationship with this student as much as possible. Visit with him/her frequently and create a more personal relationship. Doing so will help you gain the student's respect and create a situation in which he/she will want to follow your leadership.

9. Ask the student frequently to evaluate his/her own progress. Also ask the student how he/she feels about progress or lack of it.

10. Assign one task at a time. Don't overassign material, because his/her first task is to resolve his/her need for disorganization — not to show achievement. Once the disorganization is resolved, the student will be able to do more work and progress more rapidly.

11. Always ask for parental assistance. Unfortunately, you may see that there is no organization at home. If so, you will realize that *you* must be the primary helper if change is to be successful.

12. Meet with all teachers — and make a concentrated effort to work together. However, *don't* "get on" this student. It will only make him/her anxious — and make the behavior worse.

IV. MISTAKES: Common misjudgments and errors in managing the child which may perpetuate or intensify the problem.

1. Giving in and allowing an unstructured classroom situation to exist and thrive.

2. Making unrealistic demands upon this student.

3. Being extremely rigid and inflexible about work demands and assignments.

4. Issuing unclear instructions about assignments.

5. Putting too much pressure on the student.

6. Lecturing the student and confronting him/her harshly, rather than trying to set a positive example and helping the student recognize what he/she is really doing — and how such behavior is working against him/her.

7. Constantly trying to get the student to do things that he/she isn't really prepared to do; such efforts only reinforce the behavior.

8. Giving too much attention to the problem.

9. Prejudging, and failing to handle the situation privately.

SEE ALSO: • The Distracter   • The Forgetter   • The Noncompleter with Grand Plans

THE DISRESPECTFUL

I. BEHAVIOR: **Specific attitudes and actions of this child at home and/or at school.**

1. Reveals disrespect in the classroom in many ways: a pointed look, a sigh, a sneer, or a look of clear disdain.

2. Also reveals disrespect by what he/she *doesn't* do — usually through lack of common courtesy.

3. May act as if some people don't even exist.

4. May reveal disrespect in the form of ugly words.

5. Doesn't think very highly of anyone, including him/herself, even though he/she may act superior.

6. Often seems to be expressing frustration.

7. May have real problems at home or with friends.

8. May have basic primary needs which aren't being met. Appears unable to meet needs in a positive manner. Therefore, turns to disrespect out of frustration, anger, or hostility.

II. EFFECTS: **How behavior affects teachers, classmates, and parents in the school learning environment and the home family situation.**

1. Teacher may find that disrespect "gets to" him/her in a way that nothing else can, and that it takes a damaging toll. He/she may be unable to respond in any way except by being disrespectful in return.

2. Teacher may feel helpless or insignificant.

3. Worse, teacher may become hateful.

4. Teacher may even become disrespectful toward other teachers — and especially toward administrators for not "taking care of" disrespectful students quickly and harshly.

5. Peers who experience disrespect from a classmate have similar feelings. That's why the disrespectful student brings discord into the classroom.

III. ACTION:
- **Identify causes of misbehavior.**
- **Pinpoint student needs being revealed.**
- **Employ specific methods, procedures, and techniques at school and at home for getting the child to modify or change his/her behavior.**

1. Primary cause of misbehavior:

   ◆ Revenge: This student has been mistreated and therefore is mistreating others.

2. Primary needs being revealed:

   ◆ Escape from Pain: He/she is feeling a great deal of pain caused by peers, family, or educators.

   ◆ Sex: There may be a great deal of conflict between the adults in the home.

3. Secondary needs being revealed:

   ◆ Power: This student, because of his/her hurt, is hurting others as a form of power. The power is usually a demonstration against adults.

◆ Status: Because of the treatment received, the student — through disrespect — lets everyone know he/she is somebody.

4. Always remember that disrespect is never given without reason. The reason may or may not have to do with the teacher. Yet, student disrespect will never be resolved unless we realize this fact — and do something about it.

5. Adopt the strategic position of acting in a positive rather than a negative way. Don't try to fight fire with fire. The behavior of this student can't be changed with such an approach.

6. Be aware that, more often than not, the teacher is not the cause of disrespect. It's an indicator that a child has problems, is experiencing failure, has been hurt, or has been indulged too often by adults. However, a close look will reveal that disrespect is often a result of a circumstance which could be altered rather than a permanent condition. It's an instant response which the student might withdraw immediately if so allowed.

7. Try responding to the offender with "What's wrong? Did I do something to offend? If I did, I'm sorry." This can set the stage to resolve rather than fuel the situation.

8. Keep the responsibility on the student. This is an important aspect of handling the disrespectful student. Retaliating only lets him/her off the hook.

9. A public confrontation may put the student on the spot and compel him/her to act even worse to save face or retain his/her image as one who "doesn't get pushed around by anyone." Whenever you can, move to the hall or a private place in the room to handle disrespect.

10. Remember, an unprofessional reaction always reinforces negative behavior in this student. Approach disrespect as you approach other student misbehavior — professionally. Although it's normal to be offended by disrespect, returning it only proves to the disrespectful student that he/she is right and justified in the behavior. It convinces the student that the teacher does not deserve respect. That's why a private one-on-one meeting always has a better chance of success and of achieving honest communication — and a student apology. In addition, classmates will not support disrespect from another student directed at the teacher when the teacher responds respectfully to the disrespectful student.

11. Be calm, poised, and perceptive when disrespect is shown. Most disrespectful outbursts are the result of quick, unthinking, and emotional responses. They would never have been made with forethought. By remembering this reality, you'll never prolong a student's quick outburst. Rather, you'll shorten it.

12. If you believe that the disrespectful remark was completely unwarranted, say so. Simply say, "Jim — I don't think I deserve that." Follow this remark with "Now . . . tell me what's really on your mind." This is confronting in a professional and caring way. This response will produce more instant student apologies and resolve more ugly incidents than you might think.

13. Remember, disrespect is often a result of hostility and revenge. Give the student nothing more to be hostile toward, and he/she will usually cooperate.

14. Don't jump on disrespect too quickly and harshly. Doing so can turn a cornered kitten into an ugly tiger. If your reaction is negative or retaliatory, you may receive further disrespect. So be careful not to let your initial response be defensive, indignant, or attacking.

15. Don't engage in sarcastic comments, put-downs, ridicule, or barbed teasing with students, or you will probably hear similar statements made to you — openly or behind your back. There is much truth in the old cliche: Example is the best teacher. The behavior you display toward students will be mirrored. You can count on it. Remember, misbehavior can originate from both sides of the desk.

IV. MISTAKES: Common misjudgments and errors in managing the child which may perpetuate or intensify the problem.

1. Getting mad and responding accordingly. As much as we would like to understand and respond in professional ways, we may find it difficult and may react in a negative way.

2. Giving the student something to react to.

3. Reacting publicly.

4. Issuing ultimatums.

5. Failing to teach acceptable behavior.

6. Failing to show feelings of kindness.

7. Fighting for power or dominance in an attempt to change behavior.

8. Saying and doing things that we normally wouldn't.

9. Believing administrators don't respect us, or they wouldn't allow children to inflict such punishment on us. If we believe this, we may be expecting administrators to act beyond the realm of their authority.

SEE ALSO: • The Foulmouth   • "I Won't Do It"   • The Interrupter   • The Lewd
• The Loudmouth   • The Smart Aleck

THE DISRUPTER

I. BEHAVIOR: **Specific attitudes and actions of this child at home and/or at school.**

1. Disturbs teachers and students alike.
2. Always seems to want to do the opposite of what teacher suggests.
3. Gives silly, foolish, and absurd answers purposely.
4. Drops books, laughs, sighs, or makes strange noises.
5. Calls out to classmates when others are talking.
6. Changes the subject.
7. Shoots holes in every suggestion.
8. Finds fault with rules and regulations.
9. Wants to have long talks in class regarding his/her opinions.
10. Always claims he/she doesn't understand what's happening.
11. Acts hurt if reprimanded.
12. May be openly hostile or stay on the borderline of getting into trouble.
13. Usually does not achieve as well as he/she should.

II. EFFECTS: **How behavior affects teachers, classmates, and parents in the school learning environment and the home family situation.**

1. Undue attention is demanded by this behavior.
2. Classmates and teacher are very annoyed by the behavior.
3. This behavior is time consuming.
4. Attention is diverted from class discussions and class presentations.
5. A bad example is set for classmates.
6. Students who are not doing well academically are easily distracted by the disrupter's antics.

III. ACTION: • **Identify causes of misbehavior.**
• **Pinpoint student needs being revealed.**
• **Employ specific methods, procedures, and techniques at school and at home for getting the child to modify or change his/her behavior.**

1. Primary cause of misbehavior:
   ◗ Attention: This student finds many ways to get attention.
2. Primary needs being revealed:
   ◗ Escape from Pain: This person is avoiding the confrontation of pain in his/her life by being disruptive.
   ◗ Sex: This student may be seeking the attention of his/her peers and trying to establish a relationship.

3. Secondary needs being revealed:

   ▶ Achievement: It is possible for this student to find a place in the class through improved achievement.

   ▶ Gregariousness: The need to belong to a group is most important.

   ▶ Status: The disrupter needs to improve his/her feeling of self-worth in order to discontinue the negative behavior.

4. First, recognize that the disrupter has two needs which aren't being met: attention and success. This student yearns for both. In fact, he/she *hurts* for both. This student may have brothers and sisters with whom he/she finds it difficult to compete in positive ways — often because the student doesn't think he/she can.

5. Don't respond to this student's inappropriate and immature behavior with rejection. Rather, give him/her responsibilities which will offer direct involvement with you.

6. Initiate a conference daily.

7. Always investigate his/her background — and see parents as soon as problems begin.

8. Don't wait until this student's behavior has reached crisis proportions before you act.

9. Above all, never forget that it's important that you and the student agree on the exact behavior that needs adjusting. It must be clear exactly what behavior is disturbing — and to whom.

10. Too, know that this student may be struggling to attract students of the opposite sex — and doing so in a negative way.

11. Recognize that the disruptive student has not been able to meet his/her needs in a positive manner. The negative behavior is an attempt to fill his/her needs for status, gregariousness, and achievement. Therefore, provide positive experiences that might meet these needs, and you'll stop the behavior.

12. Be aware of these common causes of disruptive behavior and make sure your response matches the stimulus: First, feelings of inadequacy lead to overreaction. Second, feelings of anger lead to bullying. Third, feelings of conceit lead to show-off behavior. Listening and open communication are the best ways to begin helping this student. For best results, make sure you respond to the student's underlying feelings. Remember, it's the inappropriate teacher response that usually blocks communication — and fires rather than resolves conflicts.

13. Convince this student with the "Citizenship" technique. Remember, disagreeing with your rules does not make a student wrong, bad or insubordinate. However, when good citizens disagree with a rule, they don't defy it. They simply try — and maybe even keep trying — to get it changed. This is what the disrupter needs to be taught about class rules.

14. Never teach that your rules are perfect and must be accepted without question. Such a stance will not stop the disrupter's behavior, but rather will force the student to fight the teacher rather than fight to get rules changed.

15. Say to this student, "Without law there can be no freedom. The strong will dominate and control the weak unless there are rules to protect everybody from such chaos. Therefore, we must not look at rules as punishment. Rather, rules provide a structure that gives safety and freedom to every student, including you."

16. If a student speaks out abruptly or causes a quick disturbance, be careful about using a sarcastic retort or "jumping down his/her throat." Often, it's more effective to use calm to regain calm. Simply pause; then after a moment say, "I'm glad that's over and done with." This technique gives the student a chance to view his/her behavior objectively, regain composure, and continue appropriately.

17. Whenever possible, allow this student a choice — even if it's over minor points on how to do

an assignment or a choice between two assignments. Also, don't demand that he/she do things in a certain order. Rather, allow a procedural choice. You'll find the student's frustration level will decrease if you do.

18. Often, these students won't talk. As a result, you may have emotions which range from doubting your fairness to frustration. Try this technique for getting the student to speak. Ask for advice rather than information — and the student may loosen up. Tight-lipped disruptive kids withhold information until they see an advantage in giving in. Therefore, beginning with "What would you like to do about this?" will often get interaction rather than silence.

19. One of the best preventive discipline techniques for the disrupter relates to the placement of desks in a classroom. The arrangement of your desk relative to students' desks is important. Make sure all students can get to your desk easily. Don't create a physical situation in which the disrupter can bother everyone in the row on the way to your desk. He/she may hit, bump, poke, and irritate others all the way to your desk — and watch you continuously so as not to get caught. Fortunately, desk arrangement can curtail this problem.

20. Never reject an entire class because of the actions of the disrupter. If you do, you're in for trouble. Whenever a class thinks that you don't like them, the student-teacher relationship may be impaired to the point that you can't be effective. Don't indicate that the class as a whole doesn't have your confidence just because the disrupter hasn't earned it. You can never punish a class for the actions of a few.

21. The disrupter often feels he/she can't succeed in school — and for good reason. This student has failed in the past. Unfortunately, teachers have *told* this student he/she wasn't smart or didn't measure up. Never make this mistake if you want to be positioned to handle the disrupter. With the promise of your help and his/her effort, this student must be able to both anticipate and experience success — or he/she will fight. That's because most of these students honestly feel that they can't do schoolwork successfully alone — they need the help of their teachers.

22. Misbehavior can be the direct result of academic frustrations and failure. A student may demonstrate this frustration by swearing, crumpling papers in a ball, or slamming books shut when working on a difficult assignment. Assist this student; don't reprimand. Once the disrupter understands the task and is able to work toward its completion, self-discipline will return. The disrupter may demonstrate this behavior frequently — and need help frequently.

IV. MISTAKES: Common misjudgments and errors in managing the child which may perpetuate or intensify the problem.

1. Making threats in anger and exasperation that can't be carried out.
2. Disallowing any explanation the student may have for his/her disruptive behavior.
3. Sending him/her to the office continually.
4. Ignoring the disrupter.
5. Giving him/her negative attention.
6. Trying to combat the disrupter by disrupting his/her life in school.

SEE ALSO: • The Angry • The Authority Pusher • The Defier • The Disrespectful
• The Forgetter • "I Won't Do It" • The Interrupter
• The Last Worder • The Noisemaker • The Petty Rules Breaker
• The Smart Aleck • The Smartmouth

THE DISTRACTER

I. BEHAVIOR: Specific attitudes and actions of this child at home and/or at school.

1. Talks at inappropriate times, and gets others to join in the conversation.
2. Asks questions which are not related to the subject matter.
3. Interrupts during directions.
4. Easily distracted and may play with objects.
5. Has a short attention span.
6. Often relates better to younger students because he/she is not accepted by peers.
7. Seldom totally absorbed in the lesson.
8. Watches others more than he/she participates with others.
9. Behavior is mainly annoying. Seems to be more a social problem than a discipline problem.

II. EFFECTS: How behavior affects teachers, classmates, and parents in the school learning environment and the home family situation.

1. Instruction is impeded; learning is interrupted.
2. Teacher is always aware of the distracter's presence; this student demands individual attention continuously.
3. Both teacher and classmates are annoyed by the behavior.
4. Classroom tension can be created when efforts to get this student involved fail.

III. ACTION: • Identify causes of misbehavior.
• Pinpoint student needs being revealed.
• Employ specific methods, procedures, and techniques at school and at home for getting the child to modify or change his/her behavior.

1. Primary cause of misbehavior:
   ◗ Attention: This student is trying to gain attention through all possible channels.
2. Primary needs being revealed:
   ◗ Rest: This student might find school so difficult that he/she has to take frequent breaks from tasks.
   ◗ Escape from Pain: This student avoids the thought of failure by being a distracter.
3. Secondary needs being revealed:
   ◗ Achievement: Little successes may help reduce the distracting behavior.
   ◗ Status: The need to belong and to get attention arises from the need for status. Remember, the continuous interruptions say, "Look at me, I'm somebody."
   ◗ Power: Causing distraction is a form of power; this student's effort needs to be positively directed.
4. Get this student involved in class by giving him/her physical tasks or routine class responsibilities.

5. Give the student assignments suitable to his/her attention span; gradually increase the amount of work involved in each assignment.

6. Contract with the student for behavior required for him/her to remain in class, and offer rewards for appropriate behavior. For example, a contract might be made that the student move about or take a break after a certain amount of work is completed. This break can be a routine classroom task, such as straightening books.

7. Initiate personal conferences in order to clarify appropriate behavior. The student must be told why this behavior is important for all involved.

8. Talk with nurse or counselor about requesting that parents get the child a medical check-up. The short attention span and inability to concentrate could be the result of a physical problem.

9. When working with the parents, make sure you can document the specific behavior that causes your concern.

10. When giving instructions, stand in the distracter's area of the room and make eye contact with him/her from time to time. Use this student's work as an example. This strategic action gets him/her started automatically.

11. Use a timer when students are completing assignments. You'll find the distracter often likes "competing" against a clock.

12. Look at the distracter continuously. Call him/her to your desk periodically to check progress. The point is that he/she cannot be left unattended. Too, this student functions better with attention.

13. Discipline problems usually arise when a teacher's attention must be diverted from the lesson and/or the class. Therefore, during study or work time, the physical positioning of a teacher is important. Whether helping students individually or performing other duties during study times, station yourself in a position where students think that your attention is still on the entire class. A table for assisting students in the rear of the room during these times can be advantageous.

IV. MISTAKES: Common misjudgments and errors in managing the child which may perpetuate or intensify the problem.

1. Allowing the distracter to affect us personally rather than keeping our professional objectivity.

2. Failing to take immediate action when these problems begin to arise.

3. Calling attention to this behavior or confronting it too often publicly.

4. Explosively overreacting, losing classroom control.

5. Failing to give the distracter positive reinforcement for appropriate behavior.

6. Feeling that nothing can be done to help this student.

7. Depriving him/her of activities.

8. Fighting his/her need rather than trying to meet it.

SEE ALSO: • The Attention Demander • The Forgetter • The Fun Seeker • The Hider • The Late Arriver • The Noisemaker • The Test Challenger • The Troublemaker

THE DO-NOTHING

I. BEHAVIOR: **Specific attitudes and actions of this child at home and/or at school.**

1. Probably a high-IQ student, but a poor achiever.
2. Draws, daydreams, and walks around during class; is poorly organized.
3. Usually keeps a messy desk.
4. Socially, is a loner.
5. Would rather read or draw than complete work.
6. Never does what teacher wants him/her to do.
7. Fails to bring supplies to class.
8. Has a very limited attention span.

II. EFFECTS: **How behavior affects teachers, classmates, and parents in the school learning environment and the home family situation.**

1. Teacher feels that he/she is failing because of constant do-nothing response from this student.
2. Teacher is put under a great deal of pressure.
3. Other students try to get by without finishing assignments.
4. Teacher is forced to restructure the program of class work that has been set up.
5. Whole class is slowed down.
6. Special attention will be required for this student if any motivation is ultimately to occur.
7. Classmates feel resentful because they feel the do-nothing student is getting away with a lot.

III. ACTION: • **Identify causes of misbehavior.**
• **Pinpoint student needs being revealed.**
• **Employ specific methods, procedures, and techniques at school and at home for getting the child to modify or change his/her behavior.**

1. Primary cause of misbehavior:
   ‣ Self-Confidence: This student, for some reason, does not deal very well with him/herself. Then, he/she gets deeper and deeper in trouble because of the choice to do nothing.
2. Primary need being revealed:
   ‣ Escape from Pain: This student may be getting so much pressure from parents or dominating peers that he/she feels completely unable to measure up to expectations. The pain of "I can't be what they want me to be" leads to lowered expectations on the student's part and do-nothing behavior.
3. Secondary needs being revealed:
   ‣ Aggression: This student needs to learn to assert him/herself and find out what he/she really can do.
   ‣ Inquisitiveness: The student needs to experience the excitement of a good learning situation.

▶ Achievement: The student needs to be involved somehow and to feel success in classroom activities.

4. Seek help from support staff immediately.

5. Call parents for a conference. If this conference effects no change, call a second conference with support staff, parents, and child. This helps the child to see the efforts adults are making on his/her behalf.

6. Create a verbal or written agreement with this student to help create a stepping-stone to real progress and self-motivation.

7. Organize the school day for this student so that he/she can work on one thing at a time clearly and directly. This may mean a cooperative effort with other teachers.

8. Give this student as much positive reinforcement as possible.

9. Find the student's personal interests and use them as a catalyst to create self-motivation.

10. Talk to the student alone frequently. Check the progress of work continuously. Remember, he/she may have had pressure in the past "up to a point" — and may believe a teacher will give up and quit in a short period of time.

11. Formulate realistic goals with the student — goals which can be accomplished. However, he/she must help establish any goal.

12. If you feel it is in order, talk with nurse or counselor about a physical examination for this student.

13. Remember, the feeling of being a do-nothing is very real to this student. Don't tell the student, "I know you can do it." You must deal honestly with what he/she is feeling.

IV. MISTAKES: Common misjudgments and errors in managing the child which may perpetuate or intensify the problem.

1. Taking the behavior of the do-nothing student personally, and allowing personality clashes to occur.

2. Refusing to investigate new avenues of learning the material which would be more exciting and challenging to this student.

3. Failing to realize that this student simply is not aware of what is expected of him/her.

4. Constantly nagging, and inadvertently reinforcing do-nothing behavior.

5. Making a public issue out of this student's behavior — especially in front of the class.

6. Assuming that the student is unable to do classroom tasks.

SEE ALSO: • The Dreamer • The Goer • The Goldbrick

THE DREAMER

I. BEHAVIOR: Specific attitudes and actions of this child at home and/or at school.

1. Actions vary, but result of behavior is always the same. Usually quiet, probably an underachiever, and mentally "a million miles away" from what is happening in the classroom.

2. Sometimes just sits and looks out the window.

3. May draw, doodle, or engage in some other type of diverted, individual activity.

4. Or may appear scholarly — or try to give a serious and scholarly appearance.

5. Often carries a briefcase. Takes out his/her work, opens a book, and appears to be diligently involved in an assignment — but is not.

6. Does not really participate in class discussion. May ask a question but is not thinking about the subject the class is discussing.

7. Usually, not doing what rest of class is doing.

8. Fails to turn in daily papers or assignments.

9. Often asks for help with work that has been finished by the rest of the class long ago.

10. Seldom, if ever, volunteers to do anything in the classroom.

11. However, attendance is often regular.

12. Does not appear to realize or fear the consequences of his/her behavior.

II. EFFECTS: How behavior affects teachers, classmates, and parents in the school learning environment and the home family situation.

1. Teacher finds the need to constantly prod this student annoying.

2. Teacher must teach every lesson twice — once to the class, and again to the dreamer.

3. Teacher worries about possibility of student failing or having "a bigger problem."

4. Other students tease the dreamer.

5. Group does not accept this student; he/she doesn't "fit in."

6. Teacher may even become unaware of this student's presence because he/she is so quiet. Often, because the dreamer is not a discipline problem, teacher forgets about — or ignores — him/her.

7. Including this student in the class is not easy.

III. ACTION:
- **Identify causes of misbehavior.**
- **Pinpoint student needs being revealed.**
- **Employ specific methods, procedures, and techniques at school and at home for getting the child to modify or change his/her behavior.**

1. Primary cause of misbehavior:

   ▶ Self-Confidence: This student's self-esteem may be so low that he/she escapes to a dream world.

2. Primary needs being revealed:

   ▶ Hunger, Thirst: This student may not get the proper nutrition.

- Sex: This student may be feeling that he/she is responsible for a problem in the family.

- Rest: He/she may not be getting enough rest.

- Escape from Pain: The student's world may be so painful that he/she has become a dreamer.

3. Secondary needs being revealed:

   - Affiliation: This student needs to develop a close friendship and thus make the real world important again.

   - Achievement: Recognition for *something* may be important to change the person's behavior.

   - Power, Status: This student needs to know that he/she counts and is "somebody."

4. Remember that this student *expects* failure and is using inability or assumed inability to escape participation. He/she may have stopped trying because of repeated failure — discouragement has made the dream world happier than the real world.

5. It's easy for a teacher to err with the dreamer. Avoid continuous prodding to pay attention, get to work, and hand in assignments. Such prodding can often have a negative effect.

6. Don't tease or pick on the dreamer because he/she wastes time and does not participate in class work. Teachers have been known to be guilty of this, because this student is "different" or may be a "loner."

7. On the other hand, if the dreamer is discreet in his/her dreaming, don't allow him/her to pass from dream to dream and class to class without detection or without receiving special help.

8. Proceed on a one-to-one basis with this student. If you do, the dreamer presents an excellent opportunity for success.

9. Schedule a conference with parents. Explain that you'd like to work with this student after school, during conference period, or during study time, on a regular basis.

10. Try making special lesson plans for this student, and remember to make all goals for the dreamer short term.

11. Never force involvement with other kids upon this student.

12. Make it your major goal to get the dreamer simply to try — and then reward him/her quietly and privately for his/her effort and success.

13. Too many times this student does try — and fails; however, we aren't aware of his/her efforts. Have patience and never be discouraged when working with the dreamer. Remember that discouragement and failure are primary factors making this student happier in his/her dream world than in the real world.

14. Remember that the classroom is not a place where this student feels psychologically safe to participate. We feel this student *is* capable . . . and he/she is. We also feel the student is copping out . . . and he/she is. But there's a reason.

15. Include parents for assistance.

16. Use the *"What Is More Important Than Why"* strategic action. Ask, "What are you doing?" and wait for an answer. Then ask, "What can you do about it?" and wait for an answer. The student, not you, must initiate action and goals. Asking "why" is a major mistake. The student doesn't know "why" he/she is a dreamer.

17. Contract . . . in writing . . . for short-term goals with prestated rewards.

18. Do not use threats. They will make the student retreat.

19. Seek administrative assistance when necessary. Do not pass this student on to another grade if his/her academic work doesn't warrant it.

20. Arrange for this student to do things physically in the classroom. Do not let him/her sit. Make it a point to interrupt his/her "sitting time."

21. Direct a simple question or two toward the dreamer. This will snap the spell and bring him/her back to reality. Too, saying his/her name in the course of a sentence will gain attention.

22. If the daydreaming is excessive and you can't stop it, talk to a counselor or administrator.

IV. MISTAKES: Common misjudgments or errors in managing the child which may perpetuate or intensify the problem.

1. Taking the behavior personally and reacting personally rather than professionally.

2. Continuously prodding this student to pay attention, get work done, wake up, and hand in assignments.

3. Promoting him/her in the same condition to another teacher.

4. Allowing this student to pass from dream to dream, class to class, year to year, without intervention or help.

5. Permitting him/her to fail without teacher resistance.

6. Picking on or teasing the student because of wasted time and failure to participate.

7. Classifying him/her as "different" . . . or as a "loner."

8. Trying to force involvement upon this student.

9. Ignoring the behavior . . . or getting angry.

10. Rejecting him/her.

11. Lowering expectations for this student.

12. Giving up on attempts to help him/her.

13. Embarrassing him/her.

14. Making fun of the student in the presence of classmates.

15. Using class work as a punishment.

SEE ALSO: • The Do-Nothing   • The Shy

THE EXAGGERATOR

I. BEHAVIOR: **Specific attitudes and actions of this child at home and/or at school.**

1. Not a child we dislike — just one we don't always totally believe or trust.
2. What this student says is true — partially. But he/she makes every detail bigger, and adds something to every incident or story.
3. Often, his/her behavior leans more toward the flamboyant than a lie.
4. Credibility may be questioned in every situation unless he/she receives teacher help.
5. Wants attention.
6. Exaggerates to appear important or to make small events important. This is a vital clue in helping this student change behavior.
7. Has strong need to relate to and be accepted by others.

II. EFFECTS: **How behavior affects teachers, classmates, and parents in the school learning environment and the home family situation.**

1. Others do not take the exaggerator seriously.
2. People do not believe anything he/she says.
3. Other students often begin fabricating stories too.
4. Teacher can come to feel that everything is getting "out of control" because he/she isn't sure what is true and what is not.
5. People avoid the exaggerator.

III. ACTION:
- **Identify causes of misbehavior.**
- **Pinpoint student needs being revealed.**
- **Employ specific methods, procedures, and techniques at school and at home for getting the child to modify or change his/her behavior.**

1. Primary cause of misbehavior:
   - Attention, Self-Confidence: This student is afraid of being unacceptable as he/she is, and so "adds to" stories.
2. Primary needs being revealed:
   - Hunger, Thirst, Rest: A student whose basic needs are not being met at home may exaggerate the condition in order to have those needs met.
   - Escape from Pain: Inability to measure up to self-imposed expectations may also create an exaggerator.
3. Secondary needs being revealed:
   - Gregariousness: The student exaggerates him/herself to be important and to be accepted by peers or adults.
   - Achievement: A series of successes will limit the need to exaggerate in front of peers or adults.
   - Status: A feeling of worth will reduce the need to exaggerate stories or build him/herself up to others.

4. This behavior is easy to identify, analyze, and treat, but beware of the danger of taking action opposite from what is needed.

5. Confront this behavior considerately. By doing so, you can influence the exaggerator in a positive and constructive way very quickly.

6. The minute this student starts exaggerating, stop the student in his/her tracks. Winking, raising the eyebrows, smiling, or saying his/her name with the hint of a question mark after it will make the student stop or at least think.

7. If the student reacts to your doubts by saying, "It's really true, honest," simply take over the conversation by changing the subject or telling what you know about the situation. Don't let the student keep talking when he/she is exaggerating.

8. Privately — and at another time — talk to the student seriously and with concerned care regarding the reasons people exaggerate.

9. Don't reject this student personally. It won't be long before simply saying the student's name will make him/her check the behavior.

10. Remember, this student has a strong need for attention. If you ignore the exaggerator, he/she will tell bigger stories.

11. Always question the exaggerator about specifics first. No matter how clear-cut an issue is, ask before you leap. And remember, nobody likes a lecture. Few will accept one, until they've had a chance to say their piece — especially those who are overtly trying to be important. And if you don't have all the facts correct, a student will almost always think you are totally wrong and he/she is right, regardless of the situation. You'll get a better response from the exaggerator if you start by asking specific questions rather than stating absolutes.

12. Never forget, the best way to show respect for a student is to be empathetic. The size of his/her concern is immaterial. If this student feels that you belittle his/her concerns, the behavior will get worse. As far as this student is concerned, "If you don't respect my problems, you don't respect me." Worse, the student may think, "Do I have to have a big problem before you'll listen? Well, if you don't help me, I'll have one."

13. Never say casually to a student, "That's not a big problem," or "You can work it out." Such answers may be regarded as demeaning or taken as abandonment. Too often, these are the band-aid statements teachers use to avoid children. Many times, unfortunately, students do not have the resources for working out problems. Remember, problems are opportunities to become partners with students. A teacher can blow the partnership with a single phrase.

IV. MISTAKES: Common misjudgments and errors in managing the child which may perpetuate or intensify the problem.

1. Failing to do anything until after the fact. Too often, we do this, and it's the biggest mistake we can make.

2. Letting the child tell the whole exaggerated story and dig him/herself into a big hole — then confronting the student about all he/she said.

3. Ignoring the exaggerator. Doing so will make him/her fabricate even more. The need for attention and importance will make the student tell bigger stories — maybe for the rest of his/her life.

4. Calling the student a liar.

5. Never believing anything he/she says.

6. Laughing at the student publicly.

7. Forgetting to recognize the student after he/she has made some adjustment in the behavior.

SEE ALSO: • The Blabbermouth   • The Gossip   • The Liar
   • The Noncompleter with Grand Plans

THE EXCUSE/ALIBI MAKER

I. BEHAVIOR: Specific attitudes and actions of this child at home and/or at school.

1. Always offers reasons for not doing what he/she was supposed to do.
2. Invariably forgets books and materials.
3. Repeatedly fails to complete assignments.
4. Can rationalize inability to meet standards very easily — and thinks he/she is right.
5. Expects concessions.
6. Always has an alibi.
7. Never sees him/herself as responsible; it is always everybody else who causes the problem: "I can't help it if Mom washed my homework in my jeans."

II. EFFECTS: How behavior affects teachers, classmates, and parents in the school learning environment and the home family situation.

1. Class time is wasted.
2. Teacher must constantly repeat directions or find materials to replace those that this student forgot.
3. Teacher is frustrated.
4. Teacher wonders if the time spent coping with the excuse/alibi maker is worth it.
5. Teacher may give up — and write this student off.
6. Teacher and classmates alike develop a negative attitude toward this student and come to expect continuous excuses from him/her.
7. Classmates begin to make fun of this student.
8. Classmates do not want to work with this student because of his/her inability to complete tasks.

III. ACTION: • **Identify causes of misbehavior.**
  • **Pinpoint student needs being revealed.**
  • **Employ specific methods, procedures, and techniques at school and at home for getting the child to modify or change his/her behavior.**

1. Primary cause of misbehavior:

   ▶ Self-Confidence: If the student felt good about him/herself, there would be no need to make excuses.

2. Primary needs being revealed:

   ▶ Primary needs should be checked very carefully because this student may be experiencing problems at home, such as not eating well, not getting enough rest, or poor family relationships. Any of these could be a cause for many of the excuses at school.

3. Secondary needs being revealed:

   ▶ Achievement: The feeling of being able to do something will reduce excuses/alibis.

▶ Power: When a person feels powerless, he/she may make a lot of excuses/alibis to justify the failures.

4. Remember, alibis are quite different from objections and complaints. If they are not treated differently, big problems can result. Mainly, students offering alibis have lost interest in the activity related to the alibi. Remember this fact when handling this student.

5. The alibi is expressed by such token offerings as "I was too busy," "I'm going to do it tomorrow," or "My mother lost my notes." A teacher must attempt to analyze the *cause* of the alibi — not the alibi itself. Therefore, ask yourself: "Can the student do the work? Is the assignment missing something in the eyes of the student? Would the student do something else better?" If so, it might be much better to alter or change the assignment than hold to a dead-end course. Remember, lack of interest is the primary reason behind most alibis.

6. Until you discover the reason behind the alibi, here are some techniques you can employ to get the behavior you need: Listen closely and respond fast. If a student says, "I lost my pencil," say, "Here's another." If a student says, "I can't find my book," reply, "Here's a loaner." If a student offers the alibi, "I lost my paper," respond quickly, "You can have more time." Then, ask to see the student later to find the real cause behind the alibi. When you do this, you are positioned to deal with the real problem.

7. Have a private conference with the excuse maker to try to find out what the real problem is — and why he/she chooses not to meet his/her obligations.

8. Always remind this student a second and third time when assignments are due.

9. When counseling, never use the words "excuse" or "alibi." Rather, always use the words "choice" or "choose." Say, "Why did you choose not to bring your book?" Then, the student is held accountable for his/her behavior.

10. Give the student continuous positive reinforcement for acceptable behavior.

11. If constant excuses and alibis continue, talk with parents quickly in a caring and serious way.

12. Ask for parental assistance, even if it means a telephone call regarding assignments.

13. Put this student in a position where he/she can successfully assume responsibility for his/her obligations.

14. Never forget, it's possible that excuse makers lack ability in certain situations.

15. The teacher's task is to supervise and improve behavior, not necessarily to punish. Therefore, the next time this problem arises evaluate the situation before you act. Sometimes a student needs to be left alone — and given the freedom to do some independent thinking regarding his/her behavior. Not reacting can be a good technique to improve this behavior — if you tell the student what you're doing as well as why. Remember, however, to communicate why you're responding in this manner.

16. Look for improvement in this student, but never expect the behavior to change immediately.

IV. MISTAKES: Common misjudgments and errors in managing the child which may perpetuate or intensify the problem.

1. Encouraging the student to offer excuses by constantly repeating directions and, consequently, implying acceptability of the behavior.

2. Giving attention only when he/she has an excuse or alibi.

3. Talking to this student only when he/she has a problem.

4. Allowing this student to waste a lot of time by permitting trips to his/her locker for forgotten materials.

5. Arguing with the student in class.

6. Putting him/her down.

7. Showing disrespect.

8. Becoming hostile.

9. Treating this student as if he/she weren't part of the class.

10. Forgetting that there is no need to punish the excuse/alibi maker, as failure to produce work will be tough enough for him/her to handle.

SEE ALSO: • The Alibier • The Complainer • "I Can't" • The Objector
• The Questioner

THE EXPLODER

I. BEHAVIOR: Specific attitudes and actions of this child at home and/or at school.

1. Can lose control — completely — over a small incident.
2. Behaves unpredictably.
3. Can even "explode" while trying to do a difficult academic problem.
4. Reacts so severely that others believe the situation to be serious.
5. Almost impossible to approach when angry.
6. Afterward, may feel either justified or embarrassed.
7. Very much aware of his/her problem.
8. Probably has never received help — only punishment, rejection, or avoidance for his/her loss of control.

II. EFFECTS: How behavior affects teachers, classmates, and parents in the school learning environment and the home family situation.

1. Classmates are very much aware of the problem.
2. Peers usually feel extremely uncomfortable about this student's explosive behavior.
3. Teacher feels threatened, and may feel he/she can't control the situation.
4. Fear may dominate the classroom.
5. A crisis may be caused in the classroom.
6. Teacher worries that students — or even the teacher — could get hurt in trying to control this student.
7. Problem is hard to resolve because something very minor can cause an incident.
8. Some classmates may purposely cause this student to explode in order to disrupt the classroom.

III. ACTION:
- **Identify causes of misbehavior.**
- **Pinpoint student needs being revealed.**
- **Employ specific methods, procedures, and techniques at school and at home for getting the child to modify or change his/her behavior.**

1. Primary cause of misbehavior:
   - Self-Confidence: A feeling of inadequacy in classroom work can cause a student to become an exploder.
2. Primary needs being revealed:
   - Hunger, Thirst, Rest: Hunger, thirst, or inadequate rest can cause a great deal of internal anger and lead to disruptions.
   - Escape from Pain: Pain caused by underachievement can lead to frustration and loss of control.
   - Sex: The inability to establish or maintain meaningful relationships at school or at home can cause outbursts.

3. Secondary needs being revealed:

 ▶ Gregariousness: The need to belong to a group is very important to this student.

 ▶ Achievement: This student needs to accomplish a task with a minimum of frustration.

 ▶ Aggression: This student needs to be responsible for his/her behavior and act out frustrations in a positive way.

 ▶ Power: A positive expression of power is being able to be in control of oneself. This student needs help to be in control and needs to be rewarded when behavior is in control.

 ▶ Autonomy: The more the student demonstrates control, the more independent he/she will become.

4. First, discuss this student with your administrator. If possible, establish a predetermined course of action which can be initiated the next time signs of explosion appear.

5. If this student leaves your room in anger, don't run after him/her and demand a change in behavior or an apology. Taking such action only compounds a bad situation, and the teacher ends up looking vindictive or guilty to the class. Instead, calmly inform the office by note or by intercom and continue your class lesson as usual. Contact the student later and talk with him/her privately. The rest of the class will appreciate your minimizing rather than maximizing the situation.

6. Gently and tactfully remove this student from class — temporarily. Getting him/her out of the room until composure can be regained is best for all concerned.

7. Inform the student that this action will be taken — but that it is not a punishment. It is being done in his/her best interest. Counsel the student to look upon this strategic action as concerned help to save him/her and classmates further hurt or embarrassment. Explain gently that it's his/her behavior which necessitates this procedure.

8. Relate that you understand anger, but not his/her expression of the anger.

9. Tell this student that others get upset too, but they have learned to control their anger. He/she must do the same.

10. Remember, the student is not being *sent* to the office or counselor, but rather is being *allowed* to go. If approached in this manner, the student may be very receptive to help when he/she sees a counselor or administrator.

11. Encourage the student to seek help when he/she leaves the room.

12. When counseling, use the "Why" technique. This is the best strategic action to take because a close look will reveal that this student usually explodes when feeling "put down." The exploder is extremely sensitive — and has a low self-concept. That's why he/she says, "Nobody can talk to me like that," or "He put me down" — when such may not be the case. Asking "why" lets the student talk. It lets him/her say what's important. Letting the student decide helps the "status" need. Reprimand and punishment are simply more "put-downs."

13. Return the student to class as soon as he/she feels able to handle the situation.

14. Give no explanation to classmates when he/she returns.

15. Discuss the matter with parents.

16. Seek professional help if behavior persists.

17. As a professional teacher, never let yourself believe that it is the dark or bad side of people that is their "real" side. Usually, nothing could be further from the truth. It's an unmet personal need that brings out the bad side of people. The quick flare of temper and the negative outlook are simply defense mechanisms which cover those voids. Before commenting upon and judging a student's temperament, be sure you have focused objectively on his/her wants, needs and personality. Then you will see the need that is not being met — and can help rather than reinforce the negative side of a personality.

18. Too often, the blame for class disruptions is placed on students when the teacher is really at fault. Incomplete lesson planning, disorganization, and inconsistency are all teacher errors which lead to classroom problems. The next time "everything seems to be going wrong," take a look at yourself and what you aren't doing — and you may find a clue.

19. Over and over, assure the student that you accept and care about him/her, but do not accept the explosive behavior.

20. Always give this student room; do not crowd him/her. The emotional behavior will be reduced much more quickly if the student is given room.

21. Remember, you cannot reason with this student until the emotional state has been reduced. When he/she begins to appear calm you can begin to problem solve with him/her.

IV. MISTAKES: Common misjudgments and errors in managing the child which may perpetuate or intensify the problem.

1. Trying to use physical force to calm the explosive student. This makes the behavior worse.

2. Touching the student. *Never* touch this student during an outburst. Later, when the student has calmed down, hug him/her if appropriate.

3. Using strong verbal and emotional reactions to try to quell the situation.

4. Talking during the incident.

5. Blaming other classmates for this student's behavior.

6. Getting tough, when getting gentle would work better.

7. Shying away from this student.

SEE ALSO: •The Angry   • The Fighter   • "I Won't Do It"

THE FAILER

I. BEHAVIOR: Specific attitudes and actions of this child at home and/or at school.

1. Gets so far behind that he/she can't seem to catch up. Every class day seems to dig this student deeper into the hole of failure.

2. May fall into one of three distinct groups:

   - Has ability, but fights authority, and resents and resists school standards. Remember, people don't fight friends as readily as they do enemies. Students are no exception. If a student doesn't have any adult friends, it's easy to see why teachers might be regarded as the enemy. These students say to themselves, "If adults don't care about me, why should I adhere to their rules?"

   - Has ability, but just isn't interested. A close look will reveal that people who fail are often void of childhood dreams and goals. Unfortunately, some kids who are failing want nothing. As a result, they see no value in school for themselves.

   - Has limited ability, or has problems keeping up with the mainstream. This student has low academic aptitude, reading ability, or achievement level.

3. Likely to have a record of misbehavior.

4. May have moved from school to school or city to city.

5. May have friends who are out of school.

6. Associates with older children.

7. Likely to miss school frequently.

8. Not interested in extra-class activities, and seldom participates in student government, interest groups, music, or athletics.

9. May come from an unstable home. Parents may have little interest in the student, and he/she may receive little or no encouragement.

II. EFFECTS: How behavior affects teachers, classmates, and parents in the school learning environment and the home family situation.

1. More work is created for teacher.

2. Both teacher's and classmates' enthusiasm for class work is dampened.

3. Teacher can, after a while, become frustrated and feel that he/she is failing.

III. ACTION:
- **Identify causes of misbehavior.**
- **Pinpoint student needs being revealed.**
- **Employ specific methods, procedures, and techniques at school and at home for getting the child to modify or change his/her behavior.**

1. Primary causes of misbehavior:

   - Self-Confidence: The student's low self-esteem leads to many failures.

   - Power: Failure can be frustrating to teacher and parents and thus it becomes a negative form of power for the student.

2. Primary needs being revealed:

- Hunger, Thirst, Rest: A student deficient in these primary needs may lose interest in accomplishing school tasks.
- Escape from Pain: Inability to be recognized as a person and/or achiever in school is very painful.
- Sex: Relations in the home and/or school may be very poor and create lack of interest in school.

3. Secondary needs being revealed:
   - Affiliation: Establishing a close relationship with one teacher could be very helpful to the adjustment of this student's behavior.
   - Achievement: This student needs success — immediate success.
   - Status: Once this student is able to achieve short-term goals, he/she will gain status, thus becoming an achiever rather than a failer.
   - Gregariousness: This student needs to belong to the class and feel he/she is a part of the learning that goes on. To belong to the group is a real motivator.

4. When a student's behavior turns to misbehavior, or class performance falls rapidly, look for reasons. Don't jump to conclusions. The reasons for sudden changes vary — from a serious home problem to a fight with a friend. Approach the student with concern rather than an immediate bombardment of threats or accusations. No matter how trivial the problem appears, remember that it is significant to the student. It's important enough to cause a change in behavior or performance. If the problem is not treated seriously, the student is apt to think you "don't understand," and any suggestion you make is likely to fall on deaf ears.

5. Don't approach this student as someone who simply hasn't found him/herself yet. If you do, you may turn away rather than toward the student.

6. See that this student develops adult relationships which will help him/her with the process of self-discovery and developing interests. Otherwise, it's very unlikely that things will change for the student. Rather, he/she will search out peers without interests.

7. Don't make lesson plans and standards so rigid that compliance is the only way the student can succeed. If you do, he/she will fail. By the time the student is sixteen, he/she may quit school. If you can be flexible and individualize instruction, this student can make it.

8. Realize that this student will require a great deal of your time and guidance. Without both, he/she may not survive.

9. Look for the signs of failure, identify them quickly, and do something immediately.

10. Remember to be a caring human being and a professional educator in the process of helping — and never be the enemy.

11. Do whatever is necessary to allow this student to experience success, however small it may be initially. Remember, experiencing success will change this student. Experiencing more failure will not. The goal should be to provide a program that allows reasonable development for this student — academically, socially, and emotionally.

12. Involve the student in regular and extra-class activities whenever possible.

13. Have frequent personal conferences with this student to reinforce success. If you can, find a model he/she can identify with. It may be a teacher who has had similar experiences, or someone in the community.

14. Communicate on a friendly level with this student by finding interests and activities which he/she might enjoy talking about.

15. Think twice before creating any situation in which student success is made more difficult. Deducting grade points for misbehavior can cause a student to quit trying. Often, demerits make passing impossible in the mind of a student. Remember, when people get in a hole they

are more likely to "give up" than "dig out." That's a fact. Certainly, teacher action should never help a behavior failure become an academic failure.

16. Work hard — by word and action — to help the student realize that the only real failure is not trying.

17. If all your efforts fail, be sure to refer the student for special help as early in the semester as possible.

18. Never give up on this student. And urge the student not to give up on him/herself. A student who sees the teacher collapse under discouragement has witnessed a surrender to an enemy he/she already knows all too well.

IV. MISTAKES: Common misjudgments and errors in managing the child which may perpetuate or intensify the problem.

1. Reacting emotionally to his/her indifference.

2. Giving up and feeling there is no hope for this student to be successful.

3. Using sarcasm or ridicule openly against a student who disrupts the learning atmosphere.

4. Labeling this student a failure and causing other students to feel the same way about him/her.

5. Allowing the "failure" label to be carried on and shared with other teachers, thus perpetuating this prejudgment with colleagues.

6. Failing to contact parents and learn about what is happening outside school which might be affecting this student.

SEE ALSO: • The Do-Nothing • "I Don't Care" • The Truant • The Underachiever • The Unprepared

THE FIGHTER

I. BEHAVIOR: Specific attitudes and actions of this child at home and/or at school.

1. Continually involved in physical fights with other children.
2. Has a need to be first, best, or strongest.
3. Has a fighting mentality. Therefore, tends to fight before he/she thinks.
4. Continually complains to the teacher about other kids, schoolwork, fairness, etc.
5. Sees him/herself as being always right and never wrong.
6. Gains some pleasure from antagonizing and hurting others.
7. Likely to have very few close friends.
8. Has been taught to solve problems by fighting. A close look may reveal that the student was taught this behavior at home.
9. May act sorry, but doesn't see any alternatives to fighting.
10. Feels superior when he/she wins a fight. And, when he/she loses, talks about the "next time." Examination will reveal that some fighters seldom win. Rather, they absorb a great deal of physical punishment in every fight, yet continue to instigate more fights.

II. EFFECTS: How behavior affects teachers, classmates, and parents in the school learning environment and the home family situation.

1. Others become fearful.
2. Others are distracted.
3. Both teacher and classmates become frustrated.
4. Classroom freedom is reduced because the fighter's behavior forces teacher to issue restrictive rules which impinge on all students.
5. Learning process is constantly interrupted.
6. Someone else is always accused of starting the fight. This is how the fighter justifies his/her behavior.
7. There is always a victim or classmate involved in the fighter's behavior. Therefore, two problems rather than one are always created.
8. Teacher may find it difficult to motivate this student when it comes to learning.

III. ACTION: • Identify causes of misbehavior.
• Pinpoint student needs being revealed.
• Employ specific methods, procedures, and techniques at school and at home for getting the child to modify or change his/her behavior.

1. Primary causes of misbehavior:
   ◗ Attention: This student has found a means to get attention from peers and adults.
   ◗ Power: This student sees the strongest as having the most power.
2. Primary needs being revealed:

- Sex: By being strong, this student attracts weak people. This is one way to establish relationships.

- Escape from Pain: By making people afraid — afraid to laugh or tease — a person can prevent much painful personal abuse from peers.

3. Secondary needs being revealed:

- Power: The student may have leadership needs and qualities, but tends to exert them by trying to instill fear in people.

- Status: This student thinks that to be somebody one has to force people to look up to one with fear. Because of lack of status, he/she is easily insulted and ready to fight back at the drop of a hat.

- Autonomy: This student makes his/her own rules regarding how to act and treat people, and attempts to live by his/her own code of behavior.

   If these three secondary needs are to be met, the teacher must recognize the potential positive leadership role in this student and be willing to take the risk to allow this student to assert him/herself when given responsibilities in class.

4. When you see students quarreling or fighting, one sentence said in a calm and factual manner can produce remarkable results. Simply ask the students, "Don't you have enough trouble already?" or "You don't want more trouble, do you?" As simple as it sounds, you'll be amazed how often it works. Such statements allow one or both students to stop, make a good decision, and "save face" in the process. If you say, "Why don't you quit now before you get into real trouble?" students will often back away from a problem voluntarily.

5. Identify the problem for each of these students through a personal conference. Then, help the student see his/her behavior in action by sharing specific examples.

6. In the process, make absolutely sure the student knows fighting will not be allowed. Even if parents are supportive of fighting, this stance on the part of a teacher or school does not contradict parent teaching. The student can fight if he/she so chooses — but not in school. If the student chooses to fight, he/she can't remain in school. The fighter needs to be told this openly and firmly, and so do parents.

7. Frequently emphasize — quietly, firmly, and privately in a conference — that the fighter's behavior is unacceptable and you will not stand around and allow other students to be physically hurt.

8. Establish goals for this student that will help to reinforce socially acceptable behavior. Above all, know that this student has never been taught how to win through acceptable behavior. He/she must be taught how to change the behavior.

9. Discuss the various options and alternatives the student can use to avoid fighting. You may, for instance, let him/her use you as an excuse not to fight.

10. Outline specific methods for achieving goals in school — and even outside school — in order to help the student feel that he/she is succeeding without resorting to overt physical force.

11. Acknowledge all positive modifications and changes in behavior.

12. Try to model your expectations of behavior. If you don't want students to hit each other, for instance, don't abuse students in any way. If you want them to be courteous to each other, be courteous to students. If you want them to respect property, show respect for property. And if you want them to respect adults, give respect to young people.

13. Enlist peer support to help the student alter his/her behavior. For instance, let him/her work with quiet and serious students occasionally.

14. Never use power or threaten force. This only convinces the fighter that the person with power wins, and that, therefore, he/she needs more power.

105

15. Use the "Writing" technique. After each incident, have the student write out exactly what happened. Then, have the student write various options he/she could have chosen. This technique serves many purposes. It is an excellent way to make an angry incident a valuable learning experience. Likewise, it gives the student another "excuse" not to fight and a way to save face with peers.

16. Always contact parents about this behavior.

17. If "right and wrong" discussions don't work, use the "Dumb-Smart" approach. Talk about how dumb it is to fight. The fighter always loses — because he/she always goes to the office and gets punished. That's just *not smart.* The fighter has to stop doing dumb things — and start doing smart things. This student may not listen to "right and wrong" lectures. But there's one thing he/she doesn't want — to be regarded as dumb. This student wants to be "sharp" and "smart."

18. Before you begin talking, use silence as a communicator. Look at the student, shake your head slowly, and act disappointed. Then say, "I hate to see you do those things. It's not good, for you or anyone else." You may also repeat the student's name with the same disappointed emotions, for example, "Jimmy . . . Jimmy . . . Jimmy . . . when will we see the behavior that will help you help yourself?"

19. Go very slowly, speak quietly, and make your points regarding the "poor behavior" — but mention the potential for good in the student. Talk about the fact that the behavior he/she is displaying doesn't measure up to your high expectations for him/her.

20. Here are two alternate techniques to use with fighters: The "Walk Away" strategic action and the "Mediator and Conciliator" strategic action.

    • "Walk Away" strategic action: If possible, do not try to settle a student fight or confrontation in the presence of other students. For instance, let's suppose that you see two kids in, or about to get into, a fight in the cafeteria or on the playground. You see or hear something being said, and you move quickly to stop the problem. You break through the crowd, confront them, and they do what kids normally do. They begin to deny that anything is going on. Instead of public confrontation, try this technique: Simply walk up and request that both students be in your room in five minutes — and walk away immediately without saying a word. If they don't show up, you can always find them. And when you do, you are on even firmer ground in settling the issue with both students. After all, they now have two problems: fighting and insubordination. This technique allows you to handle a problem privately and to keep your dignity in the process.

    • "Mediator and Conciliator" strategic action: Instead of trying to figure out who's right, who's wrong, and who did what first, so that you can settle the situation — stop. Make students responsible for the solution. You can do so by assuming the role of mediator and conciliator. Tell them you aren't going to be a judge — and you won't decide the final solution. Rather, you are going to insist that they arrive at it themselves — jointly. You can't do this in all situations, of course. However, it's particularly effective in situations in which both kids are wrong and you don't have a fair answer to the problem at your fingertips, or when the same two kids are squabbling continually.

21. When students involve you in their problems with classmates, don't talk to either student separately. Get them together and let each have equal time without interruption. Then approach the problem simply and directly. Ask if they want to continue quarreling or patch things up. Say, "We can dwell on who did what to whom when — or we can lay it aside and start again." Don't minimize the problem, and always acknowledge that mistreatment has occurred, or there wouldn't be a problem. Then proceed to ask for apologies on both sides and promises to start anew. With this emphasis on "getting together" and "letting bygones be bygones," rather than on causes, effects, and punishments, kids are quick to forgive and forget. What they both need most is a teacher to bring them together.

22. Be aware that, with proper handling, fighters will try to do as you tell them to. Remember,

people act as others expect them to act. Too often the fighter fights everyone because he/she is expected to do so.

IV. MISTAKES: Common misjudgments and errors in managing the child which may perpetuate or intensify the problem.

1. Assuming that this student started any fight that arises.

2. Assuming that the student really enjoys being identified as a fighter.

3. Refusing to listen to what the student has to say when he/she is accused of starting a fight.

4. Focusing attention only on the negative behavior of this student.

5. Assuming that this student's behavior will never change and, therefore, never expecting it to change.

6. Showing disapproval of this child as a person.

7. Telling the fighter he/she is a "bad person."

8. Revealing dislike or acting hostile.

9. Failing to call parents.

10. Failing to see how this child is doing with other teachers.

11. Failing to seek the help of counselors and administrators.

12. Never giving this student any responsibility.

13. Making values an issue. Saying, "Fighting is wrong, and bad people fight." The real issue is a question of trying to solve problems by hurting other people.

14. Trying to make an example by physically hurting the fighter.

SEE ALSO:　　• The Angry　• The Authority Pusher　• The Bully　• The Defier
　　　　　　　　• The Overly Aggressive

THE FOLLOWER

I. BEHAVIOR: Specific attitudes and actions of this child at home and/or at school.

1. Is a conformist — a common type among students. The conformist is made, not born, and begins to learn this behavior very early in life.
2. Some of this student's conforming is good; some is not.
3. Always does what the group is doing.
4. Has a compulsion to see him/herself as "one of the group" or "part of the gang" — regardless of the price paid for the association.
5. Seldom contributes, and when he/she does contribute, looks to peers for approval.
6. Is never asked what he/she thinks, because this student seldom thinks.
7. Holds to opinions of the group.
8. Likes what the group likes. His/her values are those the group dictates.
9. Doesn't show much promise of being a successful adult unless his/her individuality is developed.
10. Is a conformist basically because he/she is trying to remain safe.
11. More interested in a friend or group activities than in academic activities.

II. EFFECTS: How behavior affects teachers, classmates, and parents in the school learning environment and the home family situation.

1. Cliques are formed in the classroom.
2. Teacher senses that there is a barrier between the clique and other students.
3. Classmates and teacher may be excluded because this student is loyal only to the group.
4. Teacher may feel that he/she can't reach the follower as a person.
5. Teacher feels the follower can be led to any action by his/her leader.
6. Teacher is frustrated when repeated attempts to motivate this student fail.

III. ACTION:
- **Identify causes of misbehavior.**
- **Pinpoint student needs being revealed.**
- **Employ specific methods, procedures, and techniques at school and at home for getting the child to modify or change his/her behavior.**

1. Primary cause of misbehavior:
    - Self-Confidence: The lack of self-confidence may be not in academic productivity, but in human relationships.
2. Primary need being revealed:
    - Sex: This person has a strong desire for relationships with others.
3. Secondary needs being revealed:
    - Gregariousness: This student has a need to belong to a group, especially a peer group.
    - Affiliation: The opportunity to have a close friend may well be a substitute for belonging to a group.

♦ Status: This student feels he/she can gain identity and feel worthwhile only by being a part of a group.

If the above needs cannot be met in a positive manner, the student will try to meet them in a negative way by becoming a follower. Then, nothing matters to this student but to identify completely with whatever person or persons this student chooses to follow.

4. Keep in mind that a student's fear includes more than fear of failure. It also includes fear of ridicule, social exclusion, rejection, and parental disappointment. For older students, it can mean fear regarding the future, such as not making grades good enough to win a scholarship, get into college, or get a job. Therefore, when counseling use every motivator in the book — except fear. And remember that fear in these students causes behaviors whose consequences they don't consider — until after the fact. For instance, if a student has fears about his/her ability to do math problems, he/she may cause class disturbances, create conflicts with students or teachers, or skip class if the leader so directs. Fear can even cause children to become physically ill.

5. Help this student establish goals and objectives of his/her own. Try to draw the student out; begin by discussing his/her own likes and dislikes.

6. Teach the student how to make decisions. First, the student needs to know how to gain meaningful input. Second, he/she must be helped to see choices — rather than follow someone else. Third, the student must be taught how to listen to others, especially people other than the group leader. This is the way the follower learns to respect others so he/she can act independently.

7. In the process of teaching, don't forget that conformity is fine and not a total negative. You are only dealing with the overindulgence of a normal behavior.

8. Give this student something new or different to do alone — and explain why you are doing so. As the follower begins doing things alone, he/she will become less fearful and gain the security needed to risk not conforming to the group.

9. Provide situations in which the student can check out his/her fear of the unknown.

10. Deliberately break the follower's routine. Gradually change the ways this student does things: Change his/her seat, give him/her special assignments.

11. Above all, assign this student classroom responsibilities.

12. At some point, talk to the follower about dissent. Tell him/her that "progress often stems from dissent." Remember, dissent should be an honored word rather than one that is held in contempt. This is a difficult concept for some teachers to accept. Yet, students should be encouraged to engage in dissent. After all, the opposite of dissent is conformity. And nothing could be more deadly to learning than conformity for conformity's sake. However, there's a vast difference between dissent and defiance. To improve self-discipline, young people need to be taught this difference.

13. Provide opportunities for this student to work with many students. This will help the student see that he/she does not need to follow one person or group.

IV. MISTAKES: Common misjudgments and errors in managing the child which may perpetuate or intensify the problem.

1. Viewing this student as dull and a follower of anyone, any place, all the time.

2. Simply giving up on this student after repeated and sincere efforts fail.

3. Trying to work with this student only while he/she is in a group — and not giving notice to the student's presence once he/she leaves the group. Many kids leave a gang — and then return because there wasn't anybody else "out there" for them.

4. Failing to establish a relationship with the student.

The Follower

5. Thinking that the follower *never* "feels" or "thinks" for him/herself.

6. Talking to the leader about making the follower behave.

7. Failing to see this student's academic potential because of his/her blind loyalty to a group or person.

SEE ALSO: • The Apathetic   • The Clique   • The Loner   • The Negative Group

THE FORGETTER

I. BEHAVIOR: **Specific attitudes and actions of this child at home and/or at school.**

1. Fails to do assignments.
2. Doesn't bring materials to class.
3. Forgets to meet responsibilities.
4. Tries continually to borrow materials from other students.
5. Wants to leave room to get items he/she forgot to bring to class.
6. Is upset and unnerved by forgetting.
7. Doesn't return borrowed items — whether pencils or money.
8. Fails to meet standards of the class — often because he/she *can't*.
9. Usually is "sorry" he/she forgot.
10. Expects others to remind him/her or meet his/her needs.
11. Blames others for his/her forgetting.
12. May get mad because others "didn't tell me."
13. Wants to remain dependent upon others.
14. Does everything at the last minute.
15. May be like the absent-minded professor who is thinking about many things and forgets minor things.

II. EFFECTS: **How behavior affects teachers, classmates, and parents in the school learning environment and the home family situation.**

1. Crisis is created at beginning of class; starting a class is difficult.
2. Double standards are created. There are two kinds of forgetters — the real forgetter and the one who pretends. The problem comes when a teacher lets one do something because he/she has a real problem, and refuses the second because he/she is a phony.
3. Other students are annoyed by the forgetter's constant borrowing.
4. Teacher may not have sufficient or needed supplies for this student.
5. Teacher is irritated by this behavior.
6. Classmates may begin to make excuses, too.

III. ACTION: • **Identify causes of misbehavior.**
• **Pinpoint student needs being revealed.**
• **Employ specific methods, procedures, and techniques at school and at home for getting the child to modify or change his/her behavior.**

1. Primary causes of misbehavior:

   ▶ Attention: This student really does enjoy the attention, even if it is for a negative behavior.

   ▶ Power: The student displays a form of power by continually forgetting. He/she may feel a sense of power when adults are frustrated in attempting to deal with his/her forgetting.

2. Primary needs being revealed:

   ◗ Hunger, Rest: A deficiency in these primary needs may lead to forgetfulness.

   ◗ Escape from Pain: Fear of failure with peers, parents, and/or teachers may cause such behavior.

   ◗ Sex: A desire for recognition by others may cause such behavior.

3. Secondary needs being revealed:

   ◗ Autonomy: Receiving affirmation for tasks completed will help this student gain control of him/herself in a positive manner.

   ◗ Achievement: Appreciation by others may lead to improvement of the forgetter's behavior.

4. Look for ways to change the behavior that will be effective while creating as little turmoil in the classroom as possible.

5. First, make adjustments. Provide needed material when possible.

6. Second, follow up. Have a meeting on the student's time, rather than on class time.

7. Think *tiny consequences* rather than big punishments. Then, suggest ideas that will help the student overcome the forgetting.

8. Let other students help remind this student.

9. Many teachers dislike lending pencils and other supplies. Some even forbid borrowing. Though we are all familiar with the consistent violator, making absolute rules regarding these necessities can cause many problems. In truth, enforcing these kinds of rules often causes more disturbance than the lending and borrowing. Sometimes, in our efforts to teach responsibility, we overlook some common life practices. Borrowing is a part of life. It is not wrong to borrow — it is wrong not to pay back. This is what our teachings should promote. Many simple classroom procedures can be used to handle this everyday occurrence without disturbance while providing a learning experience. One such successful approach is to keep a box of pencils that have been found, and have students put an IOU or something they value in the box when taking a pencil. When they return the pencil or repay the box with another one, they can reclaim the possession or tear up the IOU. If no pencils remain, none can be lent. Then, they must get one from a friend. In this manner, even the constant violator can be handled privately. Remember, even outside school some are not allowed the privilege of borrowing because they have a record of nonpayment. This is another lesson students need to know.

10. Don't interrupt class. Provide materials quietly.

11. Getting students to be on time or to remember to keep their appointments has long been another problem for teachers and parents alike. None of us is unfamiliar with the age-old excuse, "I forgot the time — that's why I'm late." You'll find students will be less likely to forget meeting times if the stated time is unusual. Next time you make an appointment, try telling the student you will meet at 4:03 p.m., or 3:18 p.m. It works — with colleagues too.

12. Assign special tasks to this student to help him/her develop a sense of responsibility.

13. Accept apologies from the student graciously, but have a personal and private conference with him/her about responsibility each time that forgetting occurs.

14. Work with parents to ensure that the forgetting behavior is not perpetuated at home.

15. Set down definite rules for what will happen after a given period of time if the student continues to forget his/her materials. Make the rules fair and reasonable, and then carry them out.

16. When counseling, choose your words with care. Say, "What did we say?" rather than "I told you that ..." Then, make the student relate what he/she was supposed to remember.

Revoke a privilege for each such incident, and then return the privilege when the student succeeds in behaving responsibly.

17. Don't make a big deal out of this behavior. Be patient and realize that change will not be quick; the student will forget again. Nevertheless, your counseling is a must. Help the student begin a long-term self-improvement program.

18. Don't allow yourself to get mad about his/her forgetting, and don't take it personally.

19. Remind the student of what he/she will need. You might even give the student a note. This is a form of attention.

20. Keep an actual count of how many times he/she doesn't bring materials. Remember, improvement is your goal.

21. How many times have you heard a teacher say, "I talk ... and talk ... and talk to him — but it never does any good. He doesn't hear a word I say." Yes he does — he just chooses to forget. However, this teacher's problem is that he/she talks too much. When talking to a child about misbehavior, a teacher can find it very difficult to put that conversation on a positive basis. Because most such conversations are by necessity negative, a teacher must realize that any talk beyond the minimum is, indeed, wasted. Remember to keep such conversations clear and short, and you will receive a better response. Students not only will listen better — but also will be more likely to remember what is said. People, whether children or adults, "turn off" when somebody drives a point into the ground. Many times, everything said is forgotten — even the major points.

22. Work out a contract with the student for rewards. Thus, when the student remembers, he/she is recognized.

23. Never ask this student to remember more than two items. The true forgetter finds this extremely difficult.

IV. MISTAKES: Common misjudgments and errors in managing the child which may perpetuate or intensify the problem.

1. Failing to anticipate this student's needs, and thus forcing ourselves to adjust to avoid the turmoil.

2. Getting stubborn — and refusing to provide this student's needed materials.

3. Getting mad at this student frequently.

4. Wanting to punish the forgetter beyond the point of common sense.

5. Trying to make life miserable for this student when he/she forgets.

6. "Backing ourselves against a wall" by issuing ultimatums.

7. Ignoring the student — and letting him/her "sit and stew."

8. Giving the forgetter too much attention.

9. Treating this student differently from other students.

10. Lowering expectations for this student.

11. Being too lax.

SEE ALSO: • The Alibier • The Disorganized • The Excuse/Alibi Maker
• "I Can't" • The Indifferent • "Not My Fault"

THE FOULMOUTH

I. BEHAVIOR: **Specific attitudes and actions of this child at home and/or at school.**

1. Generally loud.

2. Very offensive in what he/she says, but very defensive regarding criticism from others.

3. Attempts to impress with offensive words others don't use.

4. Seeks attention with words — continuously.

5. Appears to "know it all," especially in regard to "life in the streets."

6. Reacts negatively in group situations.

7. Tries to shock people with foul language.

8. In one-to-one situations, may be an extremely polite child.

II. EFFECTS: **How behavior affects teachers, classmates, and parents in the school learning environment and the home family situation.**

1. Others — including teacher — are subjected to embarrassment.

2. Teacher is angered.

3. Caring and considerate climate in classroom is disrupted.

4. Teacher is forced to take immediate action — or appear to condone behavior.

5. Teacher is frustrated because punishment does not seem to alter behavior.

III. ACTION: • **Identify causes of misbehavior.**
   • **Pinpoint student needs being revealed.**
   • **Employ specific methods, procedures, and techniques at school and at home for getting the child to modify or change his/her behavior.**

1. Primary causes of misbehavior:

   ◗ Attention: There is no doubt that this student gets attention with his/her foul mouth.

   ◗ Power: The foulmouth can overwhelm peers with his/her language. It represents a form of being tough. The foulmouth confuses adults and, in many ways, defeats adults in a confrontation.

2. Primary needs being revealed:

   ◗ Rest: This student may be tired and unable to control him/herself.

   ◗ Escape from Pain: He/she may find school very difficult and the foul mouth may help to keep people at a distance.

3. Secondary needs being revealed:

   ◗ Aggression: Verbal abuse is a strong form of aggression. This student must be taught positive assertiveness.

   ◗ Status: This use of language makes the student stand out in the group. Other means of attaining status must be explored.

   ◗ Power: This student needs to gain a feeling of power and of being somebody by assuming a variety of responsibilities.

4. Talk to the student privately.

5. Make no mistake — this student does not feel adequate with appropriate language. He/she feels very inferior without this club of a foul mouth. This behavior keeps others away; it's the student's protective wall. Therefore, do not respond in anger. Rather, ask if he/she wants help. If the student says, "No," respond with "Are you sure?"

6. Try to get student to reveal whether this is at-home language.

7. In private, point out the times he/she uses inappropriate words and what the words are. This student has a limited vocabulary.

8. To initiate change, offer these recommendations: First, never use such words with the opposite sex; second, never with those who would be offended; and third, never with those he/she respects.

9. Suggest "nonsense" words to substitute. Try "zitcher" or "zotch" as replacements. It works.

10. Involve the student in deciding what language is appropriate in the group setting.

11. Give the student positive attention for positive actions.

12. Remind the student that you want to help. Say, "You can do and say what you like — but not in school."

13. When such behavior occurs, respond, "I'm sorry you must use such language," and go on with the conversation. It's important to show your displeasure, but also your ability to stay on target in the conversation. This deprives the student of personal attention for his/her foul mouth, but shows your willingness to give attention to the area of importance.

IV. MISTAKES: Common misjudgments and errors in managing the child which may perpetuate or intensify the problem.

1. Using vulgar language in response.

2. Appearing to condone by action or by inaction.

3. Trying to impose moral values rather than sharing them.

4. Wasting time by preaching.

5. Calling the student "no good" or using some other put-down.

6. Believing him/her to be unworthy of help.

7. Using any of the following responses with a student under any circumstances:

   "Shut up!"

   "I don't care."

   "You'll never amount to anything."

   "You're just like your brother."

   "Get out of here!"

   "I've had it with you!"

SEE ALSO: • The Disrespectful   • The Lewd   • The Loudmouth   • The Smartmouth
            • The Snotty   • The Swearer

THE FUN SEEKER

I. BEHAVIOR: **Specific attitudes and actions of this child at home and/or at school.**

 1. Only wants to play.

 2. Wants a good time at anyone's expense.

 3. Has a great deal of difficulty staying on a subject in class.

 4. May try anything for a good time.

 5. Brags about his/her "fun" experiences to others.

 6. Generally speaking, inflates and expands on his/her experiences.

 7. Not serious.

 8. Lazy.

 9. Holds values centering on pleasure.

II. EFFECTS: **How behavior affects teachers, classmates, and parents in the school learning environment and the home family situation.**

 1. Serious class endeavors are disrupted.

 2. Students and teacher are influenced negatively.

 3. Many students are annoyed.

 4. Teacher is angered.

 5. Other students may follow the fun seeker.

 6. Teacher becomes upset and frustrated.

III. ACTION:
 - **Identify causes of misbehavior.**
 - **Pinpoint student needs being revealed.**
 - **Employ specific methods, procedures, and techniques at school and at home for getting the child to modify or change his/her behavior.**

 1. Primary causes of misbehavior.

   ‣ Self-Confidence: The student's lack of confidence in him/herself may lead to fun-seeking behavior. It becomes a good protection for someone who has little feeling of self-worth.

   ‣ Revenge: Another type of fun seeker may find his/her place in the school by being disliked. This student has fun at the expense of others, and then comments, "I was just having fun," or "Can't you take a joke?"

 2. Primary needs being revealed:

   ‣ Sex: Some people use this behavior to attract others into some kind of relationship.

   ‣ Escape from Pain: It may be very painful to be unacceptable to others and thus the fun seeker's behavior continues with more intensity.

 3. Secondary needs being revealed:

   ‣ Gregariousness: This student needs to belong to an "inner circle," and he/she is able to attract people by these activities.

   ‣ Power: The fun seeker gains power when people respond to his/her behavior.

▶ Status: This student should be given opportunities to "be somebody" in the class.

4. Give this student some serious responsibilities. The fun seeker doesn't have anything important to do. In addition, this student may have been neglected. Adults may have given him/her money, but not time.

5. Find personal interests, hobbies, and activities which the student enjoys and use them as a catalyst to get to know him/her better. Perhaps you could incorporate these interests into your classroom work.

6. Stress development of self-worth and self-value. This student wants to be important.

7. Seek help from parents, counselors, and administrators. This student might need professional help outside the school.

8. Recognize that the fun seeker is looking for something through his/her different activities. You must change the object of the "search" to something significant.

9. Harsh words and sarcastic remarks directed toward the fun seeker will never get desired results. They will only build bitterness. Be direct in your comments, but do so with firmness and kindness. A comment such as "Mary, I'm surprised at your behavior," or "John, this isn't what I expected from you" will get much better results than "Mary, that was a stupid thing to do." Remember, when we use angry words like "dumb" and "stupid," students' emotions switch immediately from their wrong to what the teacher said. Then, all is lost.

10. Always ask students to let you see what they will be working on during "free study time." Then class control is not lost, but freedom is still present. The teacher who says, "You may do anything you like for the next twenty minutes," or "You may draw or paste any picture you desire on your notebook cover" may be asking for trouble. There will almost always be some students who need teacher assistance and guidance in making appropriate choices and decisions in these situations. If you say "anything," some students will take the word literally — and you may have opened the door for trouble or embarrassment.

11. If necessary, schedule a private conference in which you define the unacceptable behavior and outline the consequences of continuing it. The student may feel he/she is being backed against the wall; however, explain that his/her behavior is interfering with your fulfilling your responsibility to teach all students.

12. Be sure to praise and encourage any behavior adjustment.

IV. MISTAKES: Common misjudgments and errors in managing the child which may perpetuate or intensify the problem.

1. Allowing this student to dominate class time.

2. Acting afraid of this student, which only encourages the behavior.

3. Overreacting to statements about what this student did or what he/she is going to do to have fun.

4. Encouraging this student to tell about his/her experiences.

5. Ridiculing the student for what he/she has done.

6. Considering this student as someone who doesn't care about school or him/herself.

SEE ALSO: • The Class Clown   • The Show-Off

THE GOER

I. BEHAVIOR: Specific attitudes and actions of this child at home and/or at school.

1. Always on the move.
2. Never wants to be where he/she should be, and is always trying to go elsewhere.
3. Seeks permission to get out of class very frequently for every conceivable reason. Asks for trips to the restroom, locker, office, nurse, counselor, or elsewhere.
4. Has repeated "emergency" situations which he/she claims *cannot* be delayed.
5. Consequently, misses much class time.
6. Makes private requests to go somewhere in the form of public announcements before entire class.
7. Brags to other students about getting out of class.
8. Tries to persuade classmates to go with him/her.
9. Likely not to be a good student.
10. Wants most to leave class before tests or when important assignments are due.
11. Thinks continuously about where he/she can go next.

II. EFFECTS: How behavior affects teachers, classmates, and parents in the school learning environment and the home family situation.

1. Teacher is irritated, often at the beginning of class.
2. A great deal of time is needlessly consumed by the goer trying to get permission to go someplace.
3. Special explanations of class activities are required when he/she returns.
4. Others are interrupted.
5. Classmates are irritated because they know the goer is lying about the "emergency" requests.
6. Academic make-up time is required.
7. Teacher must make frequent judgments on the importance of requests.
8. Teacher feels helpless, at times, to correct the situation.
9. Inconveniences are caused other teachers when this student interrupts their classes unexpectedly.
10. Establishing and enforcing rules is made fairly difficult.

III. ACTION: • **Identify causes of misbehavior.**
   • **Pinpoint student needs being revealed.**
   • **Employ specific methods, procedures, and techniques at school and at home for getting the child to modify or change his/her behavior.**

1. Primary cause of misbehavior:

   ◗ Attention: This student has to be noticed.

2. Primary needs being revealed:

- Escape from Pain: This student may have a real physical problem, and parents should be advised that a physical examination may help the situation.

- Elimination of Waste: A part of the physical problem may well be that this student is unable to control him/herself.

3. Secondary needs being revealed:

- Inquisitiveness: This student has a need to know what others are doing or to be in contact with friends.

- Achievement: With improved achievement, this student will reduce his/her need to be a goer.

- Status: A need for status with peers may cause the student to be constantly on the move.

4. Recognize that this student *must* move.

5. Remember, you must structure the movements. If not, movement will be uncontrollable.

6. Don't say "no" to every request or turn every request into a public embarrassment. You must leave yourself room to operate in order to make fair and sound teacher decisions, because there *are* times when a student must go to the restroom or see the nurse. An "automatic no" when you should say "yes" will cause all kinds of problems — with all students.

7. Here are some practices you can try to help the goer learn self-control. First, have the goer escorted on his/her next "trip." This is the best strategy, but the most difficult to arrange. Using an escort on two or three successive occasions will often solve the problem.

8. Second, establish time limits. This student does not like to hurry. Structure is what he/she is trying to avoid, so a note to be signed at his/her destination helps. The additional structure imposed by time limits and signing procedures often limits his/her requests.

9. Confer with the student privately; this is a must. The goer is usually reacted to publicly — but seldom treated privately.

10. Remember, the goer may not be aware of the frequency of his/her going. Ask this student, "What if everyone asked to leave the room as often as you do?"

11. Explain that you fear his/her falling behind will create a bigger problem. The goer needs to be confronted with this fact — for it is something he/she can relate to realistically.

12. Help the student solve his/her problem, but don't hesitate to contact parents, counselors, or administrators for assistance.

13. Remember, you need a special plan to meet this student's needs. The goer interferes more with the teacher than with classmates. Plan specific involvement for this student in your class so that he/she has some reason to be present.

14. Discuss the behavior with other teachers. This student is probably getting passes from others, and may be playing one teacher against another. For example, he/she may volunteer, "Mrs. Jones wants to see me."

15. Discuss the matter with counselor, principal, and parents before taking any drastic measures.

IV. MISTAKES: Common misjudgments and errors in managing the child which may perpetuate or intensify the problem.

1. Responding too harshly. Doing so may cause other students to fear making any request.

2. Misjudging when to say "no."

3. Reprimanding publicly.

4. Assuming other students think we are "pushovers" when we agree to the goer's requests.

5. Making rules for entire class which will be enforced for this student only.

The Goer

6. Denying every request this student makes.

7. Developing a negative attitude toward this student.

8. Allowing disruption caused by constant coming and going to take its toll on our patience.

SEE ALSO: • The Distracter • The Hyperactive • The Repeater • The Traveler

THE GOLDBRICK

I. BEHAVIOR: **Specific attitudes and actions of this child at home and/or at school.**

1. Always trying to get "something for nothing." Wants a good grade without studying, a good reputation without being nice to others, more teacher time without showing interest in class work.

2. Displays behavior that is incompatible with classroom activities, because his/her goal is achievement through nonproductivity.

3. Devotes majority of time, energy, and resources to loafing.

4. Feels "getting by with something" is an indication of cleverness.

5. Quite satisfied to continue operating in this manner.

6. Has no apparent sense of wasting his/her potential.

7. Justifies behavior to self by considering it a product of superior intelligence.

8. Unfortunately, gets a great deal of satisfaction from his/her stance.

9. Laughs at students who work hard.

II. EFFECTS: **How behavior affects teachers, classmates, and parents in the school learning environment and the home family situation.**

1. Teacher must devote extra time and attention to dealing with this behavior.

2. Conscientious students question their principles when they see this student achieve while expending no effort.

3. Class is interrupted.

4. A negative attitude is created in class.

5. Apparent importance of work is diminished.

6. Teacher efforts are demeaned.

7. Teacher becomes frustrated and very angry.

III. ACTION:
- **Identify causes of misbehavior.**
- **Pinpoint student needs being revealed.**
- **Employ specific methods, procedures, and techniques at school and at home for getting the child to modify or change his/her behavior.**

1. Primary cause of misbehavior:
   - Attention: Because of inability to be productive or a feeling of failure, this person gains attention through goldbrick behavior.

2. Primary need being revealed:
   - Escape from Pain: This person's inability to perform necessary tasks in the classroom adequately may be very painful to him/her.

3. Secondary needs being revealed:
   - Achievement: If achievement is improved, more honest effort may be seen from this student.

▶ Power: As this student gains power, he/she may feel increased responsibility toward assigned tasks.

▶ Autonomy: The goldbrick may be getting a feeling of control over his/her own life from present behavior. Every effort should be made to show the negative consequences of such behavior.

4. Don't treat this student like everyone else. This is the worst thing a teacher can do. Acceptance and tolerance only serve to strengthen the emotional needs, and make the student think the teacher appreciates his/her cleverness.

5. Make sure the goldbrick doesn't get everything he/she wants. This is the only way to change the behavior. Don't be misled: This student will work to satisfy needs — if someone makes him/her.

6. This is one of those rare times when it is in the best interest of the child to keep the pressure on — continually. Never "let up," or this student will revert to his/her old ways. Experience has taught this child that adults "let up" when he/she shows improvement.

7. Approach this case with parents' knowledge and assistance. It is vital that parents understand the reason for teacher pressure. Teacher pressure can cause problems that would be difficult to explain to uninformed parents. However, parents are probably having the same problem at home. Too, as the student becomes aware of his/her actions, it helps to have him/her hear teacher-parent conversations.

8. Remember, praise positive behavior change, but maintain firm and kind pressure so that the student will have to continue making an effort.

9. Refuse to satisfy the student's wants and needs until he/she has worked to deserve this return.

10. Make it clear that honest effort will be rewarded, but the student must do his/her best.

IV. MISTAKES: Common misjudgments and errors in managing the child which may perpetuate or intensify the problem.

1. Treating this student like everyone else. Acceptance and tolerance only strengthen his/her emotional needs.

2. Letting the student think we believe he/she is clever.

3. Treating this student as a discipline problem.

4. Easing our demands on this student before he/she has learned that real work is the only avenue through which he/she can seek satisfaction.

5. Applying pressure without explaining the situation to parents.

SEE ALSO: • "I Don't Care"   • The Irresponsible   • The Noncompleter with Grand Plans
• The Procrastinator

THE GOSSIP

I. BEHAVIOR: Specific attitudes and actions of this child at home and/or at school.

1. Always has something to tell about someone.
2. Carries stories about classmates, teachers, administrators, and parents. Even talks about his/her best friend.
3. Unfortunately, usually conveys bad news.
4. Turns any conversation to stories he/she has to tell.
5. Not concerned about the whole truth — or whether the gossip will hurt someone.
6. Seeks attention; must have it. If he/she doesn't get it in positive ways, will get it by gossiping.
7. Disloyal. Honestly doesn't know how to be loyal.
8. Worse, seeks out information to relate. Therefore, his/her mind is constantly occupied with news to tell others.
9. Likes to be with people.
10. Avid talker.
11. Tells stories about him/herself.

II. EFFECTS: How behavior affects teachers, classmates, and parents in the school learning environment and the home family situation.

1. Teacher is concerned about how other students are affected by the stories.
2. Learning climate may deteriorate.
3. Protecting rather than sharing can become the classroom condition.
4. Distrust prevails.
5. Fights between students result.
6. Friendships are broken up.
7. Exclusion is increased.
8. Classmates often "use" the gossip to relay bad news.

III. ACTION:
- **Identify causes of misbehavior.**
- **Pinpoint student needs being revealed.**
- **Employ specific methods, procedures, and techniques at school and at home for getting the child to modify or change his/her behavior.**

1. Primary causes of misbehavior:
   ▶ Attention: This student feels that if he/she can relate a story to a teacher or student who listens, he/she gains attention.
   ▶ Power: Being able to relate exclusive stories is a form of power.
   ▶ Self-Confidence: This student may attempt to enhance his/her self-concept by being "in the know" about others.
2. Primary need being revealed:

- Sex: The behavior of the gossip is an attempt to gain attention and establish relationships with others.

3. Secondary needs being revealed:

- Gregariousness: This person wants to belong, but doesn't know how to approach this need positively.

- Aggression: This person needs to assert him/herself through classroom activities and other responsibilities.

- Power: The gossip sees him/herself as having a certain amount of power. But he/she does not understand where loyalty fits into friendship and, too often, "uses up" people by discarding them when their usefulness is over.

4. Always talk privately to this student.

5. In the private conference explain the hurt that gossip may cause other persons. Also explain that your position is to help the gossip and others in the class, and that you will not allow others to be hurt.

6. In a caring way, confront specific situations in which his/her gossip has caused hurt or violated a confidence.

7. However, never generalize, and always talk about his/her strengths as well as weaknesses in any discussion.

8. Give this student tips for sharing information in a constructive way. For instance, tell the student to tell everyone his/her heart desires about good news, but to resolve not to say a word about the negative.

9. Regard each incident as an excellent opportunity to teach responsibility.

10. Look for the hidden message this student is sending you. It is usually the need to be center-stage, reveal importance, or take pressure off him/herself.

11. Always consider and try to meet the needs of the gossip rather than put him/her down. For instance, this student has a strong need to belong to a group, be affiliated with you, or acquire power or status with classmates or adults. There are countless tasks you can give him/her in the classroom to fill these needs.

12. Seat this student where he/she is close to you — or at least easily accessible.

13. Be aware that the rest of the class will be watching how you work with the gossip. It's important for classmates to see how you relate to and manage the gossip because your behavior will serve as a guide for their actions.

14. Don't use the gossip. Rather, stop this behavior when it begins. Don't wait to hear the story, then reprimand. This is treating the problem after the "horse is out of the barn." Remember, until you stop this behavior before the fact, he/she will continue to gossip.

15. As a last resort, bring this student face to face with the person he/she is talking about and have him/her repeat the story.

IV. MISTAKES: Common misjudgments and errors in managing the child which may perpetuate or intensify the problem.

1. Deciding that it's not worth spending valuable class time dealing with this problem.

2. Missing the significance of the gossip's behavior.

3. Rejecting this student or choosing to deal with gossip stories in front of other students.

4. Feeling the gossip got what he/she deserved if classmates have reacted physically against him/her.

5. Being nice in order to get information, and then scolding after we get it.

6. Failing to see the student privately.

7. Failing to call parents.

8. Forgetting there is always a victim.

9. Failing to realize the power this person has for disruption in the classroom and/or school.

SEE ALSO: • The Blabbermouth • The Exaggerator

THE GREEDY

I. BEHAVIOR: Specific attitudes and actions of this child at home and/or at school.

1. Always looking for "more." Continually pushing to see if he/she can get an extra privilege.

2. Asks teacher to repeat statements or instructions in the hope that reiteration will reflect a change that will prove advantageous.

3. Very persistent.

4. Will even talk to one teacher about what another teacher will do for him/her in comparison — hoping to gain an extra privilege.

5. Knows exactly what he/she is doing and, if the tactics work, will be back for more . . . and more . . . and more.

6. Never satisfied with the extra privileges received — because nothing is ever enough.

7. May concede if teacher becomes angry, but comes back with another request as soon as he/she feels safe in doing so.

8. Is developing a personality characteristic that makes a happy life impossible, and hurts those around him/her too. Greed is one of the worst human diseases.

II. EFFECTS: How behavior affects teachers, classmates, and parents in the school learning environment and the home family situation.

1. No matter what the teacher does, he/she can't make this student happy.

2. Others are hurt by this student's "taking."

3. Teacher and classmates alike are put on edge.

4. Others are irritated.

5. An unfair atmosphere is created.

6. Time and energy are required to deal with this student.

III. ACTION:
- **Identify causes of misbehavior.**
- **Pinpoint student needs being revealed.**
- **Employ specific methods, procedures, and techniques at school and at home for getting the child to modify or change his/her behavior.**

1. Primary cause of misbehavior:
   - Power: The more this student can get from people, the more powerful he/she feels.

2. Primary need being revealed:
   - Sex: This person assumes that his/her behavior will attract others.

3. Secondary needs being revealed:
   - Achievement: This student needs to be recognized as successful.
   - Status: This person needs to feel he/she is "somebody."
   - Autonomy: This student needs to be independent, to feel in control of his/her life.

4. First, consult with other teachers, counselors, and administrators to see if they are having similar experiences with this child.

5. Next, talk to parents. They are probably experiencing similar difficulties at home.

6. Then, arrange a private conference with the student.

7. Tell the student exactly what you see him/her doing and becoming.

8. Be very serious, and call a spade a spade during this visit. Place *all* the responsibility for future behavior on the student's shoulders. You will find an immediate improvement in his/her actions because, although this student is often confronted, most people end up trying to appease him/her rather than holding to a firm stance.

9. Remember that this student is trying to win. He/she may have become greedy without even realizing it. Too, his/her greed can be the result of competition.

10. Use the "Mature" strategic action technique. Explain the secret of maturity. It's not age or experience. Maturity is moving from being a "taker" to being a "giver."

11. Follow up by informing counselors, administrators, and other teachers regarding the conference. If the entire teaching team will follow your lead, this child will have a better chance of living a happy and healthy life.

12. Finally, be extremely kind — but firm and strong. Once this student knows your dislike for the behavior, he/she will be extremely careful.

IV. MISTAKES: Common misjudgments and errors in managing the child which may perpetuate or intensify the problem.

1. Giving in to get rid of this student.

2. Conceding anything to this student. It only fuels the problem.

3. Allowing the behavior to go unchecked. This is the biggest problem the greedy student has.

4. Arguing with him/her.

5. Letting this student justify his/her behavior.

6. Getting on the defensive rather than the offensive.

7. Thinking that if you let the behavior go, this student will change.

SEE ALSO: • The Apple Polisher • The Chiseler • The Manipulator
• The Rabble Rouser

THE GRIPER

I. BEHAVIOR: **Specific attitudes and actions of this child at home and/or at school.**

1. Gripes about everything he/she can think of — tests, grading scale, homework, etc.
2. Hangs his/her head, throws mini-tantrums, whines, cries, and mopes.
3. Even complains about relationships with others.
4. Appears very unhappy about him/herself and his/her responsibilities.
5. Hates work. Gripes about work, but doesn't do very much of it.
6. Usually claims he/she is always being picked on.
7. Fears challenge.
8. Wastes great amounts of time.

II. EFFECTS: **How behavior affects teachers, classmates, and parents in the school learning environment and the home family situation.**

1. Classmates may begin griping too.
2. Disharmony is caused in the classroom.
3. Classmates may reject — or laugh at — the griper because of his/her behavior.
4. Teacher is frustrated.
5. Teacher may eventually become angry.
6. Teacher may also be led to question him/herself unfairly.
7. Teacher may be forced to make concessions because of this behavior.

III. ACTION: • **Identify causes of misbehavior.**
• **Pinpoint student needs being revealed.**
• **Employ specific methods, procedures, and techniques at school and at home for getting the child to modify or change his/her behavior.**

1. Primary cause of misbehavior:

   ▶ Attention: The griper will use this behavior to let others know he/she exists.

2. Primary need being revealed:

   ▶ Escape from Pain: This behavior prevents people from really knowing this individual. Griping is a protection from the pains of life. In reality, it is just a screen.

3. Secondary needs being revealed:

   ▶ Affiliation: This student needs to develop a strong friendship with someone — perhaps with an adult.

   ▶ Achievement: This student may really need to achieve, but somehow feels inadequate.

   ▶ Aggression: This student may be acting out some real hostilities toward the school and attempting to beat the system in any way possible.

   ▶ Power: The griper may be attempting to let others know that he/she counts. This student wants some control over what's happening to him/her in the classroom.

   ▶ Autonomy: The griper is also demonstrating a need to be his/her own boss.

128

4. Find the reason this student is a griper. What's causing it? Is it a home situation, a health problem, or something else? Get at the roots of the griping. Do not proceed with any action until you know the cause of his/her general discontent. But don't spend time asking the student directly.

5. When you talk to the student, ask what he/she would like to do.

6. Then, adopt a "Your Choice" strategic approach. Say, "Do as you like. However, be prepared to pay the price for your choices."

7. Next, let the student know you are angry. Tell him/her, "You are ruining my teaching plan and I don't like it." Say, "If you can't do the work, ask for help, but don't gripe about it."

8. Tell the student schoolwork is not easy. Learning is hard work. Never tell this student something is easy and he/she shouldn't complain. Such tactics are a concession or apology approach — and won't work.

9. In getting this student back on the road to success, start out with simple assignments that can be completed easily.

10. Put the griper in a leadership role which will show him/her how to become responsible.

11. Continue to talk out this problem with the student, and share specific instances when the griping behavior recurs.

12. Work to improve the student's self-concept.

13. Involve parents when necessary. And be sure that the source of the problem is resolved and that there is consistency in positive reinforcement both in school and at home.

14. Have the student offer a plan for a solution to what he/she is griping about, or offer data to support his/her griping.

IV. MISTAKES: Common misjudgments and errors in managing the child which may perpetuate or intensify the problem.

1. Ignoring this student when nothing else seems to work.

2. Reacting in the same manner as the griper.

3. Becoming defensive.

4. Letting this student's behavior give other students negative ideas.

5. Making concessions.

6. Being inconsistent.

7. Refusing all gripes.

8. Babying the student.

9. Being harsh publicly rather than confronting the student privately.

SEE ALSO: • The Attention Demander • The Complainer • The Crier (Who Claims Foul) • The Disrupter • The Last Worder • The Loudmouth

THE HABITUAL ABSENTEE

I. BEHAVIOR: Specific attitudes and actions of this child at home and/or at school.

1. Misses class and school for countless reasons, from illness to the excuse that parents need him/her at home.

2. May be uneasy about his/her absence. More often than not, however, does not believe his/her absence should cause teacher any problems or upset.

3. Expects extra help.

4. Thinks he/she shouldn't have to make up work and feels persecuted if teacher thinks differently.

5. Doesn't achieve much because he/she misses so much class.

6. When present, often so far behind that he/she can't do class work.

7. Doesn't know what's going on in class.

8. One of the hardest students for both teachers and administrators to deal with. That's because this student is likely to be doing *nothing* even when he/she does come to school. In a sense, this student is absent even when he/she is present.

9. Likely to act bored by school. May be either bright or dull intellectually, and thus may be bored for either of two completely opposite reasons.

10. Usually defensive. Therefore, refuses to look at him/herself as the problem.

II. EFFECTS: How behavior affects teachers, classmates, and parents in the school learning environment and the home family situation.

1. Teacher may be upset if this student is achieving far below his/her potential.

2. Teacher is continually subjected to the inconvenience of bringing this student up to date academically. Because the student may be so far behind, this can seem insurmountable.

3. Classmates may ignore, reject, or make fun of this student.

4. Class may recognize this student only as a "partial" member.

5. Unfortunately, teacher may choose to be happy or relieved when this student doesn't show up for class, and "half mad" when he/she does. Therefore, teacher mood and disposition may be altered.

III. ACTION: • Identify causes of misbehavior.
   • Pinpoint student needs being revealed.
   • Employ specific methods, procedures, and techniques at school and at home for getting the child to modify or change his/her behavior.

1. Primary causes of misbehavior:

   ▶ Self-Confidence: This student escapes from school because of a feeling that he/she can't do the work.

   ▶ Power: Being absent continually may be an act of open dissent against the school.

2. Primary need being revealed:

   ▶ Escape from Pain: This child could be a poor student and might find it too painful to attend class. By being absent, he/she gains an excuse for being behind.

3. Secondary needs being revealed:

  ◗ Aggression: This student needs to be involved in school in some way that makes him/her feel a part of the school. Absenteeism may be a negative form of assertion.

  ◗ Power: The habitual absentee is demonstrating his/her power through the school's inability to keep him/her in school. Somehow the power need must be met by giving this student authority of some kind.

  ◗ Achievement: This student *must* experience some little successes.

  ◗ Status: Every effort should be made to make this person feel his/her importance in being present in class.

4. If you want to change the behavior of this student, you must make the most difficult professional adjustments a teacher can make:

  • Make this student an exception. If you cannot make a temporary exception for this student, he/she will have no reason for coming to class and staying. His/her hope will be gone in a short period of time.

  • Work on today's lesson only. Forget about back assignments. Working on them is self-defeating for teacher and student alike. The student may be directed to back assignments to support today's lesson.

  • Remember, the student who has fallen behind in his/her work is facing a double burden: making up the incomplete or missing work, and keeping up with the current assignments. In essence, the student is doing double work. Every teacher should keep this fact in mind. Sometimes the best way to help this student is to reduce the length of some make-up assignments. The real issue, after all, is to have the student demonstrate a competency level in the work missed. If this student is required to "complete every missed assignment," he/she may quit altogether. A teacher's hardest task is to motivate students. That's why it's important not to present insurmountable obstacles in the form of make-up work.

  • Here's a procedure for make-up work that can be an aid to student and teacher alike. Get a notebook and keep an absentee make-up book which is available for all to use. In the book, list assignments to be completed. Keep it as you go each day and leave it at the front of the room. Then, it will be available for all to use at any time. Encourage students to use it, especially if they have been absent. Not only will it keep you up to date and accurate, but it also eliminates the excuse, "I didn't know we had to do that."

5. Make your first goal getting this student to attend class. Then begin working on selection of the work he/she must make up in order to master the present curriculum. Never forget, insistence on making up all work will only succeed in driving this student away.

6. Remember, people do what works for them. And being absent *works* better for this student than attending class. Therefore, you must make coming to class work for him/her.

7. If you really want to change this student's behavior, make something happen for him/her *today*. Equally important, make *each day* important and successful.

  • Never talk about "not doing anything important tomorrow." Rather, talk about the need to be in class tomorrow. Remember, it's harder to stay away from class if something significant is happening. When the student returns, never do or say anything that implies that it's not important to be in class. Rather, do everything you can to create the feeling that something important happens in class every day. Always call home on the second or third day of the student's absence. Make it a point to visit privately with the student when he/she returns. You may improve motivation, performance, and attendance if you do.

  • To make tomorrow important, try these techniques — one at a time:

    Give the student a special assignment.

131

Plan to see him/her about something important as often as you can.

Give him/her an important daily task.

Never ignore this student.

Never fail to talk to him/her.

8. As soon as the child stops showing up for class, take quick action. Call parents immediately. Inform counselors, nurse, and administrator immediately.

9. Check with other school personnel to determine if they are aware of any special problems. If they are not, then schedule a meeting with the student to discuss the situation. Try to settle the issue quickly and positively, without fanfare. But realize that you may need to meet with parents to enlist their aid. Therefore, notify parents of the frequency of absences immediately. Above all, inform them of the steps you are taking to resolve the problem.

10. Be totally accepting and do not compare this student with classmates, especially in terms of evaluation. And don't make this student defensive about being his/her own worst enemy. This student cannot take such confronting *until* he/she is experiencing success.

11. Be aware that habitual absenteeism doesn't start overnight, and it can't be cured overnight. A check of records might reveal that absenteeism started several years ago and was allowed to go unchecked for some reason — often with parental permission.

12. Talk to parents about the importance of regular attendance. Some parents think it's OK for a child to miss school. They may even take the child out of school to go on a family trip. Emphasize that repeated absences jeopardize a student's chances to achieve success in school, and form poor habits for the world of work.

13. Make sure that this child knows you care about his/her being in class. Don't ignore this student when he/she does come. Welcoming a student back to your class after an absence can do much to build a stronger pupil-teacher relationship. Absences can become commonplace for teachers because they see so many of them during a week's time. However, for the individual student, the absence is very important. Let the student know that he/she was missed and you are glad he/she is back. Comments such as "We had a good discussion yesterday and missed your participation" or "The students needed you for their dodgeball game at recess yesterday" certainly prove that the student was missed and that he/she "counts for something." They also help the student like his/her teacher.

IV. MISTAKES: Common misjudgments and errors in managing the child which may perpetuate or intensify the problem.

1. Forming our own opinions of the validity of this student's reason for absence — regardless of the formal excuse he/she brings to class.

2. Giving the student a "disbelieving look" after reading his/her excuse, throwing it on the desk without even reading it, or saying something like "It was a good day to be sick, wasn't it?" By doing so, we may punish this student continuously in our own way — and make *coming to class* unpleasant rather than pleasant.

3. Accepting the behavior and giving up on any corrective action, including counseling.

4. Acting as if we are too busy when this student comes to us for help.

5. Getting angry — and withholding information regarding academic make-up work until the orderly learning process becomes confused and the student becomes lost academically between past and current work.

6. Postponing help, delaying a make-up test until the information gets stale, or simply "springing" the test on the student on the day of our choosing.

7. Showing that we dislike the student as well as what he/she is doing.

8. Saying such things as "You're worthless" or "You'll never amount to anything."

9. Failing to welcome the student to class when he/she comes.

10. Allowing the student's nonattendance to be our reason to judge him/her a discipline problem.

11. Allowing nonattendance to become a personal confrontation, when the absence has nothing to do with us.

12. Responding flippantly with comments such as "Well, you decided to come in today."

SEE ALSO: • The Apathetic • The Do-Nothing • The Failer • The Skipper
• The Truant

THE HATER

I. BEHAVIOR: **Specific attitudes and actions of this child at home and/or at school.**

1. Seems to dislike everything — including him/herself. Worse, wants everyone to know it.
2. Reveals hatred through aggressiveness, rigid body language, icy stares, or total silence.
3. Does not participate.
4. May refuse to work with other students.
5. Holds grudges for a long time.
6. Works poorly as a group member.
7. May have sympathetic followers.
8. Appears unapproachable.
9. Does not meet academic or rule requirements.
10. Criticizes others.
11. Questions the necessity and/or importance of teacher decisions.
12. Has frequently experienced hurt.
13. Has rarely experienced success.
14. Usually on the defensive.
15. Has a negative attitude.
16. Usually a loner.

II. EFFECTS: **How behavior affects teachers, classmates, and parents in the school learning environment and the home family situation.**

1. Teacher and classmates feel uncomfortable — and maybe a little frightened.
2. Others may ignore or avoid this student.
3. Others find this continuous and total hatred difficult to understand.
4. Academic interest is halted, to say nothing of achievement.
5. Enthusiasm for academic material is totally eliminated.
6. A negative classroom climate is created.
7. Constant tension is generated.
8. This attitude may isolate the student from the rest of the class.

III. ACTION:
- **Identify causes of misbehavior.**
- **Pinpoint student needs being revealed.**
- **Employ specific methods, procedures, and techniques at school and at home for getting the child to modify or change his/her behavior.**

1. Primary cause of misbehavior:

   ▶ Revenge: This person is expressing a lot of pain and finds satisfaction in being a hater.

2. Primary need being revealed:

♦ Escape from Pain: When a person experiences pain, inflicting pain sometimes makes him/her feel better.

3. Secondary needs being revealed:

♦ Power: Acceptance by an adult may meet this student's power needs. The acceptance of assigned tasks may be a form of power.

♦ Affiliation: This student needs to have someone he/she can trust so that some of the hate may be vented through a trusted friend.

♦ Status: An adult can assure this person that he/she counts and is an important person.

4. There are some very definite things a teacher should and should not do with the hater. First, don't try to handle the hater as you do other discipline problems, and don't ignore him/her.

5. Most important, never hate back — or you will reinforce the behavior.

6. Adopting a "special" attitude toward the hater will prove beneficial. Rather than classify this student as a hater, think of the child as someone who hasn't found him/herself yet.

7. Also, never forget that this student may have good reason to hate. If his/her hating makes sense, the behavior may be a protective wall.

8. When counseling, don't inquire about the hate. Talk about his/her "being down." The former is more private and entrenched than the latter. A student will reveal why he/she is "down" more quickly than why he/she hates.

9. Be empathetic and sincere.

10. Encourage others to give this student positive comments.

11. If you have not experienced whatever is causing this student to hate, don't say, "I know how you feel." You don't.

12. Explain that your class can be a good place for this student and that he/she can count on you. Then, keep your promise. Make school a better place than any other.

13. Try to force involvement gently and on a simple level at which success is sure and your acceptance can be revealed.

14. Inform counselors, school psychologists, and administrators, and seek their assistance.

15. Don't expect one or two sessions with you to help this student. He/she may have a reason to hate. Never forget, studies show it takes seven impressions to get people to change a strongly held attitude or belief.

16. Be aware that the key to this behavior is that the student thinks more power would eliminate his/her problem.

17. Keep a clear perspective and do not make the mistake of taking this student's behavior personally. Remain above his/her personal attacks and say, "I'm sorry. Is there anything I can do for you?" The hater has very few meaningful relationships with adults and needs you more than any other kid in school does.

18. Show that you like and accept this student for what he/she is.

19. Be flexible and know that there will be days when this student will again display vindictiveness. Remember not to reject when he/she slips on "bad days."

20. Tell the hater whenever you hear something good about him/her from someone else — even if it is something minor.

21. Seek professional counseling assistance.

22. Here is a counseling approach that is effective with the hater. Explain to the student that:

• People can help us with our hurts. They can soothe them. They can even help resolve them. This is not so easily done with hate. That's because there are many differences between hurt and hate. Others can understand, accept, sympathize, and empathize with our hurt. Truly, others can hurt *with* us. However, hate has an entirely different weight. It scares many people. Though people may accept the fact that we hate, they often don't really understand how we arrived at our position. More often than not, others don't condone our hate. In fact, they may be confused by the rationale behind our hate. How often have you heard someone say, "How can you be so angry over that?"

- A close look will reveal that our real problems may come if our hate *is accepted* by those close to us. For instance, it might seem that someone has the right to hate because of all the hurts he/she has endured. Such reinforcement may cause the person to be consumed by hate. Unfortunately, people can and do justify hate even if it doesn't make sense, and may even continue to understand someone's hate when the only outcome is chaos. After all, the vast majority of hate is illogical.

- Hate is usually the projection of hurt. The problem is that a temporary hurt can become a permanent hate for the smallest and most insignificant reason. Too, hate is often projected toward those we know. Likewise, hating people we don't know is almost always illogical, irrational, and based more on opinion and hearsay than on fact. Once we choose not to love, we have closed off many of our options. In truth, we are forced into a locked position and our choice may hurt us as much as those we hate.

23. Hurt and hate in the classroom need examination. When a child is hurt, *confusion* reigns first. Then *pride* often takes over. *Poor judgment* and *poor reactions* are likely to follow. Remember, a student will often try to make sure nobody else is aware that he/she is hurting. Don't act as if nothing is wrong, or this hurt can be transferred into hate. Someone must be sensitive to hurts. A friend or classmate should be; a teacher must be. If someone isn't there to do some protecting when hurts are revealed, hate may be the result.

24. Make sure that the hater gets special attention from you and/or another teacher. This can do more to change his/her attitude and behavior than any other technique. Many of these "hard" children are really "softies," but have had very few gentle people in their lives. Often such a child, even one who is in serious trouble with the law, will try his/her very best to achieve success in school simply because one teacher takes a personal, private, and sincere interest. Even though it is difficult for one teacher to take very many of these students, through group meetings it can be arranged to have different teachers take different children. However, *never* let the children suspect that "assignments" have been made. They don't need that kind of help. They need someone to get to know them well enough to believe in them.

IV. MISTAKES: Common misjudgments and errors in managing the child which may perpetuate or intensify the problem.

1. Trying to handle this student as though he/she were a discipline problem.

2. Ignoring the student.

3. Rejecting the student.

4. Reacting personally, returning hatred for hatred and thinking this student hates us and all our values. This reaction reinforces feelings of hate.

5. Talking *at* — rather than *with* — this student.

6. Raising our voices or yelling.

7. Failing to think in terms of goals for this student — or failing to set such goals.

8. Failing to be positive with this student in any way, or to see any good in him/her.

9. Judging too quickly.

10. Trivializing the student's problem.

11. Being impatient.

12. Dealing with this student publicly.

13. Talking about him/her to other students.

14. Thinking we know how he/she feels.

SEE ALSO: • The Agitator • The Angry •The Authority Pusher • The Defier
• The Exploder • The Overly Aggressive

THE HIDER

I. BEHAVIOR: Specific attitudes and actions of this child at home and/or at school.

1. Does not steal; rather, hides pencils, books, lunches, tickets, purses, and other items — just for fun.
2. Hides at critical times — gym clothes before P.E., lunch tickets before noon.
3. Denies the action.
4. Pretends innocence.
5. May help look for hidden items.
6. Sometimes involves others.
7. Attempts to secure approval for his/her cleverness.
8. Is hurt when others get mad.
9. Often a loner.

II. EFFECTS: How behavior affects teachers, classmates, and parents in the school learning environment and the home family situation.

1. Class is interrupted.
2. Learning time is wasted.
3. It's often difficult, if not impossible, to detect who is responsible for the hiding.
4. Victim is hurt and frustrated.
5. Teacher appears helpless and not in control of situation.
6. Atmosphere of distrust is created in the classroom.

III. ACTION:
- **Identify causes of misbehavior.**
- **Pinpoint student needs being revealed.**
- **Employ specific methods, procedures, and techniques at school and at home for getting the child to modify or change his/her behavior.**

1. Primary cause of misbehavior:
   ◗ Attention: This person needs others to notice him/her.
2. Primary needs being revealed:
   ◗ Sex: This student is attempting to establish relationships, but just doesn't know how to go about it. When someone hides another person's belongings, he/she certainly gets interaction with that other person.
   ◗ Escape from Pain: This person may have had some painful experiences with people and, for this reason, is going about causing pain to others.
3. Secondary needs being revealed:
   ◗ Gregariousness: Certain classroom activities may provide opportunities for this person to belong to a group.
   ◗ Achievement: The tasks of the classroom may appear too difficult, so the student distracts him/herself from failure by hiding things.

   ◆ Autonomy: By hiding things, this person is showing some independence. Involvement in activities could meet this need in a positive way.

4. Do not treat this behavior as stealing.

5. Make it clear the first time such behavior occurs that it is unacceptable, and why this is so.

6. Be aware that the hider often acts in the presence of another, or tells somebody what he/she has done.

7. Remember, attention is the primary motivation.

8. Instead of reacting negatively to this student's need for attention, ignoring him/her, or showing dislike, give this student as much attention as possible without overdoing it. Too often, the only attention this student receives, even from classmates, comes from hiding things.

9. Talk with this student at length, privately. Private counseling is a form of attention. Threats must *never* be a part of your talks.

10. Assign some responsibility that will provide an opportunity for this student to be recognized in a meaningful way. More often than not, if you give the hider classroom tasks and praise for his/her efforts, this student will respond quickly with acceptable behavior.

11. Use the "Immature" technique. Point out that this behavior is typical of younger children — not of students on this grade level. You can apply this technique to any grade.

12. Tell the student when you observe another's approval of him/her.

13. Give this student extra attention. A strong need for attention may be prompting him/her to seek satisfaction by hiding things.

14. Refer student to counselor.

15. Contact parents; once will often solve the problem.

16. Discuss the problem with the class — but not at the time of the disturbance.

17. If an item is permanently lost, make sure the hider assumes responsibility for replacing the item.

18. Make sure that the student knows you accept him/her, but disapprove of the behavior.

IV. MISTAKES: Common misjudgments and errors in managing the child which may perpetuate or intensify the problem.

1. Refusing to take this problem seriously enough.

2. Turning on the victim and blaming him/her.

3. Failing to explain the unacceptability of this behavior and/or the reasons for rules against it. Too often, we just treat it as a "bad joke."

4. Disciplining the entire class for the behavior of one student.

5. Making accusations, which may sometimes be erroneous and therefore damaging.

6. Ignoring or showing dislike for this student.

7. Ostracizing this student.

8. Punishing too severely.

9. Confusing hiding with stealing.

SEE ALSO: • The Attention Demander • The Con Artist • The Destroyer
               • The Distracter • The Thief

THE HYPERACTIVE

I. BEHAVIOR: **Specific attitudes and actions of this child at home and/or at school.**

1. Simply cannot sit still.
2. Moves arms, shifts body, and plays with objects.
3. Gets out of seat whenever he/she can.
4. Has a short attention span.
5. Pesters other students continually.
6. Needs and seeks attention from anyone and everyone.
7. In perpetual motion at home, too. When watching TV, fiddles with hands, picks face, or eats. And gets up during every commercial.
8. Seems unable to accept any kind of confinement or limits, no matter how reasonable.
9. Falls behind in schoolwork and, as a result, is not a good student.
10. However, in courses which require activity, may not even be noticed by teacher.

II. EFFECTS: **How behavior affects teachers, classmates, and parents in the school learning environment and the home family situation.**

1. Teacher is driven "up the wall."
2. Classmates feel tense and anxious.
3. Teacher must spend a disproportionate amount of time dealing with this behavior.
4. Classmates may misbehave more because this student acts as a catalyst for misbehavior.
5. Peers can't identify with this behavior; thus the hyperactive student may become alienated from peers.
6. Constant watching and correction become a continuous teacher activity. If a teacher corrected all this student's misbehavior that's all he/she would do.
7. Establishing standards in the classroom becomes difficult.

III. ACTION:
- **Identify causes of misbehavior.**
- **Pinpoint student needs being revealed.**
- **Employ specific methods, procedures, and techniques at school and at home for getting the child to modify or change his/her behavior.**

1. Primary cause of misbehavior:
   - This is usually not a misbehavior situation, but a physical problem.
2. Primary need being revealed:
   - Escape from Pain: This is usually a health problem. It is very difficult for this student to remain quiet or inactive for a long period of time.
3. Secondary need being revealed:
   - Autonomy: This person must be put in charge of him/herself, and must take the responsibility to move about without disturbing anyone.

140

4. Discover the cause of the student's hyperactive nature. There may be medical reasons. The student may be on some kind of medication which is controlling the hyperactivity, and the teacher must help him/her stay on schedule. Or it may be stress, family life, anxiety, or some other cause.

5. Do not force this student to sit for a long time. He/she can't.

6. Arrange for him/her to move at intervals planned by you. Movement should be the reward system you use to motivate.

7. Create short-term goals for the student so he/she can realize more successes, and find activities which will absorb the need to be hyperactive.

8. Students often instinctively call out to a friend or push the person next to them. Asking "why" won't bring an answer because there isn't one. This doesn't mean the behavior should be condoned, but it should be looked upon and understood for what it is — an act of impulse. Treat such acts as a temporary lack of self-control — which is normal. Remember, at times students will act impulsively without thinking. Correct such acts, but don't make this behavior into something that it isn't.

9. Give positive reinforcement whenever the hyperactive student is quiet or under conscious direction.

10. Make improvement your goal. Have the student keep a chart of how many times you have corrected. In the process, develop a set of hand and eye signals which will let you correct without disturbing class.

11. Give task assignments which involve activity, such as passing out papers — as long as work is being done. This will motivate him/her to work more quickly.

12. Refer this student for professional counseling when necessary.

13. Suggest to parents that the child receive a complete physical examination.

14. Try role playing in a private conference. Switch roles with the student. You become hyperactive and let the student become the teacher. This will allow the student to observe how his/her hyperactivity appears to others.

15. When necessary, create a special schedule which will allow more freedom for this student.

16. Schedule a parent conference early. Do not wait for a crisis. Ask parents for help, and express a willingness to cooperate with outside professional assistance.

17. Keep a close check with other teachers. This may be a problem in your class only.

18. Always use verbal and nonverbal communication in a slow, quiet, and patient way. Any other strategic action only increases the student's anxiety and makes the behavior worse.

19. When students gather during a class break or recess, it's not unusual for them to get "carried away" occasionally. This is the time when teacher alertness and rapport can really count. Try a quiet touch on the shoulder and a friendly "Take it easy"; this approach can work wonders in helping students keep their behavior under control. It's always more effective than shouting.

IV. MISTAKES: Common misjudgments and errors in managing the child which may perpetuate or intensify the problem.

1. Assuming that the student can control his/her behavior, and that the hyperactivity is a conscious choice.

2. Giving unfair punishments.

3. Tending to prejudge the student's behavior in all situations because of a few occurrences.

4. Attempting to humiliate the student, whether privately in conference or publicly in the classroom.

The Hyperactive

5. Failing to try to motivate this student by making his/her class work or assignments more challenging.

6. Getting impatient. This only increases the student's anxiety.

SEE ALSO: • The Distracter • The Goer • The Repeater • The Traveler

"I CAN'T"

I. BEHAVIOR: **Specific attitudes and actions of this child at home and/or at school.**

1. Approaches every task insisting, "I can't."
2. Even claims to be unable to do assignments that he/she has done before.
3. Behavior is habitual.
4. Says, "I can't" before listening to teacher explain what it is he/she is claiming to be unable to do.
5. Through teacher's cajoling, prodding, and even begging, continues to say, "I can't."
6. Acts scared.
7. Worries continuously.
8. Insecure.

II. EFFECTS: **How behavior affects teachers, classmates, and parents in the school learning environment and the home family situation.**

1. Teacher as well as the entire class is adversely affected.
2. Defeat spreads over the classroom.
3. The learning process is slowed down.
4. Classroom procedures are held up.
5. Classmates are pestered by this student's requests for help.
6. Sometimes, both teacher and classmates exclude this student.
7. Teacher may become angry.

III. ACTION: • **Identify causes of misbehavior.**
   • **Pinpoint student needs being revealed.**
   • **Employ specific methods, procedures, and techniques at school and at home for getting the child to modify or change his/her behavior.**

1. Primary cause of misbehavior:
   ‣ Self-Confidence: It's a much better defense to say, "I can't" than to attempt any task. This stance allows one to discuss all the reasons why something can't happen rather than why it can happen.
2. Primary need being revealed:
   ‣ Escape from Pain: This student may be experiencing many personal problems in and out of school, resulting in a defeatist attitude.
3. Secondary need being revealed:
   ‣ Achievement: Review this student's records, and you may discover a failure experience. This student should be taught every possible method to increase his/her successes in the future.
4. Recognize that this student needs individual attention and encouragement.
5. Remember, if you could spend your time with this student exclusively, his/her reluctance to try wouldn't be such a problem. Unfortunately, you can't. You have a roomful of other students.

143

6. Never offer bribes and rewards to get this student to try. This is easy to do because it's obvious that if the student would just try, half the battle would be won.

7. Here are four motivational techniques that can be used separately or in combination. It should be remembered that praise and other reinforcement techniques should be used following the success of motivational efforts.

   • First, try the "Assumption" technique. Stop urging, begging, and prodding. Simply present the assignment and assume through both attitude and action that the assignment can and will be done. Assume a positive "take-for-granted" position during instruction. Ignore the "I can't" — and act as if any question is a very good one. For best results, use the "Assumption" technique for short assignments. Keep a clear perspective. This student will not attempt long or complex assignments, so don't assign a difficult task until he/she has had success with simpler ones.

   • The "Choice" approach can also be successful. Simply give the student a choice of two or three things to do and walk away as soon as he/she makes a choice. The choices should be of equal value. Combining the "Assumption" and "Choice" techniques can produce good results. Remember, assignment completion is not the primary goal; trying is. Therefore, never criticize a failure to achieve. Rather, praise the student's efforts.

   • Utilize the "Minor Point" technique. Make the primary issue something insignificant, rather than the task at hand. Simply say, "Do you want to use a pen or pencil on this assignment?" or "White or yellow paper?" or "Do you want to hand in your papers in thirty minutes or at the end of the hour?" The "Minor Point" method is very effective with the "I can't" student as well as the rest of the class.

   • Also, employ the "Physical Action" technique. Do something physical to get things started and take minds away from the issue of trying. Many physical actions can be employed. Give the student the instrument or physical object necessary to do a task. Or send a student to the library to get the one thing that is needed to do the assignment easily. Talk about this one needed aid — not the task. It can be a special book, specific pages in the text, or anything else related to the assignment. This technique reduces fears and starts the physical action of trying at the same time.

8. The "I can't" habit in a student is hard to break because it works so well. Once the student finds it no longer works, he/she will abandon it, but usually only with the person with whom it doesn't work. Therefore, involve other teachers and parents in your action.

9. Make sure your expectations remain high for this student. The self-fulfilling prophecy will be a factor, and you want it to be a positive one.

IV. MISTAKES: Common misjudgments and errors in managing the child which may perpetuate or intensify the problem.

1. Accepting this student's reluctance to participate, and going on without him/her.
2. Ignoring this student.
3. Making fun of this student.
4. Comparing him/her to other kids.
5. Saying it's wrong to ask for help.
6. Helping the student reluctantly.
7. Saying, "Sure, you can." Such statements close communication, because this student believes he/she *can't.*

SEE ALSO: • The Alibier • The Do-Nothing • The Excuse/Alibi Maker • The Lazy • Satisfied with Second Place

"I DON'T CARE"

I. BEHAVIOR: **Specific attitudes and actions of this child at home and/or at school.**

1. Always says, "I don't care" to anyone who will listen.
2. Says, "I don't care" nonverbally too — through behavior and attitudes.
3. Usually fails to bring materials to class.
4. Doesn't do assignments.
5. Inattentive.
6. Shows disgust or lack of interest in class activities all the time.
7. Makes up any kind of excuse which he/she thinks will work in the situation — especially "I forgot."
8. Doesn't follow directions.
9. Doesn't listen.
10. Doesn't do well academically.
11. Often, in trouble in more than one class — and out of school as well.

II. EFFECTS: **How behavior affects teachers, classmates, and parents in the school learning environment and the home family situation.**

1. Teacher's enthusiasm, and class climate in general, are dampened.
2. Class is interrupted.
3. Time is taken away from other students.
4. "I don't care" attitude can become contagious.
5. Teacher can easily become frustrated.
6. After awhile, when no success or forward movement is seen relative to this attitude, teacher may get angry.
7. Peers can become alienated and disgusted themselves because the "I don't care" attitude often means disregard for them, too.
8. Entire class can begin to develop a low image of itself.

III. ACTION:
- **Identify causes of misbehavior.**
- **Pinpoint student needs being revealed.**
- **Employ specific methods, procedures, and techniques at school and at home for getting the child to modify or change his/her behavior.**

1. Primary causes of misbehavior:
   - Self-Confidence: This student may have such low self-esteem that he/she has reached a point of really not caring.
   - Revenge: Failure may have caused this student to give up trying, and to find personal satisfaction in "I don't care" behavior.
2. Primary needs being revealed:
   - Sex: This student may have experienced a failure in some personal relationship.

145

     ♦ Escape from Pain: Failures in academics and/or personal relationships are very painful and an "I don't care" attitude screens the pain.

3. Secondary needs being revealed:

     ♦ Achievement: This student probably arrived at the "I don't care" attitude through a series of failures. Somehow there must be some success in his/her life.

     ♦ Status: The student probably considers him/herself a "nobody." If this child becomes "somebody" to a teacher, peer, or any special person, his/her attitudes may change.

4. Be aware that the student who says, "I don't care" in a hostile manner usually *does* care. He/she may really be saying, "I don't want to get hurt." The student who appears to have given up may, indeed, have stopped caring.

5. Talk with the student individually. Ask what he/she wants — try to discover what, if anything, the student is interested in.

6. Rather than reprimand, ask, "What are you worried about?" This is the real issue, even if the student doesn't know it yet.

7. Then, talk to the student about "finding yourself."

8. Ask what his/her problem is with the class. Ask why he/she is coming to class with these negative feelings and bringing them into the open. Then, ask the student to think about these things. Say, "You do care. That's why you're acting this way." Then say, "I'm going to help whether you say so or not."

9. Always explain the consequences of "I don't care" behavior. Show the student how this attitude totally dissolves and ruins his/her effectiveness; the student will be the only loser if the behavior continues. At the same time, show the student the excitement that can be inherent in the learning process.

10. Use all modalities for learning when dealing with this child.

11. Point out the good things this student does.

12. Shorten assignments.

13. Make the goal of each assignment clearer and more immediately achievable.

14. Try to give the student choices.

15. Be aware that this student is much more difficult to work with than the cheater or the liar. The latter are at least attempting success through cheating and lying. The person who doesn't care won't even cheat or lie to get tasks completed.

16. Think twice before addressing a question to a nonlistener in order to gain attention. This technique only makes everyone aware that someone in the class isn't giving full attention. Too, the questioned student may laugh or counter with some other defensive reaction that instills a negative climate in the classroom.

17. Never reveal dislike for a student. Such dislike is very often triggered by a student's aggressive or passive defiance of teacher authority. Revealing dislike may lead to such student responses as more aggression, a retreat into despair if the student feels unworthy, or an "I don't care" attitude. Worse, other students may respond the same way because they think they may be the next target. Thus, a teacher's response of dislike can set in motion the negative feelings of a whole class. The teacher must make the initial positive move when dislike surfaces. The teacher must *understand* the causes of his/her dislike, *make* him/herself respond to student behavior rather than to the student personally, and *follow up* every difficulty with caring counsel.

IV. MISTAKES: Common misjudgments and errors in managing the child which may perpetuate or intensify the problem.

1. Not trying to find out what's really important for this child.

2. Failing to ask what really motivates or would motivate this student, what he/she would be interested in and would like to do, and how he/she would like to approach it.

3. Making the student's problems exclusively his/her own, and beginning to manifest an "I don't care" attitude toward the student.

4. Reinforcing this negative behavior in either subtle or overt ways.

5. Giving up on this student.

6. Getting tough.

7. Responding personally.

8. Failing to look for tiny improvements in the student's behavior or attempts to complete tasks.

SEE ALSO: • The Alibier • The Apathetic • The Do-Nothing • "I Can't"
              • The Indifferent • The Irresponsible • The Lazy • The Unprepared

"I WON'T DO IT"

I. BEHAVIOR: Specific attitudes and actions of this child at home and/or at school.

1. Refuses to try new tasks.

2. May start, then stop almost immediately.

3. Fearful.

4. Will only attempt lessons or tasks that appeal to him/her.

5. Often appears busy, but ends up not completing assignments.

6. Usually argumentative.

7. Always makes excuses for what he/she did or didn't do.

8. May "dare" you to make him/her do anything.

9. Appears very hostile to adults.

II. EFFECTS: How behavior affects teachers, classmates, and parents in the school learning environment and the home family situation.

1. Teacher is frustrated.

2. Teacher spends disproportionate amount of time trying to deal with this student.

3. Peers are often influenced by this negative attitude. When they see it working for a classmate, they will try it themselves.

4. A lot of teacher's time is required outside class.

5. Many times the confrontation causes a win/lose situation between teacher and student.

6. Classmates are very aware of how teacher deals with the "I won't do it" student.

7. Teacher may lose control of him/herself.

III. ACTION: • Identify causes of misbehavior.
• Pinpoint student needs being revealed.
• Employ specific methods, procedures, and techniques at school and at home for getting the child to modify or change his/her behavior.

1. Primary causes of misbehavior:

   ◗ Revenge: This student is pulling away from all adult figures and striking out at authority.

   ◗ Power: Open dissent is a form of power.

2. Primary need being revealed:

   ◗ Escape from Pain: This student could be trying to escape the pain of various concerns at home or in school. Efforts should be made to explore possibilities of underachievement in school or difficulties outside school.

3. Secondary needs being revealed:

   ◗ Status: This student might be attempting to "be somebody" by saying, "No" or "I won't do it" to adults or any kind of authority.

   ◗ Aggression: This acting out may be a negative form of aggression, and effort should be made to direct this behavior in some positive manner. This student could be allowed

148

leadership roles in the classroom, or given responsibilities on the playground or in out-of-classroom activities.

- ▶ Power: This is a need that many students do not know how to handle in a positive manner. Students refuse adults as a show of power. Every effort should be made to demonstrate to the student that such behavior causes him/her to lose power.

- ▶ Achievement: Personal as well as academic success is important to this student.

4. Make your expectations for this student very clear. State the choices that are available to the student now or later. Show him/her the ramifications of the "I won't do it" attitude. Say, "That's fine, but this is what I must do if you don't try."

5. Be sure that you and the student are clear regarding what the specific results will be.

6. Help the student to realize that your expectations are fair and reasonable. Then, follow through with the stated consequences.

7. Set reasonable goals for this student.

8. Don't expect the student to alter his/her behavior all at once.

9. Remain calm. Don't react personally. Stay professional.

10. Be consistent in the way you deal with this student. Don't show favoritism one way or the other from day to day.

11. When correcting the student, preface a negative comment with positive comments. For instance, say, "This behavior isn't typical of you; what happened?" or "You usually get along with everyone. What made you fight today?" It's easier for this student to accept teacher guidance when it's clear that you see his/her good points as well as his/her faults. Regard every correction situation as an opportunity to build relationships with the student — not to destroy them.

12. Notify parents early. Do not allow this behavior to reach an excessive level before scheduling a conference. This may be a problem at home too, and parents may be most willing to assist in working with the student.

13. Look for small improvements in the behavior of the student. Your ability to see the small positive changes will affect how you work with the student.

14. Celebrate with this student small victories and improvements in behavior. Use such comments as "You should be proud of yourself for such a positive effort on this assignment," or "Isn't it neat that this was the result of your efforts on the assignment?"

IV. MISTAKES: Common misjudgments and errors in managing the child which may perpetuate or intensify the problem.

1. Listening too much to excuses.

2. Letting this student miss activities rather than pushing him/her.

3. Taking this student's behavior personally, or allowing him/her to upset us.

4. Feeling that we have to lower standards for this student.

5. Misjudging this student's real ability.

6. Thinking this behavior is an act of defiance.

7. Losing control and physically trying to force this student to meet our demands.

SEE ALSO: • The Alibier   • The Authority Pusher   • The Defier   • The Distracter
• "I Can't"   • The Last Worder   • The Rebel

149

THE "IDIOT" SYNDROME

I. BEHAVIOR: **Specific attitudes and actions of this child at home and/or at school.**

1. Doesn't attend to assignments because, he/she claims, "I've never seen that before" or "I don't know anything about that."

2. Always raises his/her hand before, during, and after the assignment is given to ask questions that usually waste class time.

3. Asks to have directions repeated.

4. Repeatedly says things like "Do another one for me."

5. Uses expressions like "Huh?" "Why?" "I don't understand," and "I'm dumb."

6. May have low potential and use the "idiot" syndrome as a cover.

II. EFFECTS: **How behavior affects teachers, classmates, and parents in the school learning environment and the home family situation.**

1. Teacher spends disproportionate amount of time dealing with this student.

2. Other students are distracted.

3. The "idiot" type of response can be contagious.

4. Teacher frequently ends up just trying to tune out this student.

5. Teacher may become irritated after a while when no success is seen with this student.

III. ACTION:
- **Identify causes of misbehavior.**
- **Pinpoint student needs being revealed.**
- **Employ specific methods, procedures, and techniques at school and at home for getting the child to modify or change his/her behavior.**

1. Primary cause of misbehavior:
   ▶ Self-Confidence: This student has discovered a means of excusing him/herself from achieving in the classroom.

2. Primary need being revealed:
   ▶ Escape from Pain: It is much better to be an "idiot" than to face the reality that one is not a good student.

3. Secondary need being revealed:
   ▶ Achievement: The need for success is a most important need and should be met with many quick successes.

4. Reinforce positive behavior.

5. In a private conference, discuss and try to identify what the real problem is for the student by asking questions and moving toward the student's real feelings.

6. Always try to teach to each child's needs.

7. Vary the way you explain directions and give assignments to see if one way seems to be clearer than others.

8. Allow the student to feel that he/she is accomplishing, moving forward, and expanding.

9. Review the student's work with him/her privately. Make allowances for errors if effort is being made to work up to his/her potential.

10. Refer this student to the counselor in the early stages of this behavior.

11. Seek help from parents early.

IV. MISTAKES: Common misjudgments and errors in managing the child which may perpetuate or intensify the problem.

1. Believing that this student really does understand the assignments or the directions, the first time, all the time.

2. Assuming that the student operates this way simply for attention.

3. Feeling that this student acts like an "idiot" simply to "bug" us.

4. Failing to take the time to assess the true potential of the student.

SEE ALSO: • The Class Clown • "I Can't" • "I Don't Care"

THE IMMATURE

I. BEHAVIOR: **Specific attitudes and actions of this child at home and/or at school.**

1. Very self-centered.

2. Unable to think for him/herself.

3. Doesn't follow directions.

4. Demands a great deal of individual teacher time and involvement.

5. Exhibits "baby" traits or characteristics which carry over into his/her behavior — crying, pouting, foot-stamping, etc.

6. Does not relate well with peers.

7. Has a short memory concerning his/her immature behavior. This is the one sure way to identify the immature student. One minute the student seems to understand his/her immature emotions, and agrees to act better, and the next minute he/she is acting out the same misbehavior again.

8. Worse, when questioned about repeated immaturity, often acts as if unable to help him/herself or as if it's the first time he/she has ever acted this way.

9. Continues to tease, poke, touch, tap pencils, and drop books on the floor as a way of getting attention. That's why his/her immaturity surfaces continually.

10. Cannot complete daily work without constantly checking with teacher.

II. EFFECTS: **How behavior affects teachers, classmates, and parents in the school learning environment and the home family situation.**

1. Teacher finds this student is a daily thorn in his/her side.

2. Unfortunately, classmates shy away, ridicule, and are reluctant to accept this student.

3. The tantrums that this student acts out cause incredible distractions for students, teacher, and the class in general.

4. A great deal of class time is wasted.

5. Others are disturbed continually by this student's attention seeking.

6. An inferior climate is continually created.

7. Other students become frustrated and angry over this student's behavior.

III. ACTION:
- **Identify causes of misbehavior.**
- **Pinpoint student needs being revealed.**
- **Employ specific methods, procedures, and techniques at school and at home for getting the child to modify or change his/her behavior.**

1. Primary causes of misbehavior:

   ◗ Attention: This student finds it difficult to relate to peers; thus he/she seeks attention from certain adults.

   ◗ Self-Confidence: In relation to classmates, this student may feel so inadequate that he/she lacks the confidence to work on his/her own.

2. Primary needs being revealed:

   ‣ Sex: This student may be younger than most members of his/her class, and may therefore find it difficult to establish relationships with them.

   ‣ Hunger, Thirst: It is also possible that, because of a lack of proper nutrition, this student is physically smaller than his/her classmates. A complete physical exam is suggested.

   ‣ Escape from Pain: The student may feel so inadequate that it is painful to compete with peers; thus, to avoid pain he/she seeks constant help from the teacher.

3. Secondary needs being revealed:

   ‣ Status: When this student begins to find a place with others, he/she will begin to mature.

   ‣ Gregariousness: Acceptance by others will improve his/her maturity.

   ‣ Achievement: Opportunities to achieve with others and before others will improve his/her maturity.

4. Remember that the immature student is seeking more than answers from you — he/she is seeking attention. Knowing this, be sure to provide the student with attention before it is sought. You'll find two distinct advantages. First, the student will get the attention he/she needs to operate effectively in the classroom. Second, you will be helping the student build better independent work habits in the process. Try to find additional ways for the immature student to receive teacher attention and recognition throughout the day, or his/her habit of asking will continue. In a short period of time, you'll find this student will be saying, "No, thank you, I don't need any help."

5. Sit down with this student and deal strictly and directly with his/her behavior. This is the only way to deal effectively with this student.

6. Don't discuss the behavior in terms of right and wrong. Such an approach won't work.

7. Be careful about comparing the immature student with classmates; doing so may make the behavior worse.

8. When confronting, never talk about the *"why's"* associated with the behavior. Instead, get the student to admit his/her action. Talk about *what* the student is *doing* — and what you insist he/she do about it.

9. Approach this student at a level appropriate to his/her behavior. He/she needs specific instructions. It's almost a "when you quit crying you can come out of your room and play with others" approach.

10. Then use the things the student likes the most at school to get him/her to change.

11. Tell the student this behavior is totally unacceptable and that, if it continues, the privileges he/she likes the most will be lost — one at a time.

12. Follow through on your promises, and the behavior will begin to improve almost immediately. Just make sure that mature behavior brings back privileges one at a time rather than all at once.

13. Finally, remember that being immature works for this child. If being mature has no apparent advantages, he/she will revert to old ways quickly. Never forget, there are many immature 50-year-olds.

IV. MISTAKES: Common misjudgments and errors in managing the child which may perpetuate or intensify the problem.

1. Reprimanding or punishing this student in any way that reflects immature behavior on our part.

2. Showing anger, threatening, or showing open irritation. This posture won't work, but is too often our course.

The Immature

3. Expecting too much too soon; that is, expecting too quick a turn-around and resolution of immature behavior.

4. Trying to give the immature student too much help, too much reinforcement.

5. Calling attention to the "baby" ways and behaviors of the student publicly.

6. Lowering expectations for this student.

7. "Skirting the issue" with student or parents.

SEE ALSO: • The Alibier   • The Attention Demander   • The Crier (Who Sheds Tears)
• "I Can't"   • "Not My Fault"

THE INDIFFERENT

I. BEHAVIOR: **Specific attitudes and actions of this child at home and/or at school.**

1. Not interested in anything that is happening in the classroom, and not concerned about what is happening to him/her as a result of this disassociation. "He (she) just doesn't care" seems to be the best description of the indifferent student.

2. May be docile or belligerent, quiet or loud, capable or a slow learner.

3. Listens to what teacher says, but doesn't respond.

4. Doesn't display emotion.

5. Not motivated to action by teacher efforts.

6. May even tell teacher, "Do whatever you like. It doesn't matter to me."

7. One of the hardest children to help in a school situation. Unfortunately, this student will pay a tremendous price for his/her indifference.

II. EFFECTS: **How behavior affects teachers, classmates, and parents in the school learning environment and the home family situation.**

1. Classmates may be unaffected by this "I don't care" attitude.

2. Teacher may feel emotions ranging from helplessness to anger.

3. Teacher is bothered by ineffectiveness of his/her efforts. Every technique that has worked with students before is of no avail.

4. Classmates may become frustrated with the teacher's taking so much time with this student.

5. Teacher may begin to dread facing the class.

III. ACTION:
- **Identify causes of misbehavior.**
- **Pinpoint student needs being revealed.**
- **Employ specific methods, procedures, and techniques at school and at home for getting the child to modify or change his/her behavior.**

1. Primary cause of misbehavior:
   - Self-Confidence: This student is building a defense against possible failure. Such a defense is very difficult to break down because any little failure may turn the student back to the original behavior.

2. Primary need being revealed:
   - Escape from Pain: This student can escape the pain of failure by being indifferent.

3. Secondary needs being revealed:
   - Affiliation: If this person discovers a close friend in a peer or adult, it could affect his/her indifference.
   - Achievement: This student has a real need for success — both academically and personally.

4. Extend kindness, patience, and understanding to the indifferent student, even though doing so may be a strain.

5. Constantly present this student with opportunities for involvement, and search for areas of possible interest — regardless of how often such efforts are rejected. Involvement and interest are two components necessary to turn the indifferent student into a productive human being.

6. Accept two important facts in order to help this student — and keep your balance in the process. First, the teacher is the professional and must be the first to recognize the indifference. The teacher must also determine whether the indifference is only school-related. This is significant for both approach and treatment. Second, the student must recognize the problem. Never forget, indifference is a problem that must be recognized by both teacher and student — and a desire to change must be effected in the student or the indifference will continue.

7. In the process of trying to help the student recognize the problem, be aware that you are using the "Buying Time" strategic approach. You are persevering, in the hope that one day change will begin. Also, you're taking this approach knowing that if you quit, this student's whole life may be unhappy.

8. Accept responsibility for helping this student, and refuse to accept his/her rejection of your efforts. Realistically, this is the best attitude to take.

9. View this student professionally rather than personally. Don't think the indifference is aimed at you. It's not. It has to do with the student him/herself.

10. Be aware that, at some point, this student will probably move in healthier directions because of changes in time, situations, and conditions.

11. Don't do anything that will prolong the indifference or make changes more difficult or impossible.

12. Wait and talk to this student when he/she is not "on the line" for something he/she failed to do.

13. During your conversation, place the indifferent student in a position to make a decision. The best way to do this is to *ask* rather than tell. Ask questions as fast as you can, even when you don't get answers. When the student fails to answer your question, ask another quickly. Don't volunteer or suggest an answer if he/she doesn't know. Your concern is not with the answers themselves, but merely with the fact that the student is answering. Allow the student to express him/herself without your commenting on the answers.

14. If, after several visits, you feel this student has a severe emotional problem, talk to your counselor and administrator about seeking professional help.

15. Don't quit on this student, even if the student quits on him/herself. It will be significant to your mental health and professional conscience if, as a professional educator, you can say you have never quit on a student.

IV. MISTAKES: Common misjudgments and errors in managing the child which may perpetuate or intensify the problem.

1. Failing to remain involved and interested. A teacher void in this area will result in a teacher-student relationship that will discourage rather than encourage.

2. Resorting to ridicule or sarcasm; this mistake will compound the problem. Not only will any possible progress be thwarted, but a negative effect on other students is also likely.

3. Allowing the indifferent student to destroy our relationship with others or our position as classroom teachers. Remember, our relationship with one student affects our relationship with all students.

4. Becoming irate with this student. Other students identify and relate to us, as teachers and as human beings, by how we treat people. If we become irate with a student, then there is no reason for others to believe we don't have the potential to do so with them.

5. Rejecting this student by word or deed. If we do so, all is lost.

6. Choosing confrontation as our method for dealing with this student. This kind of reaction often leads to crisis.

7. Becoming angry about this student's indifference. Remember, this student truly doesn't care, and this is sad. It's an attitude that should arouse concern and empathetic understanding, not anger or hostility.

8. Failing to realize that this student needs a teacher — badly.

SEE ALSO: • "I Don't Care" • "I Won't Do It" • The Nonparticipator
                • The Unprepared

THE INFLUENCER

I. BEHAVIOR: **Specific attitudes and actions of this child at home and/or at school.**

1. Often a popular student and a natural leader. Has the power to influence.
2. Pits people against people. Will get students fighting with each other or pit class against teacher.
3. Usually very capable and intelligent.
4. Delights in "trapping" teacher or making schoolwork seem insignificant.
5. Almost always intimidates a specific group of students.
6. Causes problems in direct proportion to the number of his/her followers.
7. May even make rules that conflict with classroom or school rules.
8. Laughs at what teacher says, ridicules what teacher does, and degrades the importance of what teacher presents in class. And his/her followers listen.
9. Will not permit his/her followers to listen to anyone else, including teacher. There can be only one master as far as the influencer is concerned, and he/she must be the master.
10. Seldom disrupts directly. Rather, gets his/her followers to do it.
11. Encourages others to speak out, complain about an assignment, or refuse to comply with teacher requests.
12. Frequently, is not at the scene of the disturbance he/she promotes. If at the scene, acts like an innocent bystander, because he/she is a coward.

II. EFFECTS: **How behavior affects teachers, classmates, and parents in the school learning environment and the home family situation.**

1. Authority of teacher is undermined.
2. Teacher is embarrassed.
3. Too much attention is diverted from other students.
4. A "game" is created between teacher and the influencer ... and the class knows it.
5. Teacher experiences an uneasy feeling in class.
6. Teacher may lose control in some situations.
7. Classmates may follow the influencer's lead.
8. Followers of the influencer are often pressured by fear to take the commands of this student. This is the source of the influencer's strength and ego satisfaction.
9. Followers of the influencer, as well as other students, are distracted.
10. Neither followers nor the influencer is learning.
11. Teacher may become frustrated and angry.

III. ACTION: • **Identify causes of misbehavior.**
• **Pinpoint student needs being revealed.**

- **Employ specific methods, procedures and techniques at school and at home for getting the child to modify or change his/her behavior.**

1. Primary cause of misbehavior:

   ▶ Power: This student believes that having power over others will provide the answer to all his/her problems.

2. Primary need being revealed:

   ▶ Sex: This person may have experienced poor relationships at home as well as at school, and may be motivated to make up for such situations by becoming an influencer.

3. Secondary needs being revealed:

   ▶ Power: The influencer has a strong power need that must be met in order for him/her to adjust the behavior. This person feels very "safe" operating as an influencer of others.

   ▶ Status: The influencer knows he/she becomes "somebody" through this behavior. Somehow the same status must be achieved in a positive manner.

4. Devote your efforts exclusively to changing the behavior of either the influencer or one follower. Do not treat them as a group.

5. The behavior of the influencer offers clues on how to approach him/her. Remember, this student does things through others, and may not be at the scene of the disturbance or may act like an innocent bystander.

6. The key to changing his/her behavior is to realize that the influencer is really a coward. He/she doesn't want blame or exposure. That's why you must provide both.

7. In simple and direct terms, tell this student privately and forcefully, "I know what you're doing and will not allow it." You'll be surprised how often he/she will offer alibis, cower, deny, and apologize. If you hold firm, the influencer may shift his/her stand.

8. Don't buy the innocence role. Make sure this student knows that when something happens, you're coming after him/her.

9. The influencer will almost always abandon his/her followers for something more advantageous. This is sad, but true. Capitalize on this fact by offering this student something bigger and better, a meaningful responsibility. Offer him/her something of importance with high visibility, such as passing out papers, helping you, or working with another student. Often the influencer will take the bigger "carrot" and the problem will be resolved.

10. When the influencer has abandoned his/her followers, have another staff member ready to work with the abandoned followers and/or to straighten them out. Don't try to handle both influencer and followers at the same time.

11. Challenge this student's ability.

12. Point out that he/she always takes the "easy way out" which, in reality, is the "hard way." This student may win the battle and lose the war. Let the student know this saddens you but does not make you mad.

13. Discuss the student's future, focusing on the possibility that he/she may wind up scrubbing floors instead of using his/her potential.

14. Talk to the influencer about "using people up."

15. Explain that you are going to make sure the student lives up to his/her abilities and that, therefore, you want a private conference with him/her every day.

16. Be confident and calm and talk to him/her quietly in each conversation.

17. Be aware that this kid is very coachable.

IV. MISTAKES: Common misjudgments and errors in managing the child which may perpetuate or intensify the problem.

1. Losing control and falling into the influencer's trap of vying for control of the class.

2. Using sarcasm.

3. Overreacting with threats, possible punishments, or demerits.

4. Yelling at the student.

5. Lashing out at other students, especially this student's followers.

6. Failing to counsel this student individually and privately.

7. Rejecting the influencer personally.

8. Working on the group of followers in an attempt to weaken the influencer's power. The influencer exerts great pressure, and has told followers to expect attempts to break up the group. Thus, such attempts reinforce what followers have been told, and prove our rejection of the person they need most — their influencer.

9. Punishing by revoking privileges when there is no logical relationship to the misbehavior. Doing so may be interpreted as teacher revenge and may lead to a bigger discipline problem with all students. It's not difficult for a teacher to gain a reputation for being "unfair" in these situations. Too, the sympathies of other students will reside with the student being reprimanded and impair student-teacher relationships. A teacher must remember never to create a negative response in other students while correcting the behavior of one student.

10. Creating peer pressure in ways that can damage class relationships. This is what happens when we say, "The whole class will stay until this room is in order," rather than privately telling offenders to remain until their desks are in order. We may misinterpret what really happens when we create peer pressure which forces other students to "shape up." Usually, other students leave feeling the teacher has been unfair — to them.

SEE ALSO: • The Agitator   • The Defier   • The Hater

THE INTELLECTUAL SHOW-OFF

I. BEHAVIOR: **Specific attitudes and actions of this child at home and/or at school.**

1. Likely to be a good student.
2. Receives good grades.
3. Wants everyone to know how smart he/she is.
4. Seeks attention and admiration via class performances and test scores.
5. Acts superior.
6. Dominates and disallows others' input.
7. Displays competitive behavior — and it carries over into imposition and confrontation.
8. Struggles overtly to be accepted and to have good relationships.
9. Yet, makes fun of peers who don't know the answer to a question.
10. May be very creative.
11. Always sees a different way to do something.

II. EFFECTS: **How behavior affects teachers, classmates, and parents in the school learning environment and the home family situation.**

1. Teacher, as well as classmates, is alienated. Thus the intellectual show-off defeats him/herself.
2. Many classmates dislike this student because his/her superiority is always at others' expense.
3. Free expression in the classroom is curtailed.
4. Others begin to fear failure.
5. Teacher's time is dominated by this student.
6. Teacher may be intimidated.

III. ACTION: • **Identify causes of misbehavior.**
 • **Pinpoint student needs being revealed.**
 • **Employ specific methods, procedures, and techniques at school and at home for getting the child to modify or change his/her behavior.**

1. Primary causes of misbehavior:
   ◗ Attention: This student uses his/her knowledge to get attention.
   ◗ Power: He/she also uses knowledge to gain power.
2. Primary needs being revealed:
   ◗ Sex: This student may experience many disappointing attempts to establish relationships, and may exhibit intellectual show-off behavior as a result.
   ◗ Escape from Pain: People don't like those who make an issue of their intellectual abilities. Thus, this student's behavior leads to more rejection, and he/she retreats further into show-off behavior to escape the pain.

3. Secondary needs being revealed:

   ◗ Gregariousness: This student uses knowledge to become a part of the group, only to realize that many times the group rejects such behavior.

   ◗ Inquisitiveness: This student has a need to communicate with people, and uses his/her knowledge as a foundation for such communication.

   ◗ Power: This student tries to demonstrate through knowledge that he/she counts and is "somebody."

4. Recognize that this student does have something to offer.

5. Look beneath the behavior, and you'll see that attention is the motivator.

6. Work with the student privately regarding how to contribute via behavior that is acceptable to others. It is very easy to show the student how present behavior is working against him/her. In truth, it is giving the student a kind of recognition which is forcing people away from him/her.

7. Take an indirect rather than a direct strategic approach with the intellectual show-off. Say, "I appreciate your interest and knowledge, but in order to teach everyone effectively, there are some specific things I want you to do in class discussion. If you do these things, you'll be able to help others more, and others will see that you have something worthwhile to offer and share." The student will usually listen closely to this rationale — and for good reason. This approach offers the student the initiative to choose to change the behavior without lowering his/her self-worth. Likewise, it does not deny him/her attention.

8. Be specific regarding how the student should operate — and explain the reasons behind all your requests.

9. Always give the student leadership roles — rather than follower roles — if he/she complies with your requests. Make sure the student is aware of this stance on your part. It is the kind of reward system he/she needs.

10. Finally, quickly acknowledge all behavior improvements. Tell the student, "I appreciate your helping us have a better class." This strategic approach gives this student what he/she wants: attention and admiration.

11. Don't respond negatively or sarcastically to a student response. How you respond to the questions and answers of this student affects the motivation of all students. Even if the question or answer is not a good one, your response is important. Remember, other students may be thinking, "If she thought that was a dumb answer, she should have heard mine. I'm not saying anything in this class unless I'm sure I'm right." Students learn from everything a teacher does — especially from the way he/she responds.

IV. MISTAKES: Common misjudgments and errors in managing the child which may perpetuate or intensify the problem.

1. Becoming so alienated that we don't see this student's potential — or his/her real problems.

2. Confronting the student directly by calling him/her a "show-off."

3. Becoming sarcastic or hostile, or putting the student down.

4. Letting this behavior go unchecked.

5. Thinking this student motivates and stimulates other students.

6. Using him/her as a model for comparison purposes.

SEE ALSO: • The Know-It-All • The Show-Off • The Smart Aleck • The Smartmouth

THE INTERRUPTER

I. BEHAVIOR: **Specific attitudes and actions of this child at home and/or at school.**

1. Makes comments, states opinions, or asks questions that take class attention and discussion off the subject immediately.

2. Needles or badgers others.

3. Mumbles and makes noises and crude remarks.

4. Laughs and talks at inappropriate times.

5. Actually requests a change of topic — and makes a scene if it is denied.

II. EFFECTS: **How behavior affects teachers, classmates, and parents in the school learning environment and the home family situation.**

1. Learning situation is disrupted.

2. Negative teacher behaviors, such as power struggles, may be promoted.

3. Chain reactions in class discussion — both positive and negative — may be initiated.

4. Regaining attention becomes difficult.

5. Sequence of teaching and learning is disrupted.

6. Some classmates are annoyed; others are delighted.

7. Teacher is likely to regard any interruption — whether caused by a student, colleague, or administrator — as a form of insult. Teacher may be angered by the insult and may sometimes respond negatively as a result.

III. ACTION:
- **Identify causes of misbehavior.**
- **Pinpoint student needs being revealed.**
- **Employ specific methods, procedures, and techniques at school and at home for getting the child to modify or change his/her behavior.**

1. Primary causes of misbehavior:

   ▶ Attention: This person is getting desired attention from adults and peers.

   ▶ Power: The student may see his/her interrupting as a way of gaining status with peers.

2. Primary need being revealed:

   ▶ Sex: This student is attempting to establish relationships and chooses to make him/herself known by interrupting in class.

3. Secondary needs being revealed:

   ▶ Aggression: This person is struggling to assert him/herself through constant interruptions. The student must be taught to meet this need through positive involvement.

   ▶ Status: The message is loud and clear: "Recognize me, I'm here." It's important that the student know that others think well of him/her. If the student knows this before he/she begins to interrupt, then the need to do so is reduced.

   ▶ Autonomy: This student should be allowed to act out the need to be boss by being given assignments that involve responsibility.

4. Whenever possible, continue teaching, and confront the student only if the behavior stops the flow of the lesson.

5. After the second or third incident, stop the interrupter dead in his/her tracks. Simply say, "Let's stay with the topic at hand. And I will see you . . ." Then, have a private conference at the first opportunity: recess, lunch, after school, or your planning period.

6. In private conference, tell the interrupter that, whether this student knows what he/she is doing or not, the effect is the same: He/she is disrupting the class. You may present the student with the reality that both the teaching and learning sequences are being broken — and you will not allow either. Make sure the student knows you are dead serious.

7. Next, approach the *possibility* of the student's "game playing." Mention this as your final thought. You can make your point effectively enough by saying, "If, by chance, you are doing this purposely, then we have a bigger problem than I think you can handle." If you use this strategic action, the student will most likely apologize and try to convince you that he/she did nothing purposely, and will be very careful.

8. Look for improvement and give positive feedback to the student.

9. Request help from parents. Be careful to explain that if this behavior continues, it will be difficult for you to teach, classmates will withdraw socially from this student, and soon his/her schoolwork will be affected.

10. Arrange an eye or hand signal that will help the student to recognize the unacceptable behavior.

IV. MISTAKES: Common misjudgments and errors in managing the child which may perpetuate or intensify the problem.

1. Giving this student the attention his/her interruptions demand.

2. Letting this student get by with sarcasm.

3. Continually sending this student out of the room to get rid of him/her.

4. Losing our temper, or showing considerable anger.

5. Punishing wrongly.

6. Failing to explain why he/she can't interrupt.

7. Failing to have a private conference.

SEE ALSO: • The Last Worder • The Loudmouth • The Objector

THE IRRESPONSIBLE

I. BEHAVIOR: Specific attitudes and actions of this child at home and/or at school.

1. Doesn't complete assigned tasks.
2. Doesn't bring materials to class.
3. Daydreams constantly.
4. Disturbs others.
5. Doesn't make effective use of his/her time.
6. Always gives excuses and blames others.
7. Refuses to accept accountability for anything.
8. Inconsistent.
9. Has poor self-discipline.
10. Disorganized with regard to his/her desk, personal belongings, or even the rest of his/her life.
11. Has a poor self-image.

II. EFFECTS: How behavior affects teachers, classmates, and parents in the school learning environment and the home family situation.

1. Teacher and classmates are irritated.
2. Unequal distribution of teacher time is required.
3. Classroom activities invariably slow down.
4. Classroom enthusiasm is lost when time is spent dealing with this student's failure to meet obligations and commitments.
5. Peers become resentful and bored.
6. Teacher's credibility is undermined.
7. Responsible students may become irresponsible themselves.
8. Teacher may feel that this student just doesn't care about anything.

III. ACTION:
- **Identify causes of misbehavior.**
- **Pinpoint student needs being revealed.**
- **Employ specific methods, procedures, and techniques at school and at home for getting the child to modify or change his/her behavior.**

1. Primary cause of misbehavior:
   ▸ Self-Confidence: This student expects everyone to abandon him/her because of his/her failures.
2. Primary needs being revealed:
   ▸ All primary needs should be checked; in particular, the nurse or counselor should be approached about the need for a physical examination for this student.

165

3. Secondary need being revealed:

   ◗ Achievement: With success comes responsibility. Achieving a measure of success is a must for this student.

4. Create contracts with this student in order to start developing a more responsible behavior gradually over a period of time. Once a contract is made and agreed to, make the student live up to it.

5. Create concrete learning situations with hands-on experience.

6. Utilize audiovisual material.

7. Praise this student for any appropriate behavior, regardless of how small.

8. Create short-term goals to provide immediate success.

9. Be careful about withdrawing privileges. It's a punishment which can curtail motivation. Withdrawing gym, art, music, or recess can be the beginning of academic problems. Here's a tip: When you see behavior slipping, think in terms of dispensing responsibilities rather than withdrawing privileges. Ask this student to run errands, help clean up, take care of pets, or work on special projects. Restore acceptable behavior through responsibility.

10. Create extra jobs or responsibilities which you can give this student immediately to help him/her become more responsible.

11. Look for improvement. Behavior adjustment will be slow.

12. Inform parents of the student's behavior. They may not be able to understand or help with the situation at school, but they should be informed.

IV. MISTAKES: Common misjudgments and errors in managing the child which may perpetuate or intensify the problem.

1. Embarrassing the irresponsible student in front of peers.

2. Nagging this student constantly.

3. Being inconsistent in dealing with this student; for example, making threats and then not following through on them.

4. Failing to recognize the honest efforts of this student to correct irresponsibility and create acceptable behavior.

5. Failing to investigate the child's home environment as a causal element in the irresponsible behavior.

6. Trying to lay the entire blame on parents.

7. Assuming that this student simply doesn't care at all.

8. Failing to see that we may be responsible for some of this student's behavior.

SEE ALSO: • The Dreamer • The Influencer • The Noncompleter with Grand Plans

THE KNOW-IT-ALL

I. BEHAVIOR: Specific attitudes and actions of this child at home and/or at school.

1. Acts as if he/she has all the answers to everything.
2. Refuses to be told anything.
3. Always wants to talk.
4. Has a superior attitude toward teacher and classmates.
5. Argumentative.
6. Difficult to talk to; gives his/her answers or opinions before the other person finishes speaking.
7. Likely to be bright, and usually participates.
8. Acts as if he/she is doing teacher a favor by being in the class.
9. Very critical of others' responses — regardless of whether they're those of another student or of an adult.
10. May be sarcastic and even get nasty, but reflection will reveal that he/she seldom loses self-control.
11. Thinks he/she is better informed than other people.
12. May be described as a "bigmouth" by peers.
13. A poor listener.
14. Tries to impress peers.
15. Likely either to be a loner or to band together with other know-it-all students.

II. EFFECTS: How behavior affects teachers, classmates, and parents in the school learning environment and the home family situation.

1. Classroom conversations are monopolized.
2. Demands are made on the time of others.
3. Teacher and classmates are irritated.
4. Classmates know their responses are likely to be answered or contradicted by the know-it-all.
5. Classmates and teacher like to see this student put down or put in his/her place. When the know-it-all fails, others are happy.
6. Teacher and classmates may be threatened by this student's know-it-all attitude.
7. Individual participation is restricted because other students feel intimidated.
8. Classmates like to urge this student on because they get excitement from seeing a teacher or another student put down by the know-it-all's behavior.
9. Resentments can build in class among students and teacher.

III. ACTION:
- **Identify causes of misbehavior.**
- **Pinpoint student needs being revealed.**
- **Employ specific methods, procedures, and techniques at school and at home for getting the child to modify or change his/her behavior.**

1. Primary causes of misbehavior:

   ▶ Attention: This person draws a lot of attention by demonstrating his/her knowledge.

   ▶ Power: Knowledge is power, but the use of such power can cause resentment from other students and adults.

2. Primary need being revealed:

   ▶ Sex: This student uses his/her knowledge to attempt to establish relationships with peers and adults.

3. Secondary needs being revealed:

   ▶ Gregariousness: This student has a strong need to belong to a group and is using his/her knowledge to establish relationships.

   ▶ Achievement: The student has a need to demonstrate his/her knowledge.

   ▶ Power: Using his/her knowledge to help other students, or to help the teacher in classroom activities, would provide this student a positive form of power.

   ▶ Status: The use of knowledge lets people know he/she is "somebody."

   ▶ Autonomy: The ability to obtain knowledge provides independence for this student.

4. Study this child carefully before selecting a technique to change the behavior. From an examination of the primary and secondary needs, it can be noted that the know-it-all is many different persons.

5. Remember, this student is likely to be very intelligent. Therefore, approach him/her from an intellectual point of view. Talk about the fact that the best minds need to be leaders of people.

6. There's one way this student doesn't want to appear to anyone — dumb. Herein is the key to getting the student to listen to you. Tell him/her it's not very smart to do things that turn people off. Say, "There's one thing that an intelligent person knows — how to relate to people."

7. The student will accept what you are telling him/her, but will need help with practical examples and suggestions. Explain that the student must work at taking other people's ideas and experiences as seriously as his/her own.

8. Explain that the student has been foolish in not seeing how other people respond to his/her behavior. With the realization that it's advantageous to work with others rather than against them, the student's intellect will help him/her resolve this problem because of the strong need for acceptance.

9. Allow this student to be a class helper, and give him/her jobs.

10. Give this student special projects to work on.

11. Motivate this student to run for a class office or other positions in extracurricular groups or student council.

12. Don't be afraid to admit what you don't know.

13. Establish a meaningful relationship with this student, but don't assume a position of superiority. This child probably has few meaningful relationships with adults.

14. Show this student the effect of his/her attitude and how others feel about this behavior.

IV. MISTAKES: Common misjudgments and errors in managing the child which may perpetuate or intensify the problem.

1. Ignoring this student completely.

2. Reacting sarcastically or reacting competitively with the know-it-all student.

3. Trying to play other students against him/her.

4. Allowing this student to dominate the classroom situation.

5. Feeling a sense of inferiority and displaying these feelings in our reactions.

6. Attempting to put the know-it-all in one slot and failing to realize that there are many kinds of know-it-alls.

7. Failing to realize that this student really may "know it all," but just doesn't know how to relate to people.

8. Failing to utilize this student as a resource in the classroom.

9. Trying to show this student that he/she doesn't have all the answers. If the know-it-all is actually covering up a fear that he/she doesn't know enough, such an approach only proves to the student that his/her fear is grounded, and thus increases rather than eliminates the fear. Instead, counsel the student and help him/her take a more realistic view.

SEE ALSO: • The Intellectual Show-Off • The Last Worder • The Snob • The Talker

THE LAST WORDER

I. BEHAVIOR: Specific attitudes and actions of this child at home and/or at school.

1. Simply has to have the last word with classmates, teacher, or parents.
2. Persists in saying *one more* thing, or laughing, sneering, or sighing — even when he/she knows this behavior will lead to trouble.
3. Seeks attention at any price.
4. Tries to prove points.
5. Rude and inconsiderate.
6. Shows this behavior constantly — not occasionally.
7. Even while apologizing, thinks the other person is wrong — and will try to tell him/her why.
8. Finds ways to force showdowns.

II. EFFECTS: How behavior affects teachers, classmates, and parents in the school learning environment and the home family situation.

1. Classmates think the teacher cannot handle this student, and they may be challenged to "test" the teacher as well.
2. Time is stolen from lessons . . . and from other students.
3. Teacher may be unnerved to the point of ineffectiveness, or put in a bad mood for the rest of the day.
4. Both teacher and students may think, "This is a bad class."
5. Teacher's control may be diminished or lost completely.
6. Other students are drawn into discussions with the last worder.
7. Many classmates are irritated.

III. ACTION:
- **Identify causes of misbehavior.**
- **Pinpoint student needs being revealed.**
- **Employ specific methods, procedures, and techniques at school and at home for getting the child to modify or change his/her behavior.**

1. Primary causes of misbehavior:
   - Attention: This student gets attention by continually confronting the teacher.
   - Power: The need for power causes this disruptive behavior.
2. Primary needs being revealed:
   - Hunger, Thirst, Rest: This student may be eating poorly and not getting enough rest, which causes his/her frustrating behavior.
   - Sex: Home or peer relationship problems may cause such behavior.
   - Escape from Pain: The student may feel he/she is academically inadequate, and in order to hide this pain becomes the last worder.

3. Secondary needs being revealed:

   ◗ Aggression: This student's actions continually separate him/her from the teacher and most classmates. Some way should be found to channel his/her assertiveness in a positive direction.

   ◗ Power: The student is attempting to obtain power with peers, and must be helped to find other ways to meet his/her power need.

   ◗ Autonomy: To be independent or one's own boss does not mean one must be anti-authority. Finding ways for students to meet the need to be in control of themselves and stay within the limits of the classroom is a challenge to educators.

4. Remember, as an attention getter, this behavior works for the student.

5. Don't try to talk to the last worder at the time of the incident. This student doesn't want reason; he/she wants attention — at any price. You must talk to this student privately.

6. During the incident in class, try to remain calm, poised, and completely professional — even if you're "burning up" inside. Give a quick smile in his/her direction, and turn immediately to another student or subject. Remember, total attention will only give this student what he/she wants — and motivation for further misbehavior. Therefore, allow this student to have the last word — for the moment.

7. Later, talk to the student privately, and use the "Major Issue" technique. Tell the student you recognize his/her need for attention; such a move renders the student neutral. Then explain how the student can get attention in ways that are acceptable — both to him/herself and to others. Even ask the student what kind of acceptable attention he/she wants.

8. Tell the student the effect his/her behavior has on the class in specific terms: "It is hurting others. It is stealing class time from them." Explain the student's responsibility to him/herself and to classmates to function on a more mature level. Then, talk about your responsibility to this student and to the class. Say, "Even though I don't want to embarrass you publicly, I cannot tolerate behavior that steals time from classmates."

9. Inform the student that if the problem is not corrected immediately, you will ask for parental assistance. This should help you get immediate results. Oddly enough, the parents of many of these students would not tolerate such behavior at home.

10. This student probably is not mean, but just doesn't know the difference between assertion and aggression. Therefore, talk to him/her about the difference. Through assertion one speaks out without hurting others; through aggression one infringes on the rights of others and betrays his/her insecurity.

11. Stay professional at all times. Do not allow this student's needs to affect you personally.

12. Above all, try to build a relationship rather than avoid one.

13. Refrain from any drastic action in the presence of others.

14. Display liking and strength in the student's presence. Remember, the last worder makes prejudgments about who "likes me" and who "doesn't like me" as well as who is strong and who is weak. He/she will behave better with those regarded as strong and with those regarded as liking the student.

15. Be aware that if the student does not attempt to make any adjustment in the behavior, the situation could become win-lose. In a private conference, explain that in such a situation you will not be the loser, and then in specific terms outline your expectations in the classroom.

IV. MISTAKES: Common misjudgments and errors in managing the child which may perpetuate or intensify the problem.

1. Attempting to discipline the student at the time of the interruption.

2. Stopping class to compete with this student in a verbal duel.

3. Responding in a way that tends to perpetuate an argument.

4. Becoming sarcastic.

5. Responding disrespectfully by saying such things as "Only one mouth can go in this room at a time" or "When I am talking, keep your mouth shut." This kind of statement can create and perpetuate problems with the last worder — and destroy relationships with other students in the process.

6. Degrading ourselves by unfair remarks or immature reactions which cause other students to lose sight of the original problem.

7. Showing anger, frustration, or both.

8. Getting angry at the student instead of at his/her behavior.

9. Taking out anger on other students and/or another class.

10. Thinking of this student as a spoiled or smart-aleck kid rather than a student needing to fill some serious needs.

SEE ALSO: • The Agitator   • The Defier   • The Interrupter   • The Talker

THE LATE ARRIVER

I. BEHAVIOR: Specific attitudes and actions of this child at home and/or at school.

1. Last to do everything; late to class and last in line. Often lags behind everyone else.

2. Pretends to be in a hurry. Yet, is always late.

3. Acts sincere in trying to be on time or get things done. However, is "just *so* busy" he/she can't.

4. May be seeking attention or may be fearful.

5. Enters the room quietly because of embarrassment or fear — or enters noisily, seeking attention.

6. Often appears completely disorganized.

7. Usually a poor student.

8. Behind in his/her work.

9. Often appears to have good potential.

II. EFFECTS: How behavior affects teachers, classmates, and parents in the school learning environment and the home family situation.

1. Class is disrupted by late arrivals.

2. Others are forced to wait for this student. Often, it's the whole class.

3. Others are annoyed by the behavior — especially the excuses for being late.

4. Classmates' attention is distracted from the lesson.

5. Additional explanations and time are required.

6. Teacher may lose control of class.

7. Other students begin to adopt the behavior if they see that it is working for one student or a few students in the class.

III. ACTION:
- **Identify causes of misbehavior.**
- **Pinpoint student needs being revealed.**
- **Employ specific methods, procedures, and techniques at school and at home for getting the child to modify or change his/her behavior.**

1. Primary causes of misbehavior:

   ▶ Attention: This student has a strong need for attention.

   ▶ Self-Confidence: This person uses this behavior to cover for low self-esteem.

2. Primary needs being revealed:

   ▶ Sex: Poor relationships with parents and/or teacher may cause this person to feel very insecure.

   ▶ Escape from Pain: It may be painful for this person to attend class, and indecision may cause him/her to arrive late.

3. Secondary needs being revealed:

   ♦ Achievement: The more confidence this student gains through academic achievement, the more his/her self-esteem will be raised.

   ♦ Status: The knowledge that he/she is "somebody" could be important to the late arriver.

4. Realize that change will be slow.

5. Use the *"What Is More Important Than Why"* technique. Don't ask the student why he/she is late. He/she doesn't know why. Rather, ask, "What did you do, and what are you going to do about it?" "What" is a positive and demands action. Asking "why" will just bring excuses.

6. Recognize that you're dealing with a habit, not a behavior, and that habits need substitutes.

7. Talk to the student about how destructive habits can be, rather than just about the need to change this particular habit.

8. Examine the reason behind the student's tardiness. Knowing and understanding the student's lifestyle often provides valuable clues. A student usually develops this habit because there is no organization in his/her life outside school. There is not an established bedtime, mealtime, or time for other family routines. Therefore, you must realize that this student needs extra guidance to organize time and meet responsibilities.

9. Normally, there are some things you can do in the meantime. Once a student has established a pattern of tardiness, assume this student is late — not absent — if he/she is missing when class begins. When passing out supplies, distributing notebooks, or passing out daily work, put these things on the desk of the late student even though he/she isn't there. Then everything is waiting when the student arrives. This practice minimizes classroom disruption.

10. Seat the late arriver close to the door so that he/she can enter quietly and with the least possible disturbance.

11. Don't give the student attention for arriving late, or make his/her arrival unnecessarily unpleasant. If you do, the problem will intensify. Usually, the student's style of seeking attention, and not your class, is the reason for tardiness. Therefore, fill this student's need for attention in positive ways.

12. Do not talk to the student when he/she arrives. Rather, wait for a study or conference time for private consultation. The late arriver definitely needs counseling, but not on class time. Counsel the student privately regarding the importance of dependability as well as his/her responsibility to the class.

13. Allow another student to help the late arriver learn to be more organized.

14. Notify the office, but be aware that sending habitual late arrivers to the office compounds the problem.

15. If lateness continues after a student conference, notify parents and arrange a meeting with them and the student.

IV. MISTAKES: Common misjudgments and errors in managing the child which may perpetuate or intensify the problem.

1. Assuming that the class is as disturbed by the behavior as the teacher.

2. Sending the student to the office. This wastes time and causes a second interruption when he/she returns.

3. Ridiculing the student. This makes arriving in class an unpleasant experience.

4. Treating this student differently by issuing special orders to him/her.

5. Anticipating that the student will not be on time, and prejudging him/her.

174

6. Reprimanding the student when he/she arrives, thus intensifying and prolonging the interruption.

7. Assuming that he/she is uninterested and doesn't care.

8. Concluding the student doesn't want to do anything about the problem.

9. Giving up attempts to solve the problem after a certain point.

10. Allowing ourselves to fall into the habit of getting to class late, taking students to lunch late or bringing them back late, being late to assemblies, or allowing students to go late to special teachers. Doing so may cause students to feel we are part of the reason for disciplinary and other problems. We must respect the fact that what we do affects others.

11. Failing to see that regularly beginning class on time may help late arrivers get to classes on time.

12. Creating inconsistent rules for admittance to class.

13. Failing to make a clear definition of our expectations regarding when students should arrive.

14. Continually ignoring the student's lateness. Doing so may impair our position with other students.

SEE ALSO: • The Tardy

THE LAZY

I. BEHAVIOR: Specific attitudes and actions of this child at home and/or at school.

1. Shows a very low level of interest.
2. Wastes time.
3. Lacks goals.
4. Perpetually disorganized.
5. May love to talk in group discussions, whether he/she knows the material being discussed or not. But is likely to get the group off the subject at hand.
6. Many times acts as if to say, "I don't care," and may say so openly.
7. Often fails to bring materials to class or to do assignments.
8. May make up any kind of excuse to cover his/her behavior. Herein lies a valuable clue for identifying the lazy student.
9. May exhibit this behavior either occasionally or habitually.

II. EFFECTS: How behavior affects teachers, classmates, and parents in the school learning environment and the home family situation.

1. Teacher's time and effort with this student during class most commonly meet with failure.
2. Classmates mimic the lazy worker's behavior.
3. Class work may be slowed as a result of his/her presence.
4. Classmates may adopt similar attitudes if the lazy student is allowed to be assertive.
5. Teacher may begin to develop a defeatist attitude.
6. Everyone's enthusiasm is dampened because the "I don't care" attitude is contagious.

III. ACTION:
- **Identify causes of misbehavior.**
- **Pinpoint student needs being revealed.**
- **Employ specific methods, procedures, and techniques at school and at home for getting the child to modify or change his/her behavior.**

1. Primary cause of misbehavior:
   - Self-Confidence: This student may feel that he/she is a failure in everything and that being lazy eliminates the risk of further failure.
2. Primary needs being revealed:
   - Hunger, Thirst, Rest: The physical needs of this student may be contributing to the problem.
   - Escape from Pain: Being lazy is a way to escape pain of family or school problems.
3. Secondary needs being revealed:
   - Gregariousness: This student's exclusion from social groups could be a reason for laziness.
   - Achievement: Little successes may become very meaningful to this person.
   - Power: This student may feel that being lazy is a form of power over adults. The power need should be met through achievement.

▶ Status: Every effort should be made to help this student feel that he/she is a worthwhile person in the eyes of peers and adults.

4. Take care to evaluate what "lazy" means relative to each individual student.

5. Encourage parents to get a full physical examination for this student.

6. Don't overlook any factor in attempting to motivate this student. Remember, all behavior, including laziness, has a purpose. Delve thoroughly into the various responsibilities, including jobs, that this student may have outside school. The keys to changing this behavior lie in many places.

7. In the process of trying to determine *why* the student is lazy, rather than simply how laziness is demonstrated, don't misjudge the student's abilities or label him/her. If you do, you keep the student boxed in a corner.

8. Recognize that a health problem may cause lazy behavior. Therefore, be careful, or you may fail to identify the source of the problem.

9. Above all, recognize that a poor self-concept indicates *fear of failure,* and this usually lies at the root of laziness. By not participating, the lazy student avoids the possibility of failure — and keeps his/her pride. Therefore, to reach this student, try different approaches which promote a positive self-image.

10. Remember, people do what works for them. The lazy student may have been taught that it's easier to get people to do things for him/her. Therefore, being lazy works for this student — and becomes a strength. That's why you must take some definite steps to change the behavior.

11. Above all else, make this student work.

12. Stay with the student regardless of the difficulty of your effort. Don't give up on this student, regardless of his/her behavior.

13. Never forget, the lazy student isn't a procrastinator. A procrastinator will do the job eventually. The lazy student may not — unless he/she is motivated.

14. Try to find out what's really important to this student. It may be comfort, prestige, or autonomy.

15. Directly ask the student about likes, interests, and preferences, but never talk about dislikes. Remember, he/she knows the negative side of everything. Dwelling on it is part of the problem. Unless you ask about the student's likes, you may spend the entire year trying to find out — unsuccessfully. And remember, this student *may not* believe you really care. If you don't ask about his/her interests, you reinforce the negative behavior in both subtle and overt ways. To find areas of interest or ways to motivate this student, you may have to seek help from colleagues.

16. Confront laziness in the classroom — consistently. Don't ignore it. Confront parents about this issue as well.

17. Capitalize on *any* interest, regardless of how remote it may seem. In the meantime, continue to insist that the student work — and never let him/her slide.

18. Give smaller, more short-term assignments in which immediate success can be readily attained.

19. Always impose time limits. You might even set up contracts with the student.

20. Give this student alternate work time — even if it's before or after school.

21. Give rewards for accomplishments. Otherwise, motivation may not continue.

22. Talk with the student privately; inquire about the successes he/she is experiencing in school, at home, and with friends.

23. When counseling, always point out this student's strengths — because the lazy student honestly doesn't think he/she has any. Finally, try to give the student choices — and explain the consequences of laziness in the process: The lazy student will be the only loser. And your "I care" attitude should openly state that you don't want any student to be a loser in your class.

IV. MISTAKES: Common misjudgments and errors in managing the child which may perpetuate or intensify the problem.

1. Using our own value system to condemn.

2. Failing to delve into the home environment of this student.

3. Failing to consider the jobs or responsibilities that the student may have outside school.

4. Misjudging the lazy student's abilities, labeling the student, and therefore keeping him/her boxed in a corner.

5. Improperly identifying the source of the problem.

6. Failing to recognize a health problem at the root of the student's behavior.

7. Putting the student down or being sarcastic.

8. Expecting too much from this student.

9. Failing to try different approaches to reach this student.

10. Failing to promote a positive self-image, which is truly necessary for this student.

11. Giving up on this youngster because of his/her wasted potential and refusal to produce in the classroom.

SEE ALSO: • "I Don't Care" • The Noncompleter with Grand Plans
• The Nonparticipator • The Procrastinator

THE LEWD

I. BEHAVIOR: **Specific attitudes and actions of this child at home and/or at school.**

1. Rude and discourteous.

2. Unconcerned and uncaring.

3. May lack visible motivation (for example, cleanliness).

4. Habitually absent or tardy.

5. Uses vulgar language.

6. Wears clothing such as T-shirts with sexual messages.

7. Displays such behavior overtly and in a way that is intrusive to others.

II. EFFECTS: **How behavior affects teachers, classmates, and parents in the school learning environment and the home family situation.**

1. Teacher and classmates are embarrassed.

2. Other students believe that teacher or administration lacks control.

3. Teacher and classmates are angered by this student's disrespect.

4. Others' moral principles are challenged.

III. ACTION:
- **Identify causes of misbehavior.**
- **Pinpoint student needs being revealed.**
- **Employ specific methods, procedures, and techniques at school and at home for getting the child to modify or change his/her behavior.**

1. Primary causes of misbehavior.

   ◗ Attention: This student is using every negative means to gain attention.

   ◗ Power: The student is using this behavior to gain control over peers and adults.

2. Primary needs being revealed:

   ◗ Sex: This student's home situation or personal approach to establishing relationships may be very negative.

   ◗ Escape from Pain: Lewd behavior may be a protective device to avoid the risks involved in forming relationships.

3. Secondary needs being revealed:

   ◗ Gregariousness: In spite of all the negative behavior, this student may have a strong need to belong to a group.

   ◗ Aggression: This student may feel lewdness is a good way to demonstrate how very grown-up he/she is, and the desire to be treated as such.

   ◗ Power: This person may see him/herself as meeting a real power need through his/her lewd behavior.

   ◗ Status: This behavior may make the student feel that he/she is "somebody," and may give him/her prestige with certain peers.

4. Don't ignore this behavior. Pretending that you don't notice only strengthens this student's attention need.

5. For best results, do not talk to the student alone. Rather, have three or four teachers discuss the issue and approach the student jointly.

6. Talk to the student about his/her language and behavior, how it is offensive, and why. The "why" of your strategic approach is "fairness." Tell the student that it's fine to do as he/she chooses, but it wouldn't be fair for you not to explain the effect it has on others. Next, explain that it's not fair to impose his/her language, dress, or behavior on others.

7. Provide consequences for rude or lewd language, behavior, or dress.

8. Realize that this student may well have the approval of many peers. Therefore, see parents.

9. Talk to both parents together. Do so in a caring, gentle, and helping way. Use the same strategic action approach: fairness. Also, tell parents that the impression they give to people is the one people will remember. ("Do you want people to think your child is rude and crude?")

IV. MISTAKES: Common misjudgments and errors in managing the child which may perpetuate or intensify the problem.

1. Ignoring the problem.

2. Allowing the student to get attention from peers through such behavior.

3. Getting angry.

4. Trying to take away the student's status and prestige.

5. Using vulgar language around students at any time.

6. Making statements like "I don't know what I'm going to do with you." Such statements place us in a position of assuming all responsibility for a student's behavior. Teacher efforts should place the student in a position in which he/she must accept this responsibility.

SEE ALSO: • The Attention Demander   • The Foulmouth   • The Rude   • The Swearer

THE LIAR

I. BEHAVIOR: Specific attitudes and actions of this child at home and/or at school.

1. Fabricates and tells unbelievable stories, even when he/she knows others won't believe them.
2. Exaggerates even the smallest detail.
3. Lies about what he/she has done, and about what he/she hasn't done.
4. Tries to improve his/her own image in the eyes of others by telling falsehoods about others — and about him/herself.
5. Likely to be a loner.
6. Will not accept blame for his/her own actions. Rather, makes up stories to "cover" the matter being questioned.
7. Tries to persuade others to support his/her lies — including parents, classmates, teachers, counselors, and administrators.
8. Attempts to receive special treatment or get away with something by lying.
9. Accuses others of injustice when confronted with a lie.
10. May lie to teacher about parents — and to parents about teacher.

II. EFFECTS: How behavior affects teachers, classmates, and parents in the school learning environment and the home family situation.

1. A negative climate is created; teacher and classmates are continually aware of the liar's presence.
2. Others are uncomfortable and continually on guard.
3. Teacher and classmates withdraw or want to exclude this student.
4. Teacher and classmates may become defensive in his/her presence.
5. Teacher may feel the situation is hopeless and the student can't change.
6. Feelings of dislike — even hate — may take root in the classroom. Nobody likes a liar, and this fact accents the problem.
7. Teacher is saddened.

III. ACTION
- **Identify causes of misbehavior.**
- **Pinpoint student needs being revealed.**
- **Employ specific methods, procedures, and techniques at school and at home for getting the child to modify or change his/her behavior.**

1. Primary causes of misbehavior:
   - Attention: This student gains attention by always having something to say, true or false.
   - Self-Confidence: When a person has to lie, it is usually because what is real gives him/her little prestige, or because the lie makes the person feel better about him/herself.
2. Primary needs being revealed:
   - Sex: This student may have poor relationships at home and school, and may desire to obtain any kind of relationship.
   - Escape from Pain: Failure at home or at school may be so painful that this student lies to cover the pain.

3. Secondary needs being revealed:

   ◆ Gregariousness: The behavior may be intended to win friends or obtain approval from parents or teachers.

   ◆ Aggression: By lying, the student may be pretending to act out his/her aggression positively.

   ◆ Status: Lying makes this student the center of attention. Thus, in the student's mind, he/she has earned prestige.

   The liar is usually a person who desires to have any of the secondary needs met in his/her life. He/she may lie in order to feign achievement, power, status, or independence.

4. Remember, the continuous liar is looking for a chance to be successful, and an alert teacher can help stop the lying.

5. Don't ignore the lying. Experience will reveal that the student will tell "bigger" stories if you do.

6. Discover the reason for the behavior; it's usually low self-esteem. This is a problem of identity and self-worth. A student might also lie in an attempt to be successful or to gain attention and protection. Thus, lying may be a self-preservation device.

7. Don't apply rational thoughts to lying. Rational thoughts can't be applied to irrational behavior.

8. Try to discover what pressures may be causing the student to lie.

9. Use the "Deviation" strategic technique when possible. Simply deviate the lying by giving the student attention in a manner which interrupts the lie. Say, for example, "I'm sorry, Johnny, would you please get me those books?" Use the student's *name* with interruption techniques. Do not listen to the lie before you correct; rather, correct immediately. This technique allows you to *give attention* without hearing the lie.

10. Also, use the "Repetition" strategic technique. Simply ask the student to repeat the remark which you recognize as a lie. He/she will usually say, "Never mind" or "Forget it, it wasn't important." A student who lies will usually not repeat the story if you raise your eyebrows, give a knowing look, and say, "Will you tell me that again?"

11. If lying is excessive, counsel in the presence of a counselor or administrator. Make sure you do most of the talking so that the student knows you can handle the situation and are prepared to do so.

12. Work to build a relationship rather than reject the student. Show that you like the student, but dislike the lying.

13. Never call the student a liar. He/she may be hurt beyond repair, or may deny emphatically that he/she is lying.

14. Occasionally, allow the student to lie. This gives you an opportunity to show that you don't accept the lie, thereby revealing that the behavior is not working for him/her.

15. Remember, the only reasonable goal is *improvement*. You have to buy time, stay with the student, and refuse to give up.

16. Touch the hurt ... in a gentle way. Do as little damage as possible. Talk about *telling stories, imagination,* and *protection* rather than lying.

17. Be aware that lying can be a result of severe personal problems which require professional help. Refer when necessary.

18. Relating to a student who is lying is difficult. We can best help these students if we continually remind ourselves *why* people lie. Mostly, students lie to protect themselves. As teachers, we tell children that it is always best to tell the truth, no matter what the consequences. Yet, we must recognize that a child might be thinking, "Why risk getting in

trouble for telling the truth when I might completely escape punishment by telling a lie?" That's protective rationale. When confronting a child about a situation you didn't witness, establish a basis of trust. If he/she trusts you to understand the circumstances — and to help him/her cope with the wrongness of the behavior — then there is less reason to lie. If you don't establish this basis of trust, however, you may unwittingly put the student in a position to lie.

19. Recognize that lying is a cry for help.

20. Remember, the liar needs to succeed. Otherwise, there would be no need to lie.

IV. MISTAKES: Common misjudgments and errors in managing the child which may perpetuate or intensify the problem.

1. Calling the student a "liar."

2. Ignoring the lies — and the student.

3. Developing an actual dislike for the student because of one behavioral characteristic.

4. Purposely avoiding all contact with this student.

5. Immediately suspecting a lie — or accusing the student of lying — whenever he/she relates anything.

6. Failing to try to help the student because we fear that we cannot cope with the lies.

7. Failing to contact parents, administrators, and counselors to seek their help.

8. Refusing to help the student develop friendships because we have determined that he/she doesn't deserve friends.

9. Assuming that nothing this student says is the truth.

10. Making rules to cover future lying.

11. Issuing threats, or promising punishments for future lying.

12. Failing to realize that the liar desires to be successful in meeting one or more of the secondary needs.

SEE ALSO: • The Cheater   • The Excuse/Alibi Maker   • The Gossip

THE LONER

I. BEHAVIOR: Specific attitudes and actions of this child at home and/or at school.

1. Seems to shy away from everything and everyone. Easy to identify; even a classroom visitor can pick out the loner during first observation.

2. Walks alone in the halls.

3. Always extremely quiet.

4. Shuns participation of any kind with others.

5. May be a good or poor student.

6. Seems to "crawl" in and out of classroom unnoticed by classmates and teacher alike. May pass from year to year unnoticed.

II. EFFECTS: How behavior affects teachers, classmates, and parents in the school learning environment and the home family situation.

1. No one is bothered by this behavior. However, when others do notice, they think something is wrong.

2. Teacher may feel sorry for this student.

3. Teacher may feel very frustrated.

4. Teacher may ignore the behavior.

III. ACTION: • Identify causes of misbehavior.
• Pinpoint student needs being revealed.
• Employ specific methods, procedures, and techniques at school and at home for getting the child to modify or change his/her behavior.

1. Primary cause of misbehavior:

   ▶ Self-Confidence: Care must be taken in assuming that lack of self-confidence is the cause of the behavior. While some loners do lack self-confidence, others have a great deal.

2. Primary need being revealed:

   ▶ Escape from Pain: This student may feel inferior to others.

3. Secondary needs being revealed:

   ▶ Affiliation: This student may need to develop a close friendship with a peer.

   ▶ Status: Many of these students will continue to be loners, but they might like to receive recognition of their existence.

4. Before you decide on any tactic that will involve the loner in class activities, observe him/her closely for several days.

5. During the observation period, "go slowly" and speak to the student quietly.

6. Remember that this child is not an extrovert. When you involve him/her with classmates, pick quiet students and quiet activities. Placing the loner with extroverts will only make him/her more withdrawn.

7. Proceed quietly and slowly. When the student finds the people and situations with which he/she feels comfortable, he/she will begin to "come out of the shell."

8. Discuss this student with your counselor and administrator in case professional help is needed.

9. Don't jump to conclusions. This student may be fine. The loner can do what most kids can't do — be with him/herself.

10. Set aside a special time each day to think about how to reach and give attention to your timid, quiet students. A good time to do this might be on the drive to or from school, or those first few minutes after students are dismissed.

IV. MISTAKES: Common misjudgments and errors in managing the child which may perpetuate or intensify the problem.

1. Overlooking the loner from day to day — and then from year to year — because we have so many other things to do and because this student isn't troublesome. We may not even remember the student's name two weeks after the grade or course is completed. This is a tragedy.

2. Approaching the loner too quickly or with the wrong technique. A desire to be alone is a personality characteristic of long standing.

3. Singling out this student in the presence of other children.

4. Telling other children about this student or urging classmates to "help" him/her. They already know the loner's desire to be alone, and the loner will be quick to realize what you have done — and resent it. At this time, the student might not want to be with anyone even though he/she may need to be.

5. Overreacting. Remember, this student may just enjoy solitude.

SEE ALSO: • The Apathetic • "I Don't Care" • The Indifferent • The Shy

THE LOUDMOUTH

I. BEHAVIOR: Specific attitudes and actions of this child at home and/or at school.

1. Never talks softly. Everything he/she says is said so that everyone can hear.

2. If some don't hear, says it again louder.

3. Even behaves loudly. Bursts into the room, slams doors, walks heavily, and falls into furniture.

4. May try to be loud in order to be tough.

5. Seems to consider being loud an opportunity to enhance his/her personality.

6. An extrovert.

7. Seems to say, in all he/she does, "I won't let you forget that I'm here."

II. EFFECTS: How behavior affects teachers, classmates, and parents in the school learning environment and the home family situation.

1. Teacher and classmates are usually annoyed, distracted, and irritated by the loud student.

2. Teacher is irritated because everything from class discussions to classroom order is interrupted.

3. Students are irritated because they feel that the loud student is trying to "hog the show."

4. Some classmates are amused by this behavior — as long as it's directed toward someone else.

III. ACTION: • Identify causes of misbehavior.
• Pinpoint student needs being revealed.
• Employ specific methods, procedures, and techniques at school and at home for getting the child to modify or change his/her behavior.

1. Primary cause of misbehavior:

   ◗ Attention: This student needs attention, and cries out for it with every action.

2. Primary need being revealed:

   ◗ Escape from Pain: The school or home situation may be very painful, and the student may be using loud behavior to protect him/herself from others.

3. Secondary needs being revealed:

   ◗ Gregariousness: Belonging to some group is vital to this person.

   ◗ Status: This student needs to be noticed and recognized. He/she is trying to be "somebody" through negative behavior.

4. Be aware that this student is loud because being loud works; it gets him/her noticed, while being quiet doesn't. To the student, being loud seems to enhance his/her personality.

5. If the student is being loud in order to appear tough, be aware that it is just a bluff.

6. Appeal to the loud student in this way: Recognize his/her loudness as "frankness" and "honesty" when you discuss the behavior. However, show the student how much more effective this frankness and honesty could be if a mature approach were employed.

7. Counsel this student privately — repeatedly.

8. Never, never be loud with this student. Don't try to fight fire with fire — it won't work. It will only convince the student that he/she is right, in other words, that the louder one is, the more one can dominate. Then the student will believe that you dominated the situation because you were "the loudest."

9. Encourage the student repeatedly. He/she requires redirection. Always tell the student when he/she demonstrates mature behavior.

10. Appeal to the student's maturity, and give recognition in a quiet, mature manner. This will give the student the attention and recognition he/she requires.

11. Be aware that this student is one of the easiest to help, because he/she would like to change. Loudness causes the student too much trouble and embarrassment. And he/she knows that the situation gets worse as he/she gets older. Your time, patience, and direction are all that's needed.

IV. MISTAKES: Common misjudgments and errors in managing the child which may perpetuate or intensify the problem.

1. Trying to avoid this student, or not dealing with the problem at all.

2. Getting mad.

3. Continually issuing punishments.

4. Making the student feel immature.

5. Failing to counsel privately.

6. Thinking he/she is just rude, ill-mannered, and inconsiderate.

7. Yelling at the student.

8. Pointing out the loudmouth behavior to other students.

SEE ALSO: • The Attention Demander   • The Blurter   • The Last Worder
• The Smartmouth

THE LOVER

I. BEHAVIOR: **Specific attitudes and actions of this child at home and/or at school.**

1. "Hangs on" to his/her girlfriend or boyfriend everywhere he/she goes, in or out of school. Appears unable to keep hands off the other person. Keeps arms around shoulder or waist, or holds hands. Sits or stands as close as possible to the other person.

2. Has little concern about what people think of him/her or the girlfriend or boyfriend.

3. Appears, through gestures, to be claiming, showing, and demanding ownership, rather than showing affection.

4. Becomes very annoyed and indignant when attempts are made to correct this behavior. Says, "I'm not hurting anybody." Feels adults just "don't like anything I do."

5. May be a loner or a poor student, as may his/her girlfriend or boyfriend. Thus, when they "find" each other, they just can't let go.

6. Generally, doesn't do anything significant but continually touch his/her girlfriend or boyfriend.

7. Generally speaking, does not participate in class or school activities.

8. Doesn't get anything from school because of this intense involvement — and neither does the other person.

II. EFFECTS: **How behavior affects teachers, classmates, and parents in the school learning environment and the home family situation.**

1. Teacher and classmates are often embarrassed by this behavior.

2. Others are irritated and disgusted.

3. Jealousy, conflict, and misunderstanding may result between the couple and other students. Classmates who are involved in boy-girl relationships may be disgusted by this couple's behavior. On the other hand, those who don't have such a relationship may simply wish they did.

4. Others are excluded. The couple keep their world very small.

5. Classmates may reject the lover and leave the two to themselves.

6. Teacher finds it difficult to motivate this student.

7. Classmates receive the impression that "this is what a boy-girl relationship is all about."

III. ACTION: • **Identify causes of misbehavior.**
• **Pinpoint student needs being revealed.**
• **Employ specific methods, procedures, and techniques at school and at home for getting the child to modify or change his/her behavior.**

1. Primary cause of misbehavior:

   ▶ Attention: This student may gain the attention he/she needs by finding someone to be his/her lover.

2. Primary needs being revealed:

   ▶ Sex: This person may need a relationship with someone *now,* and may be willing to pay any price for it.

◗ Escape from Pain: There may be no relationship in the home, or this student may be excluded from relationships at home. The student feels the answer is to find someone and, at any cost, to keep the relationship in order to avoid the pain of being without someone who cares.

3. Secondary needs being revealed:

◗ Affiliation: This student may need to feel that he/she is needed by a very special person, and to be near that person continually.

◗ Status: This student has a strong need to feel worthwhile. Being a "lover" makes him/her meaningful to someone. If this behavior is rejected by adults, either at home or at school, he/she will move closer to the person who makes him/her feel special.

4. Do not tell the student that what he/she wants to do is abnormal. It's not. Likewise, don't try to tell the student that expressions of caring are private and should not be demonstrated.

5. Try to show empathy and express the importance of caring. However, explain that some behavior is mature and appropriate in public, while some behavior isn't. Therefore, it's important to understand that one can't actually do everything he/she wants. This stance must be a part of your strategic action.

6. Discuss what is important to this student. Use this approach: "If you really care about Mary, you should show more respect and mature caring for her. And you should have some concern about what others feel about her."

7. Talk to each of them separately in a private place. Tell them, "No more." Sometimes, you will have to describe the exact behavior you expect from a student. Your expectations should be clear and you should have the student respond as to whether your expectations are clear to him/her. For instance, holding hands may be approved. Kissing and inappropriate touching may not. Simply say, *"Your* rules outside school — school rules on the campus."

8. If the behavior continues, ask for help from parents.

9. Remember, there is a certain amount of prestige in having a special person when many other students do not have someone special. Therefore, involve this student in activities or with classmates. Otherwise, the situation will continue.

10. Attempt to find other avenues to meet the student's needs. When the student can find acceptance from teachers and classmates by performing certain tasks successfully or forming other relationships, he/she will find a need to be with others — not just a girlfriend or boyfriend.

11. Try to demonstrate that these two students' world does not end with each other. It is important to have friends and other relationships that will actually help their relationship grow.

IV. MISTAKES: Common misjudgments and errors in managing the child which may perpetuate or intensify the problem.

1. Trying to break up the couple.

2. Assuming the worst about these two students.

3. Embarrassing the students by making sarcastic remarks about the relationship.

4. Confronting these students in a discourteous manner and thus perpetuating the problem.

5. Telling one or the other that they are bad for each other.

6. Rejecting them.

7. Failing to teach mature behavior.

8. Trying to prevent any and all physical contact.

SEE ALSO: • The Animal • The Attention Demander

THE MANIPULATOR

I. BEHAVIOR: Specific attitudes and actions of this child at home and/or at school.

1. Uses people.

2. Tries to get others to do his/her work.

3. Very persuasive.

4. Likely to be articulate.

5. Has leadership skills.

6. Often tricks people into doing something for him/her. Will use any means to manipulate others, including guilt, false compliments, and a pretense of caring.

7. Never admits to being at fault. Tries to place blame on others.

8. Rather than perceive the reality of the situation, believes that he/she is more intelligent and clever than others. In truth, has a false sense of superiority.

9. Not truthful.

10. Wants his/her way, and will do anything to get it.

II. EFFECTS: How behavior affects teachers, classmates, and parents in the school learning environment and the home family situation.

1. Others feel duped.

2. Teacher and classmates are often embarrassed.

3. Teacher becomes angry.

4. Teacher may tend to label this student as deceptive and untruthful, and respond accordingly.

5. Teacher may carry a grudge into every aspect of his/her relationship with this student.

6. Teacher may not realize the power this student holds and the impact he/she has on classmates.

7. An atmosphere of distrust and guardedness is created.

III. ACTION: • Identify causes of misbehavior.
• Pinpoint student needs being revealed.
• Employ specific methods, procedures, and techniques at school and at home for getting the child to modify or change his/her behavior.

1. Primary cause of misbehavior:

   ▶ Power: The need for power causes this student to use people, and to feel a sense of accomplishment when he/she is successful.

2. Primary need being revealed:

   ▶ Escape from Pain: Rather than be open and honest with people and take the chance of rejection, this student escapes the pain of rejection by manipulating others.

3. Secondary needs being revealed:

   ▶ Status: This student wants to know he/she counts. The teacher must find positive ways for the student to count in the classroom.

◗ Autonomy: This student manipulates in order to gain assurance of being his/her own boss, and of the ability to get others to do what he/she wants. Some positive way to demonstrate leadership is needed. This student will change the behavior if he/she finds something better.

4. Move closer to the student personally. This is the first step in getting the student to change his/her behavior.

5. Position yourself to counsel the manipulator privately.

6. Remember, this student will not listen to you unless he/she respects you. With respect, the student may do what you ask — even if he/she really doesn't think you're right.

7. Keep in mind that this student doesn't see — or doesn't want to see — what he/she is doing. Admitting what he/she is doing is even more difficult. Herein lies a clue to curtailing the behavior.

8. First, talk to the student gently regarding the fact that he/she is *not* learning how to do things. Talk about others getting ahead of — and outgrowing — him/her.

9. Also, talk to the student firmly about the fact that he/she is using people — and using them up. Let the student know that you don't believe in using people.

10. Above all, talk about honesty. The manipulator is not being honest with him/herself or with others.

11. Make sure that doing for him/herself works for the student; otherwise, he/she will revert to manipulating. With counseling regarding healthy and honest leadership, this student will begin to change, but it will take time because he/she is lazy — and manipulation has worked so well.

12. Never pull away. Position yourself to counsel this student continuously.

13. Be firm, but take great care not to be dictatorial. All children need firmness and limits. However, they don't need domination, and they will fight teacher domination overtly or behind the scenes. Students don't learn anything from teacher domination — except perhaps to try to outwit the teacher. Efforts to teach acceptable behavior must promote self-discipline, which will eventually enable students to behave without constant supervision.

14. Don't use bribes or promises to achieve control or ward off discipline problems. Such techniques may offer short-term relief, but are a sure way to create long-term problems. Allowing students five minutes extra at lunch or recess, or promising no test or a class party if their deportment is without incident, only sets the stage for future problems and disrespect. Students will soon pick up the same techniques and apply them in their own lives to use people.

15. Remember, if you don't care about this student, you are manipulating him/her.

IV. MISTAKES: Common misjudgments and errors in managing the child which may perpetuate or intensify the problem.

1. Failing to realize that some kids are willing to be manipulated by this student.

2. Believing he/she is *never* on the giving end.

3. Trying to manipulate the student.

4. Getting angry.

5. Displaying sarcasm or vindictiveness.

6. Rejecting this student or saying we want nothing to do with him/her.

7. Failing to mold and develop his/her leadership skills.

SEE ALSO: • The Apple Polisher • The Crier (Who Claims Foul)
• The "Idiot" Syndrome • The Sidetracker

THE NAME CALLER

I. BEHAVIOR: Specific attitudes and actions of this child at home and/or at school.

1. Calls others names.
2. Makes fun of others' weaknesses.
3. However, cannot take the same treatment he/she dishes out.
4. Denies his/her involvement in starting incidents.
5. Regards punishment for his/her behavior as unfair, and will do anything to avoid it.
6. Often involved in physical fights.
7. Does not limit name calling to enemies. Even calls his/her friends names.
8. Doesn't know when to stop.

II. EFFECTS: How behavior affects teachers, classmates, and parents in the school learning environment and the home family situation.

1. Others' feelings are hurt.
2. Classmates become angry.
3. Teacher is irritated and angered.
4. Cooperation and harmony in the classroom are destroyed.
5. Teacher may feel that he/she is not doing a good job with the class because of inability to control and direct the behavior of the name caller.
6. Classmates may develop a poor self-image because of such a student.
7. Classmates may adopt name-calling behavior.

III. ACTION:
- **Identify causes of misbehavior.**
- **Pinpoint student needs being revealed.**
- **Employ specific methods, procedures, and techniques at school and at home for getting the child to modify or change his/her behavior.**

1. Primary cause of misbehavior:
   - Power: It gives a person a feeling of power to see others' reactions to name calling. This student is actually able to govern the feelings of other students.
2. Primary needs being revealed:
   - Hunger, Thirst: This student may have a need for food and drink, and may be covering this need by name calling.
   - Rest: The home situation may be so unstable that this student does not get proper rest.
   - Sex: This student may feel that he/she is an outcast or cannot make friends. He/she attracts attention from peers through name calling.
   - Escape from Pain: The home situation or inability to make friends may cause this student to name-call in order to keep others from perceiving his/her pain.
3. Secondary needs being revealed:

▶ Status: Through this behavior the student is saying, "I'm here and I'm somebody to be reckoned with. Recognize me!"

▶ Affiliation: A close relationship with someone may reduce this student's need to call others names.

4. Take immediate steps to stop the name calling. Although it can be just a passing behavior, it can also become constant or repetitious if ignored.

5. Talk to the class about name calling. It is such a common behavior that it can be dominant at any time.

6. Allow the class to establish rules regarding this behavior. Your goal is to make name calling socially unacceptable.

7. Suggest this rule: No disrespect for people or property.

8. Regardless of the rules regarding name calling, establish a procedure for due process. Listen to both sides.

9. Have the class suggest consequences of breaking any rules that are set up concerning name calling.

10. Praise the name caller when his/her behavior begins to change.

IV. MISTAKES: Common misjudgments and errors in managing the child which may perpetuate or intensify the problem.

1. Thinking that this student name-calls more than he/she actually does.

2. Punishing students for name calling without knowing both sides of the story.

3. Initiating name calling ourselves.

4. Calling names in response to students' name calling.

5. Punishing inconsistently.

SEE ALSO: • The Foulmouth   • The Loudmouth   • The Smartmouth

THE NEGATIVE GROUP

I. BEHAVIOR: **Specific attitudes and actions of this group at home and/or at school.**

1. Usually a small group of students.

2. May or may not have a recognized leader.

3. Do everything together, especially socially.

4. Stick together on every issue.

5. Act bored, disinterested, or imposed upon by teacher ideas, suggestions, or requirements.

6. Involve themselves in each other's problems; therefore, perpetuate each other's problems.

7. Claim loyalty and righteousness if reprimanded. All the interference they cause is in the name of friendship.

8. Likely to confront teacher as a group when one member has been disciplined.

9. Usually uncooperative, and possibly hostile.

10. As a group, likely to be either very good or very poor students.

11. Conduct themselves as though no other individuals exist in the school, including other students.

12. Not objective. They turn off — to everything — sometimes without even knowing what they are doing.

II. EFFECTS: **How behavior affects teachers, classmates, and parents in the school learning environment and the home family situation.**

1. Other students are excluded.

2. Others feel inferior or insignificant.

3. Others are infected with negativism. Negative people can enter a day, cloud it immediately, and then walk away apparently unaware of the effect they have had.

4. Resentment is caused.

5. Teacher — and sometimes classmates — is target of open dislike and disapproval.

6. Correction of group members on a one-to-one basis becomes very difficult, because the group may interfere in matters that involve only one member.

7. Other students feel either left out or rejected by this group, especially if they feel that the actions and behavior of the negative group are something admirable.

8. Other students are often intimidated by this negative group.

9. Teacher may fear to contend with or approach any group member for fear of repercussions.

10. Teacher may even pretend agreement rather than risk disagreement.

11. Negativism may emerge as the strongest and most powerful force in the classroom if these students aren't changed — or at least neutralized — by those who are positive.

III. ACTION: • **Identify causes of misbehavior.**
• **Pinpoint student needs being revealed.**

194

- **Employ specific methods, procedures, and techniques at school and at home for getting the child to modify or change his/her behavior.**

1. Primary cause of misbehavior:

   ▶ Power: Each of these students may feel powerless alone, but as a group they are powerful.

2. Primary need being revealed:

   ▶ Escape from Pain: The negative group member may have many poor relationships with family and peers, but the negative group helps him/her escape the pain of the failures of these other relationships.

3. Secondary needs being revealed:

   ▶ Gregariousness: People unable to get attention in a positive manner turn to a negative approach. The negative group fulfills the need to belong to an "inner circle" of people. But members would prefer a positive relationship. Therefore, if a relationship between a negative group member and nonmembers improves, the member may leave the group.

   ▶ Aggression: The negative group provides opportunities for students to fill aggressive needs that they cannot fill alone. The teacher should provide opportunities for these students to be assertive in classroom situations.

   ▶ Achievement: Students who cannot achieve through schoolwork may attempt to meet the need for achievement through the negative group.

   ▶ Power: If students are allowed to have input and some say in classroom governance, they will be able to meet a power need outside the group.

   ▶ Status: The negative group gives members status. They will be more likely to leave the group if this need can be met elsewhere. Parents may be able to help if they are made aware of such a need.

4. Be aware that, once membership is established, a student is usually more *like* than *unlike* the group of his/her choosing. The likeness doesn't have to be overt to be present. In truth, the student *is* the group; the group won't allow continued membership if the student's identity isn't genuine. Too, the student may join a particular group because of inability to find, or be accepted by, any other. Regardless, the student is there because of a need.

5. Don't reject or "write off" a student because he/she has chosen a group that is "bad" by teacher standards. Likewise, don't try to force participation in a "good" group. The student must be allowed to make the choice. However, it may be helpful to continue to advise and counsel if you think the choice was a bad one.

6. Don't allow negative attitudes to remain unchecked; they influence the teacher as well as the class. Most negative people will readily admit that negativism is their biggest liability and the one they most want to change.

7. Attempt to *defuse* the situation immediately; nothing positive can happen until this is accomplished. Arrange a meeting with the group, with the stated purpose of listening to and gathering information. You'll be amazed at the alienation on both sides that will surface. Be open and available to the group, but make it clear that you must examine the information and investigate. In a second meeting, it may be possible to use the group to work for you rather than against you.

8. Schedule a private conference with each member; this is an absolute necessity. If you are going to have any students leave the group, make sure the discussion focuses *only* on the student involved and his/her behavior, and never on the student's membership in the group or on other group members. A student will leave the group if his/her needs can be met in another way.

9. When talking to a student, always pinpoint exactly what he/she has done. Back up your

statements with factual data. Do not make inferences or generalizations. Remember, the student will always return and tell the group everything that happened.

10. If confronted by the group, remind them that you cannot talk in the presence of the whole group about what happened because it would violate all confidentiality as well as show disrespect. Group members will understand this approach — even if they don't like it. If a student chooses to tell the group everything that took place in a conference, that's the student's choice, but you cannot discuss the business of one student with another.

11. Always handle the negative group in a highly professional manner, because there are many people involved and they support each other in confrontations. It is vital to deal with the individual alone and never consider attacking the group.

12. Do not overreact and assume the negative group actually encompasses the whole class.

13. Refrain from becoming emotional.

14. Realize that this behavior is not reserved for you personally. These students treat everyone this way — classmates, teachers, parents.

15. Contact each set of parents. Discuss their child only — with the administrator informed prior to action.

16. Seek administrative assistance if trouble continues.

17. Talk with your counselor. A good counselor can make groups work in positive ways through challenge.

18. Remember, to get these students to function independently, you must meet their needs on an individual basis.

19. Be aware that it is very difficult for anyone to operate always from a negative position, because it is so self-defeating. It's important to remember that, as a teacher, when you offer a negative you offer nothing. But with every positive you propose, you suggest a course of action.

20. Make sure your contacts with students are positive. A student has a positive or negative experience every time he/she looks into the face of a teacher. As simple as it seems, eye contact and a smile show a person he/she is worth smiling at, and the first positive step — acceptance — has been made. Being positive gives students a sense of well-being in the teacher's presence.

21. Remember that, generally speaking, people will act as they think others expect them to act.

22. Be aware that freedom to choose which group to belong to is one way students learn to make choices. Whether the student's choice appears good or bad to others, it may turn out that a particular group isn't what the student is really looking for. However, by trying it, the student can arrive at that conclusion through experience.

IV. MISTAKES: Common misjudgments and errors in managing the child which may perpetuate or intensify the problem.

1. Failing to recognize an individual student's need for group membership.

2. Discussing the problem with the entire class present.

3. Demonstrating open anxiety, disapproval, or hostility toward students in the group.

4. Allowing them to work together.

5. Discussing one member by name with another member.

6. Trying to pit one member against another.

7. Thinking classmates sympathize with the group.

8. Confusing the group with the class.

9. Punishing or establishing rules for the entire class because of the behavior of the group.

10. Insulting other students by including them as members of the group through such phrases as "my bad class."

11. Responding to the group rather than handling situations on an individual basis.

12. Not giving the group a chance to be heard. The benefits of holding a structured, open meeting, at which all group members are present and may speak, should not be overlooked.

13. Talking only to representatives of a group rather than the whole group.

14. Failing to recognize the influence such a group can exert.

15. Being surprised at the presence of a pressure group, and unprepared to deal with it.

16. Discussing students' problems with others, except in a professional setting designed for the purpose of providing positive help. Confidentiality is a must. If a student hears that a teacher has made him/her the subject of a public discussion, the relationship will probably be impaired permanently.

17. Reading to the class student notes that are found or intercepted. In fact, it's good teacher policy not to read the notes at all. Often, only embarrassment for both teacher and students results.

18. Telling a group or a class, "You had better be good in assembly or you'll hear from me when you return," or "If you don't behave in the halls while passing to lunch, I'll deal with you personally." Such an approach only lets students know that we don't expect mature and responsible behavior.

19. Imposing our negative feelings on students. If a teacher sighs often and treats the whole process of teaching as a wearisome "nonevent," students feel and accept a sense of responsibility for this teacher attitude. Unfortunately, they can't know that it has little or nothing to do with them.

SEE ALSO: • The Clique • The Follower

THE NOISEMAKER

I. BEHAVIOR: Specific attitudes and actions of this child at home and/or at school.

1. Makes strange sounds or noises in the classroom. Hums, whistles, creates throat noises, drops books, taps the desk, and does other things which create odd noises.
2. May not always know that he/she is making noises.
3. Tries to disguise the origin of the noise.
4. Then puts on the "innocent" act when teacher looks in his/her direction or asks him/her to stop.
5. Seeks attention via this behavior.
6. May lack motivation; may, in fact, be a bright student who is underachieving.
7. Delights in engaging in these kinds of devious activities, and may do so purposely to annoy the teacher.

II. EFFECTS: How behavior affects teachers, classmates, and parents in the school learning environment and the home family situation.

1. Teacher is forced to stop class.
2. Teacher must interrupt study time.
3. Classmates are irritated and disturbed.
4. Lesson plan is interrupted.
5. Other students are encouraged to make noise.
6. Teacher is annoyed and frustrated.
7. Classmates — as well as the noisemaker — are prevented from achieving.

III. ACTION:
- **Identify causes of misbehavior.**
- **Pinpoint student needs being revealed.**
- **Employ specific methods, procedures, and techniques at school and at home for getting the child to modify or change his/her behavior.**

1. Primary cause of misbehavior:
   - Attention: This student needs to be recognized, and any source of recognition is satisfactory to him/her.
2. Primary needs being revealed:
   - Sex: This student feels uncomfortable in establishing relationships, and is attempting to use noisemaking as a way to form relationships.
   - Escape from Pain: This behavior may be a retreat from the pain of academic failure.
3. Secondary needs being revealed:
   - Gregariousness: This student may be trying to be recognized and to be included in a group.
   - Aggression: This person has a difficult time making contact with another person. Such contact would provide another way to gain inclusion in the group.
   - Status: The noisemaker lets everyone know he/she exists.

4. Recognize that the noisemaker must receive recognition from peers and adults through positive involvement in the class. When these needs are met, the noisemaking will be reduced.

5. Remember, this is a social problem, not a discipline problem.

6. Be aware that this behavior disturbs and annoys the teacher much more than the class.

7. Plan your actions. With foresight, you can neutralize this student.

8. Seat this student in the front of the room, close at hand, where you can keep an eye on him/her.

9. Always seat the student away from friends and near more serious students. When it becomes apparent that the immediate audience is not receptive to his/her usual behavior, the student will change to other disruptive actions, and then eventually give up the disruption altogether.

10. When the student begins changing his/her actions and behavior to other antics, don't be disturbed. The battle is half won.

11. Always counsel this student privately. This is a necessity.

12. Talk to the child about maturity. Try to reach the student with reason and explanation. If he/she is indifferent to these approaches, seek counseling assistance. This student is in need of professional help.

13. Explain that the behavior cannot continue because it impairs the class's ability to function.

14. Refrain from revealing frustration.

15. During the private conference, focus on the student's actions, not on the frustrations he/she is causing you.

16. During the conference, use direct questions: "Do you realize what you are doing?" "Do you feel left out of class?" "Do you realize what your classmates think?" "What can I do to help you?" Questions like these will help the student to put his/her behavior into perspective and see what is happening from your point of view as well as that of others.

17. Whatever you do, make the student a part of your corrective action. This includes changing seats. Then the student can regard your action as teacher assistance rather than a punishment.

18. If the student laughs at these approaches and shows an evident dislike for you personally, contact your administrator and the student's parents immediately. The student is not defying you in this case, but rather is asking you for help.

19. Try this technique the next time the student is making noise. As you do, proceed *very slowly* and *quietly* so that he/she can see what you are going to do — and don't say a word. Put your finger to your lips, and walk over and quietly take the object that the student is playing with — slowly and gently. Touch the student's moving hands. Most important, give the object back after class or after school. If you don't, the student will make an issue of the fact that you took something from him/her. Remember, this student wants attention.

20. If the noisemaker resists this gesture, don't make an issue of it. Rather, say softly, "OK — but you'll have to keep it quiet." This approach works better than confronting a student or publicly embarrassing him/her.

21. Reinforce any positive behavior. The student must change his/her behavior before any improvement in attitude can take place.

22. Explain your responsibility toward the rest of the class. Discuss the opinion others will have of this student for disrupting their serious endeavors.

23. Teachers should be very aware of the "noise level" they create. Often the teacher who requires the strictest classroom discipline code and is the most intolerant of student noise in the classroom is the real source of classroom noise. This teacher yells every instruction, slams

books and drawers, and makes presentations that can be heard in the next classroom. This mode of operation is the exact opposite of the climate the teacher is attempting to create. If you think you might be contributing to a high noise level, ask your department head or administrator for an honest evaluation.

IV. MISTAKES: Common misjudgments and errors in managing the child which may perpetuate or intensify the problem.

1. Overreacting and losing our dignity because of the annoyance this pupil causes.

2. Making threats that are impossible to carry out.

3. Behaving in a hostile manner with the student.

4. Becoming impatient and irritable with the entire class, especially those who think this student is funny.

5. Failing to confront the real problem.

SEE ALSO: • The Blurter   • The Fun Seeker

THE NONCOMPLETER WITH GRAND PLANS

I. BEHAVIOR: Specific attitudes and actions of this child at home and/or at school.

1. Never finishes a project.

2. Always has assignments close to completion ... but unfinished.

3. Never accepts personal responsibility for actions.

4. Often has goals that are too high for successful achievement.

5. Often demonstrates an attitude of superiority rather than inferiority.

6. May frequently urge teacher and classmates to take on a big project — when he/she can't finish a homework assignment.

7. Hogs the show when a project is being planned.

8. Often begins enthusiastically, but loses interest before the end. This is one of the reasons he/she fails.

9. Often criticizes teacher for being unimaginative and failing to accept anything that would be fun.

10. Yet, usually leaves his/her own grand plans for others to finish.

11. Ridicules the conservative and applauds the grandiose.

12. Lacks perspective regarding what's involved in reaching goals.

13. Is usually fantasizing when he/she offers ideas.

II. EFFECTS: How behavior affects teachers, classmates, and parents in the school learning environment and the home family situation.

1. Classmates dislike this student.

2. Teacher tends to stereotype this student by his/her failures.

3. Other students may adopt similar practices — or seek concessions.

4. Classmates may lose enthusiasm for future projects when they have to do the work of the noncompleter.

5. Teacher is put on the defensive when this student begins to set goals.

6. Other students who work with the noncompleter may get in trouble for not completing tasks.

7. Teacher's time is diverted from helping other students.

III. ACTION:
- **Identify causes of misbehavior.**
- **Pinpoint student needs being revealed.**
- **Employ specific methods, procedures, and techniques at school and at home for getting the child to modify or change his/her behavior.**

1. Primary cause of misbehavior:
   - Self-Confidence: This student does not believe he/she can complete the assigned tasks.
   - Attention: This student is probably seeking attention through his/her grand plans.

2. Primary needs being revealed:
   - Sex: This student seeks recognition from peers and adults, and hopes his/her behavior will bring friends and respect.
   - Escape from Pain: The student believes that, if people recognize him/her for the grand plans, maybe they won't notice any inability. The grand plans give the student an excuse for failure.

3. Secondary needs being revealed:
   - Affiliation: If someone accepts this student unconditionally, he/she may feel no need to make grand plans and then fail.
   - Achievement: In order for any other needs to be met, this student must experience achievement. With achievement, other needs will be met.

4. Establish a close relationship with this student. It will help provide the attention he/she is seeking.

5. Use the "Minor Point" technique. Say, "Do you want to use a pen or a pencil on the assignment?" or "Do you want to turn your paper in at 2:00 p.m., or 3:00 p.m.?"

6. Also, use the "Choice" technique. Say, "Will your report be from a text or a magazine?"

7. Support this student, but in a positive manner. Help the student readjust goals.

8. Make sure the goals are obtainable, especially in the beginning.

9. Make sure short-term goals are set for various stages of completion of projects.

10. Recognize achievements.

11. Encourage positive support from other students.

12. Remember, this isn't necessarily a discipline problem.

13. Check with the student's other teachers, as well as previous teachers.

14. Seek help of counselor and parents.

15. Be aware that this student is not the same as the procrastinator. This student can be helped because he/she is likely to have leadership characteristics. That's why he/she wants attention. If the student feels like an integral part of the class, and has a close relationship with the teacher, he/she will be unlikely to put him/herself in a position which would change this status.

16. Help the student see the enormity of his/her suggestions. When he/she suggests something, say, "Let's list what we'll have to do to get this done." Then, allow classmates to offer input about the plan. Do so in a positive and helpful way.

17. If the plan is to be undertaken, break it down into stages. By doing so, you can reduce the size of the goal and supervise achievement.

18. Don't give additional homework as a punishment for not completing tasks. Rarely does this discipline technique change misbehavior to acceptable behavior. Remember, a behavior problem is not necessarily an academic problem. Requiring a child to complete unfinished work at home is fine — but don't think for a minute that extra work will eliminate behavior problems. More often than not, such action will compound the problem. In addition to detracting from the learning value associated with homework, it may cause a child to detest your class. This is when the real problems will begin.

19. Avoid "doubling" penalties with the noncompleter. Many teachers have "dug their own graves" by issuing demerits or hour penalties — then doubling or tripling these punishments

to the point that they approach the ridiculous. This will only cause the noncompleter's behavior to worsen. There isn't an administrator in the world who can enforce or defend this type of teacher punishment. A teacher must seek the help of a counselor or administrator long before this type of situation develops.

IV. MISTAKES: Common misjudgments and errors in managing the child which may perpetuate or intensify the problem.

1. Failing to recognize leadership potential in this student.

2. Using sarcasm.

3. Allowing the student to fail without making sure he/she learns something in the process.

4. Ignoring the student and his/her suggestions.

5. Treating this child as a disruptive student who is attempting to take power away from the teacher.

6. Discouraging or making fun of his/her grand plans.

SEE ALSO: • The Alibier • The Con Artist • "I Don't Care" • The Lazy
                  • The Procrastinator • The Underachiever

THE NONPARTICIPATOR

I. BEHAVIOR: **Specific attitudes and actions of this child at home and/or at school.**

1. Isn't learning.

2. Falls farther behind in class work every day.

3. Displays varying degrees of boredom and indifference. These are the first signs of nonparticipation.

4. Fails to bring materials to class or to turn in assignments; becomes preoccupied with other interests. These may be the first overt clues.

5. By and large, just sits in class and does nothing.

6. Wants attention; actually hopes for teacher attention.

7. Suffers from three personal voids: safety, esteem, and self-actualization.

II. EFFECTS: **How behavior affects teachers, classmates, and parents in the school learning environment and the home family situation.**

1. Teacher has trouble understanding the reason behind this student's behavior, and has trouble knowing how to approach the student. That's why handling students who won't participate is one of the biggest problems for teachers.

2. Teacher must take a great deal of extra time for additional instruction.

3. Classmates resent the extra time given to this student.

4. Teacher may be angered by this student's refusal to participate in class.

5. Teacher may become resentful of this student's being in the class.

6. Classmates become tired of this student getting so much attention.

7. Classroom climate may be adversely affected.

III. ACTION:
- **Identify causes of misbehavior.**
- **Pinpoint student needs being revealed.**
- **Employ specific methods, procedures, and techniques at school and at home for getting the child to modify or change his/her behavior.**

1. Primary causes of misbehavior:

   ▶ Self-Confidence: This student does not feel capable of accomplishing the tasks of the school. Rather than disclose this feeling to peers and teachers, he/she does not participate.

   ▶ Attention: This student may be asking to be noticed by being a nonparticipator.

2. Primary needs being revealed:

   ▶ Escape from Pain: The student may be very fearful of failures and thus may withdraw from active participation in the class.

   ▶ Parents should be consulted concerning the need for a physical check-up. The primary needs of hunger, thirst, air, rest, and elimination of waste should be investigated.

3. Secondary needs being revealed:

   ▶ Inquisitiveness: This student needs to know that he/she can do the work and can be in control of his/her learning.

   ▶ Achievement: Care should be taken that tasks assigned can be completed by this student. The student needs to feel and know that his/her efforts will be accepted and appreciated.

4. Approach the warning signs of boredom and indifference immediately. Without a quick counseling, two behaviors may follow. The student may begin coming to class late, then not coming at all. Most research on drop-outs indicates heavy absence began in elementary school. In addition, once the student gets behind, he/she often becomes defensive. As the year progresses, the child may become hostile. Then you will *know* this student is in class.

5. As a beginning, be aware of the absolute need to give this student a degree of academic leeway and flexibility. If you don't, experience reveals that the nonparticipator usually begins to display three attitudes: feeling confined, comparing school with serving a jail sentence, and showing contempt for authority.

6. Never move away from this student emotionally. Rather, move in and ask, "Why?" Say, "I don't understand, but I'm going to try," or "You may give up on yourself, but I'm not going to give up on you."

7. Remember that there is usually a deeper problem underlying the surface behavior. Failure is a cause and so is the fact that this student will do anything to avoid his/her real problems, whatever they are. That's why the student says, "Nobody likes me" and "Everybody gives me a hard time."

8. There's an aggression in this student's refusal to participate which dares and challenges. Don't rise to that bait, however, or the war will have been won by the student.

9. Always use acceptance as your strategic action approach. Fortunately, there's one action this student can't handle — your refusal to reject or condemn. The student expects both because he/she sees good reasons for you to disapprove. Your refusal to quit offers the best chance for success.

10. First and foremost, establish contact with this student. A close look will reveal that the nonparticipator has few, if any, meaningful relationships with other adults.

11. In order to heighten the self-concept of the nonparticipator, share with this student the contribution he/she makes to the learning that goes on in class. Establish the kind of atmosphere in which the student feels comfortable in depending on you for help — and giving help as well. The student must feel the teacher is there to create a climate of mutual dependence.

12. Your first help should be private. During this first meeting, confront in a caring and factual way. You may say, "I'm not going to allow you not to participate. If I let you get behind, you won't catch up." Only after a relationship is firmly established can the student be told, "If you want to stay in class, you must do assignments, be on time, and bring materials." It's amazing to find out how much the nonparticipator wants caring demands from teachers after a relationship is established.

13. Every nonparticipator experiences failure in the classroom setting. The student will feel safer if he/she can ally with the familiar and secure. Therefore, whether this student likes snakes or cars, adjust your teaching efforts to his/her secure interests.

14. Likewise, make sure lack of interest or absence is not linked to insecurity. Remember, if coming late to class is unpleasant, the student won't come.

15. Establishing a relationship rather than rejecting will help give the student esteem and prestige with classmates and may prevent others from teasing or looking down on him/her. Remember, self-actualization can only be realized by inclusion.

16. Remember, right and wrong cannot be the issue if you want to change this behavior. If you hold fast to class rules, you may never get the opportunity to win with this student.

17. Don't refuse to give this student supplies when he/she doesn't bring them to class. If you do refuse, a bigger problem may loom ahead.

18. Ask yourself two questions: "Do I really want this student here?" and "Do I want to drive him/her away?" These questions must be answered before you can help the nonparticipator. Your answers will determine your actions. If you really want to hold this student in school, you'll be able to make the necessary adjustment. If you don't, you won't be able to do any adjusting.

19. Be flexible with the nonparticipator.

20. Remember to call on those students whose hands are not raised to volunteer answers. Don't form any prejudgments because some students lack the confidence to volunteer participation. They may be sitting at their desks during discussions *hoping* to be called upon. Few of us have not had the experience of wanting to say something when we didn't — and wishing later we had. A watchful eye would have noticed our partially raised hands, our eagerness, or the look of involvement on our faces. Only by watching those you teach can you develop the potential of all students — not just those who repeatedly assert themselves.

21. Helping the nonparticipator takes time. Therefore, develop a willing attitude about giving your time. Otherwise, little change is possible. This student needs a relationship with an adult.

22. Make time to talk with and listen to students who are not participating. Many of them feel removed from their teacher and classmates. Class study time is an ideal opportunity for such contact. First, identify the nonparticipants. Second, make sure you have private words with them at least once each week. You may find your private efforts result in better participation as well as the development of closer teacher-student relationships. However, keep in mind that the privacy of students should be protected. Therefore, make sure that classmates do not know what you are talking about, or your efforts will not produce the desired results.

23. Remember, without giving attention, it is often difficult to maintain good adult-child relationships. This is especially true regarding relationships with the nonparticipator. You must be careful not to shut this student out of your mind. Remember, "out of mind, out of expectations" can happen easily with a student who doesn't do well academically. Never forget, this is the kid who needs you the most. The student knows it — and so should you. If you don't, the student is likely to believe that he/she shouldn't be in school.

24. You may find that class discussion periods are times when you exert increased control of student behavior. If this is the case, examine the types of questions you are using to stimulate discussion. Ask yourself, "Do the questions I ask generally terminate group thinking and involve only the one student being questioned?" Good questions provoke, elevate, and sustain thought from all students in the class. When the level of questioning is elevated beyond simple recall responses, there is increased participation by all students and the teacher will have fewer management difficulties.

IV. MISTAKES: Common misjudgments and errors in managing the child which may perpetuate or intensify the problem.

1. Failing to notice student indifference immediately. Because the nonparticipator is often quiet, he/she can go unnoticed.

2. Failing to approach this student as long as he/she doesn't create a disturbance.

3. Trying to relate to this student as we do to other students. We can't do this and win. If, for instance, make-up work is an absolute we just won't disallow, many nonparticipators may try to catch up. However, most won't be able to — and they'll quit. Denying them security,

esteem, and self-actualization will guarantee that they will quit because of their inability to cope.

4. Taking the attitude "If the student doesn't try, I won't try."

SEE ALSO: • The Apathetic • "I Can't" • "I Don't Care" • The Indifferent • The Shy

"NOT MY FAULT"

I. BEHAVIOR: **Specific attitudes and actions of this child at home and/or at school.**

1. Always defensive.
2. Fears responsibility.
3. Replies, no matter what has been said, "It wasn't my fault" or "I wasn't talking to Johnny. Johnny was talking to me."
4. Chooses what he/she considers the easiest way out.
5. Will stick to his/her guns and wait for teacher to give up in despair.
6. Never understands why teacher is "picking on" him/her.

II. EFFECTS: **How behavior affects teachers, classmates, and parents in the school learning environment and the home family situation.**

1. Everything is thrown into confusion by this student's alibis.
2. Teacher finds it impossible to get to the real issue because of the denial.
3. Teacher is frustrated and angered.
4. Classmates are very distrustful because they know this student will seek to place blame on others.
5. Teacher may tend to assume this student is negative in all behavior.

III. ACTION: • **Identify causes of misbehavior.**
   • **Pinpoint student needs being revealed.**
   • **Employ specific methods, procedures, and techniques at school and at home for getting the child to modify or change his/her behavior.**

1. Primary causes of misbehavior:
   ‣ Attention: This student has a need to be recognized, but does not seem to understand or care about what procedures are used to gain recognition.
   ‣ Self-Confidence: The student finds it difficult to get positive attention because of his/her low self-esteem.
2. Primary need being revealed:
   ‣ Escape from Pain: This student refuses to take responsibility for his/her behavior because refusing responsibility makes it less painful if something goes wrong.
3. Secondary need being revealed:
   ‣ Aggression: This person needs to assert him/herself in a positive way and be responsible for his/her actions. Once over that hurdle, the student can go about meeting the need to be an achiever.
4. Remember, the good classroom isn't based on an attitude of accusation. Therefore, consider charges carefully before stating them.

5. Long before it's necessary to make a charge, make sure there has been a class discussion about the destructive use of blame as a way to get rid of problems. This is a lesson students need to be taught if they are to be expected to accept responsibility for their actions. We talk a lot about self-discipline. However, self-discipline can never be learned without this lesson.

6. Let children know that your primary concern is not to place blame but to solve the problem through mutual input. Then, the biggest hurdle has already been crossed.

7. Remember, no one likes to be accused. Students are not the exception, especially this particular student. Keep in mind that accusation almost always guarantees a defensive reaction, and you will carefully choose positive ways of solving problems.

8. Never set up a confrontation with this child in front of the class. The student's stubborn insistence will stand like a rock no matter how much evidence accrues against him/her. The class is not benefited, the student is not benefited, and the teacher's position certainly is not benefited.

9. Instead, talk to this student privately about why he/she feels the need to take this untenable stance when it just isn't necessary. However, remember that defense is sometimes the only option a student has with you. Never forget, it's the frightened, uncertain, and insecure child who assumes this position.

10. When this student offers a straight-on challenge, he/she is merely reinforcing this defensive position. Therefore, don't feel threatened when the student does deny.

11. Be aware that the student's response sounds silly to classmates. If you pick it up and respond badly, then there are two people who look silly to the class. There is no danger with such a student unless the teacher reacts poorly.

12. Remember, it all comes down to one fact: Situations that result from accusation can be avoided by not accusing in the first place. However, there are some techniques that can be used with all students which are very effective.

13. If you want to teach students to admit their mistakes, learn from them, and go on, then you must adopt two attitudes toward this kind of excuse. Think *tiny* consequences and *fast* chances. The tiny consequence is self-explanatory. Just don't make a big deal out of any kind of excuse. The fast chance is easy to interpret too. It means giving students a quick way to mend a fence or correct a situation. Too often, teachers do just the opposite. It's OK sometimes to think in terms of punishment and reprimand to teach a lesson. The mistake lies in the *big* punishment and the *big* reprimand.

14. Finally, give students options. Don't let them stand alone. Rather, help them seek solutions in order to learn. Remember, the "I did not" — "you did so" teacher-student argument only reinforces a negative behavior or forces capitulation — maybe without learning.

15. Realize that it is only human to defend oneself, even if the defense is a poor one. That's why students say, "It wasn't my fault." However, teachers know that little growth can result unless we are able to overcome our own human weakness and get students to accept responsibility for their own actions.

16. Rather than pointing fingers outward, point inward. The next time this excuse is offered, don't chew out the student. Rather, try taking a little of the blame. Likewise, when things are going right, take a smaller share of the credit. If you do, student relationships will benefit — and so will you.

IV. MISTAKES: Common misjudgments and errors in managing the child which may perpetuate or intensify the problem.

1. Making a big deal out of such excuses. This makes it harder to teach and harder for our lessons to take effect.

2. Reacting in anger or disgust.

3. Punishing severely.

4. Handling this behavior publicly.

5. Deciding to be judge and jury over the student behavior, and not listening carefully to *all* sides of the situation.

SEE ALSO: • The Alibier   • The Complainer   • The Do-Nothing
           • The Excuse/Alibi Maker

THE OBJECTOR

I. BEHAVIOR: **Specific attitudes and actions of this child at home and/or at school.**

1. Always has some extenuating circumstances which prevent him/her from doing something.
2. Objects to classroom rules, claiming they're "unfair."
3. Objects to changes in routines.
4. Objects when teacher won't accept excuses he/she considers valid, such as "My mother 'washed' my paper in my clothes" or "I can't find what I need in the library."
5. Not prepared to do what the class is doing.
6. Behind everyone else.
7. Borrows frequently.
8. Needs more time.
9. Makes objections rather than alibis, excuses, or complaints. Make no mistake — there is a difference.
10. Objects to assignments as too long or as interrupting his/her busy schedule.

II. EFFECTS: **How behavior affects teachers, classmates, and parents in the school learning environment and the home family situation.**

1. Time is wasted.
2. Class is interrupted.
3. Extra time and attention are required.
4. Classmates are disturbed.
5. Teacher is pestered by this student's requests for extra help.
6. Teacher may become angry because of this student's continuous objections.

III. ACTION:
- **Identify causes of misbehavior.**
- **Pinpoint student needs being revealed.**
- **Employ specific methods, procedures, and techniques at school and at home for getting the child to modify or change his/her behavior.**

1. Primary cause of misbehavior:
   - Attention: This student may feel that he/she is not getting the proper amount of attention.
2. Primary needs being revealed:
   - Sex: This student is unable to establish peer or adult relationships.
   - Escape from Pain: He/she may feel unable to achieve academically, and may object in order to cover the pain of not being a good student.
3. Secondary needs being revealed:
   - Achievement: This student needs some success with adults, either at home or at school. The objector is not so concerned with peer relationships.
   - Autonomy: The objections may be a way for the student to say, "I exist," or just to have some control over his/her own life.

◗ Power: It is possible that power contests with adults are created by constant objection. If this is true, the student is actually operating from a weak position, and care should be taken in dealing with this problem.

4. Student objections usually contain the word "but." They are expressed by such phrases as "But . . . I don't know how to do it," or "But . . . you didn't say I had to do it today," or "But . . . I didn't have time." Be aware that, in reality, the response is caused by a student wanting or expecting more — whether it's more teacher help, more information, or an extended date for turning in an assignment.

5. Of paramount importance, objecting students *may* still have an interest in class work. This is vitally important to the teacher handling the objection. Therefore, analyze the reason for the objection. Ask yourself four questions which will guide your approach with the objecting student:

   • Is the objection intelligent?

   • Is ignorance revealed by the objection?

   • Is the objection emotional?

   • Is the objection analytical?

6. Listen to every objection. If the objection has merit, share points of agreement. But the benefits of your rationale must outweigh the student objection, or the objection cannot be overcome.

7. If the student is wrong, educate the student and let him/her down gracefully. This is a must.

8. In either case, ask questions rather than tell, give benefits rather than ultimatums, and relate assurances rather than demands. Using these three techniques will allow more success in handling objections.

9. Don't feel you must respond to this student's actions or words with either approval or disapproval. Often, a nonjudgmental response which intimates neither praise nor criticism is the best secondary course of action a teacher can take with this student. This stance allows the student to form his/her own judgments — which may be more harsh and lasting than those a teacher would offer. Therefore, before you jump on this student, try the "Nonjudgmental Response" technique with the objector.

IV. MISTAKES: Common misjudgments and errors in managing the child which may perpetuate or intensify the problem.

1. Showing emotion.

2. Reacting as if the objection were a personal affront.

3. Punishing the objector.

4. Threatening to tell parents.

5. Saying this student is going to fail.

SEE ALSO: • The Complainer   • The Excuse/Alibi Maker

THE OVERLY AGGRESSIVE

I. BEHAVIOR: **Specific attitudes and actions of this child at home and/or at school.**

1. Approaches others by attacking.

2. Usually highly emotional and quick-tempered.

3. May or may not be a good student academically. If a good student, usually very ambitious regarding grades or personal achievements. If a weak student, attempts to intimidate to get higher grades.

4. Often has less classroom success than might be expected of someone who pushes so hard.

5. When confronted about behavior, usually claims he/she never gets a fair deal or that others pick on him/her. Uses this explanation as an excuse for aggressive behavior by saying, "If I don't look out for myself, nobody will."

6. Knows what he/she wants. Just doesn't know how to get it in socially acceptable ways.

7. Often, however, not a serious student academically.

8. May be anti-class, anti-school, and anti-teacher.

9. Tries to get others to go along with acts of aggression.

10. Easily demonstrates verbal or physical abuse.

11. Seeks attention and recognition in forceful ways.

12. Often openly defiant.

13. Has constant conflict with specific students whom he/she dislikes. These classmates are usually opposite this student in achievement, values, and behavior.

14. Usually has a poor attendance record.

15. Lacks a personal sense of success by appropriate adult standards.

16. Often appears unhappy, even when getting his/her way.

17. Will venture into places and situations where he/she has no business at all.

II. EFFECTS: **How behavior affects teachers, classmates, and parents in the school learning environment and the home family situation.**

1. Classroom climate is one of alienation, disruption, and constant conflict.

2. Teacher becomes angry.

3. Learning process is disturbed.

4. Other students are intimidated; aggressor tries to use power to control others.

5. Teacher's attention is distracted from what should be happening in the classroom.

6. Teacher may even be afraid of the aggressor — or his/her behavior.

7. Teacher may lose control and act in unprofessional ways.

8. Sympathies of the class are divided.

9. Fear is felt in the classroom.

III. ACTION:
- **Identify causes of misbehavior.**
- **Pinpoint student needs being revealed.**

- **Employ specific methods, procedures, and techniques at school and at home for getting the child to modify or change his/her behavior.**

1. Primary causes of misbehavior:

   ▶ Revenge: This student may find success by being disliked. Failure has made him/her turn to being mean and violent.

   ▶ Self-Confidence: It should be understood that this student has a very low self-esteem and covers it up with aggressive behavior. If we are willing to work and take time with the aggressor, he/she will reveal this lack of confidence.

2. Primary needs being revealed:

   ▶ Hunger: This student might be an abused child who has not eaten regularly.

   ▶ Sex: He/she may be experiencing poor relationships with parents, peers, and others. These poor relationships may cause feelings of "not measuring up" — and can cause a person to be very aggressive.

   ▶ Escape from Pain: One of the most effective ways to hide pain is to be very aggressive. This kind of behavior causes other people to avoid one.

3. Secondary needs being revealed:

   ▶ Gregariousness: The aggressive child needs to belong, and thus creates a following of weak persons.

   ▶ Aggression: This student doesn't know how to assert in an acceptable manner and win.

   ▶ Power: Aggression is a way of letting other students and adults know that the aggressor counts.

4. Slow down, and don't be aggressive in return. The aggressive student has a conflict with timing; his/her sense of timing is impaired by the drive to make maximum use of time, or get what he/she wants. Remember, this student thinks aggression is the way to get what he/she wants.

5. Remember that an aggressive reaction is different from a hostile response. The aggressive student often does, or threatens to do, two things: act against all other ideas, and change loyalties and friends. His/her stance is: "If you go against my wants, you go against me."

6. Realize that it's normal for students to see "how far" they can go with a teacher. However, it's abnormal when children find a teacher who "lets them go" — and they know it. Therefore, don't get upset when you are tested by your students. Rather, be upset with yourself if you fail the test.

7. Don't stop communication with this student — increase it. Private conferences are an absolute necessity. In the process, develop a relationship rather than merely an association. This means involvement is a necessity, not merely "lecture counseling."

8. Don't get into a power struggle. You have the power as a teacher. Once you acknowledge a struggle, you have automatically given the student power.

9. Ask the student, "Why do you trespass on other people and their business?" Then, talk about what he/she believes "my business" and "other people's business" is. The aggressor has never made this distinction.

10. Next, talk about privacy and respect from different viewpoints such as: respect for time, privacy, and courtesy. He/she does not understand these concepts.

11. Always ask him/her, "How are things going for you?" and keep asking until you start getting good answers.

12. Always volunteer to help. Remember, everyone else fights this student.

13. Provide opportunities for success. Remember, lack of success is what is making him/her vengeful.

14. At conferences, identify the problem by talking about specific instances which have occurred.

15. Avoid generalization about behavior or incidents. Talk specifics. Most people can't do this because they "judge" — but don't talk to — the aggressor. Herein lies part of the problem which causes the student to be more aggressive. He/she never wins with acceptable approaches, but rather is ignored when *not* aggressive.

16. Therefore, try to find out what is really causing this student's aggressive behavior.

17. Use the "Promise" technique when counseling. Whenever possible, make a promise regarding action you will take to help the student if he/she makes a sincere effort to improve the behavior. This student will need help because others will try to take advantage of him/her.

18. Always show sincere concern — and never return his/her bad manners or behavior. If you do, you only prove that a lack of power is the cause of all his/her problems. Also, you show that the aggressor's kind of power is working and he/she is in control of the confrontation.

19. Think adjustment, and you'll help the student be less aggressive. Remember, if you're rigid and have resolved to hold fast and not capitulate, the student will become more aggressive. Therefore, he/she may need your time, attention, and help at times when you're not prepared to give it.

20. If it is absolutely necessary to remove the student from the classroom, try to isolate him/her in class first.

21. Reinforce any positive behavior and transformations which occur. Tell the student specifically and pointedly the changes that you have been able to observe in his/her behavior. Above all, explain the benefits of these changes and how they are working for the student.

22. Seek help from counselors, administrators, or community services.

23. Contact parents early about this student behavior. However, be careful to explain specific behavior along with your expectations for the student to remain in class. Always ask if they are having similar behavior at home. Then, be prepared to hear them "pour their hearts out" if they feel safe in talking to you.

24. Work out joint home/school action whenever possible.

25. Never get mad at this student. Do, however, show strong displeasure with the behavior, and relate how the behavior is working against him/her.

26. Explain the difference between assertion and aggression. It's a lesson that must be taught. The difference lies in the fact that with aggression, we walk over people to get what we want. It's fine to assert because such behavior hurts nobody.

IV. MISTAKES: Common misjudgments and errors made in managing the child which may perpetuate or intensify the problem.

1. Physically handling the student.

2. Reacting aggressively in return.

3. Feeling that the techniques we can employ are limited and, as a result, letting the behavior go, or making a public example of this student.

4. Overreacting and automatically giving power to this student's negative behavior. When we overreact, we put this student in the limelight whether we want to or not.

5. Creating consequences or punishments — consciously or even unconsciously — so that we might "get even" with this student.

6. Punishing the entire group for the aggressive behavior of one or two students.

7. Putting ourselves in a precarious professional position by making threats, and then not being able to back them up.

8. Using poor grades as punishment.

9. Showing dislike in open and obvious ways.

10. Avoiding this student openly and purposely.

SEE ALSO: • The Agitator   • The Angry   • The Bully   • The Defier   • The Fighter

THE PEST

I. BEHAVIOR: Specific attitudes and actions of this child at home and/or at school.

1. Has a hundred ways to seek attention, from harassing classmates to "hanging around" the teacher. This student isn't bad, just annoying.
2. Usually lonely.
3. Harasses members of the opposite sex.
4. Commits only minor, disturbing infractions.
5. Constantly "horse-playing" — trips others, teases classmates, makes smart remarks.
6. Seeks attention . . . or friendship.
7. Minds everyone else's business.
8. Touches other students and their personal belongings . . . continually.
9. Talks incessantly . . . or is deliberately silent.
10. Asks questions at the wrong time and place.
11. Doesn't listen . . . or hangs on every word.
12. Often behind in work in comparison to the rest of the class.
13. Sometimes stays after class or school and won't leave.
14. Very much aware of how others feel about him/her, and will even say that he/she is a pest.
15. Will seek the attention of others at any price. It's better than being lonely.
16. May be a whiner or complainer.
17. Often picks a popular student or teacher to pester or hang around.
18. Appears compulsive in this behavior.

II. EFFECTS: How behavior affects teachers, classmates, and parents in the school learning environment and the home family situation.

1. Classmates and teacher are annoyed.
2. Entire class, as well as teacher, is distracted.
3. Others, especially those of the opposite sex, prefer not to be around this student.
4. Classmates react negatively. They don't want teacher to put down the pest, even though they don't like what the pest is doing.
5. Others shy away from the pest — or avoid him/her outright.
6. Classmates complain to teacher and request that something be done. Likewise, classmates' parents may complain about this child.

III. ACTION:
- **Identify causes of misbehavior.**
- **Pinpoint student needs being revealed.**
- **Employ specific methods, procedures, and techniques at school and at home for getting the child to modify or change his/her behavior.**

1. Primary cause of misbehavior:
   - Attention: The pest may have little or no relationship at home, and a strong need for attention at school.

2. Primary needs being revealed:
   - Sex: This person does not understand how to establish relationships with the opposite sex.
   - Escape from Pain: The loneliness of this person is very painful, and he/she will do almost anything to relieve that pain.

3. Secondary needs being revealed:
   - Affiliation: The student needs to have *one* close friend and, many times, his/her choice is the teacher.
   - Gregariousness: In addition to a close friend, this student needs to belong to a group — any group. This may mean selecting a group that would "use" this person.

4. Don't reprimand, reveal irritation, or treat this behavior as a discipline problem. These approaches will not prove effective. Remember, the pest knows how others feel. But his/her behavior is impulsive. Attention at any price is better than feeling lonely.

5. This student needs attention, affection, and a friend. Therefore, focus your efforts on showing him/her how to get these things in acceptable ways.

6. Seat the pest near a serious student at the front of the classroom — never in the rear of the room. If this student is ignored or isolated, his/her behavior may turn obnoxious. Therefore, ignoring the student and urging classmates to do the same may result in behavioral problems.

7. Develop a close relationship with the pest.

8. In private conference, don't dwell on what the student is doing — the student knows. Rather, give suggestions for changing the ways he/she tries to relate to others.

9. Give this student class responsibilities and include him/her in activities to provide a feeling of being needed and important. Exclusion magnifies the problem; involvement helps eliminate the behavior.

10. Don't forget, this student may "cling" to you for a time. After all, you may be his/her only friend. However, involvement will bring confidence, and it won't be long until this student finds a friend his/her own age. Even here, a teacher can give a gentle nudge. In the meantime, don't force this student to be a pest to get attention.

11. Initiate conversations with this student, and never let classmates think you regard him/her as a pest. If you do, they will emulate your behavior and a real problem can develop. Likewise, do not ever *call* this student a pest.

12. Overlook some of this student's behavior; doing so causes less distraction.

13. Give this student lots of attention, especially when the behavior is positive and appropriate to the situation.

14. Be on the student's side. You'll realize when you talk to this student that he/she is aware of being a pest and doesn't want to be one.

15. Tell the student you'll give a signal (nod, etc.) when he/she is "distracting others," instead of embarrassing the student in front of the class.

16. Make it clear that, although you're willing to help the student meet his/her responsibility to self, you also have a responsibility to the rest of the class.

17. Contact parents.

IV. MISTAKES: Common misjudgments and errors in managing the child which may perpetuate or intensify the problem.

1. Ignoring the pest, and urging students having problems with the pest to do the same.

2. Being too loud or harsh with this student.

3. Punishing for insignificant acts.

4. Failing to show patience.

5. Overreacting to what this student does.

6. Acting as if this student should be disliked.

7. Making fun of the student.

8. Trying to get rid of this student by urging him/her to leave or by saying, "I have a meeting."

9. Being sarcastic.

10. Disliking this student.

SEE ALSO: • The Attention Demander   • The Noisemaker   • The Whiner

THE PETTY RULES BREAKER

I. BEHAVIOR: **Specific attitudes and actions of this child at home and/or at school.**

1. Continually disobeys school and class rules.
2. Chews gum or eats candy in class.
3. Wears coat, hat, or some other inappropriate apparel in class.
4. Argues that other teachers allow this behavior.
5. Offends more by frequency than by seriousness.
6. Uses the excuse "I forgot" continuously.
7. May think he/she is clever in getting by with breaking a rule.

II. EFFECTS: **How behavior affects teachers, classmates, and parents in the school learning environment and the home family situation.**

1. Teacher finds it difficult to choose appropriate punishment because misbehavior is so insignificant.
2. Classmates ask why this student is allowed to break rules.
3. Classmates are influenced to make a mockery of rules, as this student does.
4. A question is created in the minds of teacher and students as to whether a rule is needed or justified.
5. Class activities are interrupted when this student's behavior must be handled.
6. Teacher may appear incapable of insisting that small rules be enforced, or may appear petty in trying to enforce them.
7. Teacher is frustrated.
8. Teacher is annoyed.

III. ACTION:
- **Identify causes of misbehavior.**
- **Pinpoint student needs being revealed.**
- **Employ specific methods, procedures, and techniques at school and at home for getting the child to modify or change his/her behavior.**

1. Primary cause of misbehavior:
   - Attention: This student is seeking attention through refusal to obey minor rules.
2. Primary needs being revealed:
   - Escape from Pain: This student becomes a petty rules breaker to relieve the pressures of home or school.
3. Secondary needs being revealed:
   - Achievement: An opportunity for achievement could reduce the need to break rules.
   - Power: The student could be attempting to gain some ownership or authority, and the breaking of rules is a negative way to meet this need.
4. Do not send the petty rules breaker to the office. Rather, seek counsel from administrators and follow their suggestions.

5. Although there may be many forms of petty rules breaking, careful teacher examination will usually reveal that each individual violator consistently breaks only one or two of the rules. Therefore, never approach the student with broad generalizations about breaking "all the rules" unless you have documented evidence. Then reveal each item, one by one.

6. Sit down with the student privately and discuss the situation calmly. Pinpoint the exact violations. Even if other infractions are noted, talk only about one or two specific things during the first visit.

7. Never accuse this student of purposely violating a rule. Instead, appeal to him/her in a way that indicates that you want to help rather than reprimand.

8. Listen to the student's reason. Don't tell him/her what to do until you ask questions. The reason may be a health problem, a feeling that teacher or classmates are unfair, a belief that everyone else is breaking the rule, or a failure to see the need for rules.

9. Work on only one rule at a time with the student.

10. Be firm, but polite.

11. Always remain calm.

12. Talk in a quiet voice.

13. Be aware that this student has no adult guidance in his/her life. Remind the student that if you didn't care, you would ignore him/her. Talk about the student's potential. Center conversation on the positive, rather than on the infraction.

14. Be patient.

15. Get both viewpoints. First, reveal what you see as the problem. Second, ask what the student sees as the problem. The student probably sees the problem as the teacher picking on him/her and being unfair. Therefore, listen to the student's reason for disobeying so that you can work on the right problem.

16. Don't make a big deal out of a little deal. Say, "Do we have to make a big deal out of this or can we handle it ourselves?"

17. Explain your obligation to apply the same rules to everyone and to be fair to every member of the class.

18. Explain the necessity for some rules, the problems that would arise if there were none, and the practical need for a particular rule.

19. Classroom rules that do not allow flexibility are targets for trouble. For instance, making rules that pencils can be sharpened only before class, and that no restroom privileges are allowed during class time, is asking for trouble. Guidelines should be stated, of course. However, know that there must be exceptions to rules, and leave yourself room to make good decisions. Never think that a hard and fast rule will allow you the flexibility you need to operate in the classroom. It won't.

20. Remind the student that you would not offer guidance if you did not care about his/her potential and future.

21. Contact parents.

IV. MISTAKES: Common misjudgments and errors in managing the child which may perpetuate or intensify the problem.

1. Believing this student's actions are open insubordination.

2. Ignoring the infraction.

3. Failing to punish or correct this student consistently.

4. Deciding to allow the behavior since we don't agree with the rule either.

5. Overreacting and thus accenting the problem.

6. Failing to re-evaluate rules periodically — and objectively.

7. Sending the student to the office and thus making a major offense out of a minor infraction.

8. Getting angry.

9. Degrading or belittling the student in the presence of others.

10. Trying to handle this matter before the entire class. The teacher who walks angrily into class and writes a new rule or command on the blackboard accomplishes little. Such action irritates students who rarely need discipline, because they feel the teacher doesn't care enough about them to handle the matter privately with the offenders. Furthermore, those to whom the message is directed seldom realize it is meant for them. Private conferences with those who need disciplining or a brief explanation to an entire class can make the difference between a situation in which teacher control is paramount and one in which orderly learning is paramount.

SEE ALSO: • The Excuse/Alibi Maker • The Forgetter • The Immature
• The Irresponsible

THE POUTER

I. BEHAVIOR: **Specific attitudes and actions of this child at home and/or at school.**

1. Sulks.

2. Attempts to get his/her way with immature, improper, and even unfair behavior.

3. Refuses to participate if unable to get his/her way.

4. Responds to the failure with hurt.

5. Takes the situation personally and withdraws. Makes sure everyone knows he/she is upset through body and facial expressions or talking under his/her breath.

6. Worse, tries to make everyone feel guilty regarding his/her decision to disagree, but never deals with the reasons behind his/her inability to convince.

7. Can't be consoled. Even if we talk about trying again, the student says, "No," and holds on to his/her hurt.

8. May get what he/she wants, but others dislike the pouter more after each incident. This behavior is unique: It works both for and against the student.

II. EFFECTS: **How behavior affects teachers, classmates, and parents in the school learning environment and the home family situation.**

1. Others are drawn into conflict.

2. In the classroom, someone is always mad — either the pouter or a classmate.

3. Constant commotion is caused.

4. Others may feel teacher is unfair.

5. The democratic process in the classroom is destroyed.

6. Both teacher and classmates get disgusted at this type of behavior — and more so with each incident. Therefore, bad feelings are caused in the classroom.

7. Classmates say this student acts like "a big baby."

8. Teacher becomes angry.

9. Classmates may bait this student to get him/her to pout.

III. ACTION:
- **Identify causes of misbehavior.**
- **Pinpoint student needs being revealed.**
- **Employ specific methods, procedures, and techniques at school and at home for getting the child to modify or change his/her behavior.**

1. Primary cause of misbehavior:

   ▶ Self-Confidence: This student perceives every failure as an attack on him/her personally.

2. Primary need being revealed:

   ▶ Escape from Pain: This student may have experienced failure many times and may use pouting to control people and relieve the pain of failure.

3. Secondary needs being revealed:

   ▶ Affiliation: A strong, positive close friend could change the behavior of the pouter.

223

♦ Achievement: Achievement in classroom, home, or playground could bring an end to the pouting behavior.

4. Be aware that this student responds in two ways to the usual efforts: The pouter continues pouting unless you give *more* than he/she wanted in the first place, and he/she refuses to change no matter what you do.

5. Don't ignore this behavior. Make it clear to the student that the behavior is unacceptable. Don't expect him/her to get your message from the way you act.

6. Recognize that this behavior is caused by a need for improved self-esteem that stems from fear of rejection.

7. Don't try to quiet every fear and give the student too much attention. This approach will make the behavior worse.

8. Never forget this fact: If pouting gets the student what he/she wants, then the student will pout.

9. Never say you don't approve of the student — say you don't approve of the behavior and will not reward it.

10. Tell the pouter privately that you'll not allow such a selfish and immature behavior to work.

11. Explain that every time the student gets his/her way by pouting, he/she always loses with people.

12. Be prepared to put the student through a couple of pouting incidents. When confronted in a caring and logical way, it won't take the pouter long to realize pouting is a poor choice for trying to get his/her own way.

13. Give this student immediate feedback when you see improvement in his/her behavior. This kind of positive attention can help the student to make a quick adjustment in behavior.

IV. MISTAKES: Common misjudgments and errors in managing the child which may perpetuate or intensify the problem.

1. Ignoring this student.

2. Consoling him/her.

3. Being unfair by treating this student differently from others.

4. Believing he/she is spoiled, and blaming the home.

5. Failing to recognize that this behavior serves to meet needs that could be met positively.

6. Mocking the behavior or even encouraging classmates to mock the behavior.

SEE ALSO: • The Attention Demander • The Distracter

THE PROCRASTINATOR

I. BEHAVIOR: Specific attitudes and actions of this child at home and/or at school.

1. Long on talk and enthusiasm but short on work and success.
2. Always puts things off.
3. Has no sense of urgency.
4. Usually "talks a good game," but accomplishes little. To hear this student talk, one would think he/she couldn't wait to get to work, or to put into practice what he/she has learned.
5. Often the first to volunteer for a task. Says, "Oh, I'll do it." Unfortunately, never says when.
6. Never gets anything done; is always "going to get it done tomorrow."
7. Does seem to have a need to please and usually does want to get the job done.

II. EFFECTS: How behavior affects teachers, classmates, and parents in the school learning environment and the home family situation.

1. Others become very angry when they depend on the procrastinator and he/she lets them down.
2. Others tend to doubt all of this student's intentions.
3. Others express low expectations of his/her attempts to do a task.
4. Classmates usually do not want to work with him/her.

III. ACTION:
- **Identify causes of misbehavior.**
- **Pinpoint student needs being revealed.**
- **Employ specific methods, procedures, and techniques at school and at home for getting the child to modify or change his/her behavior.**

1. Primary cause of misbehavior:
   - Attention: The procrastinator gains some recognition for always saying he/she will get to something, even if it never gets done.
2. Primary needs being revealed:
   - Sex: This student is making every effort to establish relationships with adults and peers alike, but in the wrong way.
   - Escape from Pain: This student may be attempting to cover his/her inability to achieve.
3. Secondary needs being revealed:
   - Aggression: The need to be taught how to be assertive is important to this student. His/her actions are attempts to be assertive and responsible.
   - Power: This student may desire power, and may need to be taught the responsibility that must go along with that power.
4. Don't beat around the bush. Tell the student exactly what he/she is doing. The student already knows he/she is a procrastinator.
5. Talk about the fact that putting things off is a natural human tendency. This approach will allow you to achieve the best results with the procrastinator.

6. Show the student how this behavior is giving him/her a reputation opposite the one he/she so desperately wants.

7. Show, by example, how waiting to complete tasks hurts the student personally.

8. Explain how this behavior affects the feelings of others toward the student — and the student's own feelings toward him/herself.

9. Help the student change by assigning dates for partial and total completion of any assigned task.

10. Talk to the student about being only as good as his/her word. Likewise, talk about developing a sense of urgency.

11. Encourage the procrastinator to complete one project before he/she volunteers for another. In the process, make sure the hard parts of tasks are done *first*. Give the student immediate instructions to begin. Have him/her give you step-by-step progress reports.

12. Always remember this student's tremendous need and urgency to please. Capitalize on this need by checking work and giving praise. With teacher understanding, patience, and guidance, the student can overcome this problem.

IV. MISTAKES: Common misjudgments and errors in managing the child which may perpetuate or intensify the problem.

1. Getting mad.

2. Failing to see this student's desire to please.

3. Putting the student down publicly, and not helping privately.

4. Letting the student take on more than he/she can handle.

SEE ALSO: • The Dreamer • The Noncompleter with Grand Plans
• Satisfied with Second Place

THE QUESTIONER

I. BEHAVIOR: Specific attitudes and actions of this child at home and/or at school.

1. Asks an abnormal number of questions — about every conceivable subject. Displays a particular type of student questioning that is abnormal.

2. Has his/her hand up in the air continually.

3. Asks questions even when he/she knows the answer.

4. Interrupts with questions.

5. Often interrupts with a question that the teacher may be answering at the moment.

6. Appears not to listen.

7. Asks to have instructions repeated immediately. After instructions have been given, says he/she couldn't hear or didn't understand.

8. Even while the question is being answered, seems to be thinking of what he/she can ask next.

9. Doesn't work well independently.

II. EFFECTS: How behavior affects teachers, classmates, and parents in the school learning environment and the home family situation.

1. Teacher and classmates are annoyed. Classmates may groan when this student asks another question.

2. Proceedings are interrupted.

3. Time is stolen from other students because the questioner requires "double instruction."

4. Serious discussions are distracted and even prevented.

5. Teacher is diverted from following lesson plan.

6. Teacher may feel this student is attempting to trap him/her with this continual questioning.

III. ACTION:
- **Identify causes of misbehavior.**
- **Pinpoint student needs being revealed.**
- **Employ specific methods, procedures, and techniques at school and at home for getting the child to modify or change his/her behavior.**

1. Primary cause of misbehavior:
   - Attention: This person wants people to know he/she exists, and may consider continually asking questions a very legitimate behavior.

2. Primary need being revealed:
   - Sex: The questioner uses this behavior to establish relationships with peers and adults. This behavior may be used to "impress" others or to get their attention.

3. Secondary needs being revealed:
   - Inquisitiveness: The student may question because he/she really has a need to know.
   - Aggression: The questioner may be a brighter student who is looking for ways to express knowledge. If so, this student may need guidance in asserting in the classroom.
   - Power: This student may be attempting to demonstrate authority or even a desire for more responsibility.

227

4. Give this student special and individualized attention. He/she sincerely needs it. The secret to handling the student who asks continual questions is to recognize his/her need for attention.

5. Make this student feel involved. It is a need he/she must have fulfilled.

6. Look directly at this student as often as possible. Place the student in the front of the room and, if possible, where you are usually directly in front of him/her. If you have a natural tendency to look at the second row, place the questioner there.

7. However, do not answer every question he/she asks.

8. Frequently, refer the student to certain books and ask him/her to report findings to the class the next day.

9. Too, tell the student that, in the interest of time, you will see him/her privately after the class has started the assignment.

10. Above all, do not allow yourself to become detached from the student or his/her questions. How you handle this student's questions will have a great bearing on how other children feel about asking questions in your class.

11. If you think that the questioner is putting you on, take his/her questions professionally rather than personally. If you feel duped, use your intelligence and turn a ridiculous question into a good one.

12. Field all questions kindly so that other students will not anticipate and fear negative reception to their questions. Make it clear — by action — that you will be patient with each individual, even with the questioner who annoys you and everyone else. Other students will learn quickly that if you have time for this student, you have time for them.

13. Do not allow classmates to "moan" over any question, including those of this student.

IV. MISTAKES: Common misjudgments and errors in managing the child which may perpetuate or intensify the problem.

1. Responding by repeating instructions.

2. Answering every question this student asks.

3. Prejudging this student to be actually uninterested and simply pretending interest.

4. Becoming angry, raising our voices, and intimidating. This action does intimidate serious students who have legitimate questions.

5. Ignoring this student.

6. Reprimanding or "putting down" publicly.

7. Treating this student with less than usual consideration. Doing so may cause him/her to feel justified in quitting in this class, and in using this treatment as an excuse to others for his/her quitting.

8. Failing to follow up with counseling.

9. Failing to recognize this student's potential and failing to direct him/her to further enriched learning experiences.

10. Failing to recognize that the student may be only testing us. If we assume all the questions are legitimate, we may get manipulated in a way that's not good for us or the student.

SEE ALSO: • The Agitator • The Apple Polisher • The Manipulator
             • The Test Challenger

THE RABBLE ROUSER

I. BEHAVIOR: **Specific attitudes and actions of this child at home and/or at school.**

1. Usually regards him/herself as leader of a "cause."
2. However, as often as not, leads classmates against teacher or against petty grievances.
3. Will pit students against teacher, kids against each other, and teacher against teacher.
4. Most important, encourages others to get involved in negative actions.
5. When big trouble arises, however, may act like an innocent bystander.
6. With either stand, regards him/herself as a champion of students.
7. May be lazy.
8. Wants to stir up trouble and avoid responsibility.
9. May believe strongly in what he/she is doing.

II. EFFECTS: **How behavior affects teachers, classmates, and parents in the school learning environment and the home family situation.**

1. A climate of distrust is created.
2. People are divided and the learning environment is disturbed.
3. Other students are drawn into trouble.
4. Time and energy are wasted.
5. An argumentative attitude is created among students, because the rabble rouser is searching for trouble.
6. Teacher is frustrated.
7. Teacher may lose composure.
8. Teacher may react negatively toward other students.

III. ACTION:
- **Identify causes of misbehavior.**
- **Pinpoint student needs being revealed.**
- **Employ specific methods, procedures, and techniques at school and at home for getting the child to modify or change his/her behavior.**

1. Primary cause of misbehavior:
   - Attention: This behavior may be a very positive way for the student to meet the need for attention, if he/she can be taught to operate within the system.
2. Primary needs being revealed:
   - Sex: This student may find it difficult to establish relationships, and may attempt to do so by being a rabble rouser.
   - Escape from Pain: The rabble rouser may be hiding a great deal of pain. The pain may

229

result from inability to achieve in school, from a home situation, or from inability to form peer relationships.

3. Secondary needs being revealed:
   - Gregariousness: The person may want to belong to, or even lead, a group within the school or classroom.
   - Aggression: Through acting out with peers and/or adults, the student may be expressing a real need for involvement in certain courses of action in a group.
   - Inquisitiveness: This student may be filling a need to deal with issues of right and wrong, rather than just causing trouble.
   - Achievement: The feeling of inability to achieve causes this student to direct his/her attention to achievement through rabble rousing. Certain academic successes may reduce such behavior.
   - Power: This person may see his/her ability to disrupt as a form of power. He/she should be directed to more responsible forms of power.
   - Status: Recognition from peers and adults enhances this student's self-esteem.

4. Be aware that this student is easier to handle than you may suspect. However, definite steps must be taken quickly before he/she gathers momentum for the cause from classmates.

5. First, identify the issue quickly. Don't let the student generalize. Be specific. This makes the student *weak* rather than allowing him/her to stir up others. For best results, make the student pinpoint his/her complaint.

6. Next, define the problem as belonging to the student.

7. Finally, make the student work for a solution to his/her complaint privately.

8. When you see this student causing problems, call him/her in for a private conference immediately.

9. Tell the student, "If you want to involve others, I will. This means administrators and parents must be called — if that's what you want. You have the right to complain; you don't have the right to be a rabble rouser. Therefore, do you want to solve this problem — or just cause trouble?"

10. Be firm; call a spade a spade. Be very serious and businesslike. Tell the student, "We'll solve this issue, but we're not going to involve the whole class or detract from the learning environment. Do you understand?" He/she will. Say, "This means neither of us talks to others about this."

11. Recognize this student's leadership potential, but react to it in a professional rather than a personal way.

12. Remember, up to this point, this child has not been made responsible for his/her actions. Given good advice and ways to demonstrate responsible behavior, the student will become more responsible. With this one dimension, he/she will look at things differently.

IV. MISTAKES: Common misjudgments and errors in managing the child which may perpetuate or intensify the problem.

1. Ignoring the rabble rouser until his/her behavior is out of hand.

2. Refusing to deal with the issue.

3. Letting this student get attention and power in irresponsible ways.

4. Failing to confront him/her.

5. Failing to realize this student's power to appeal to other students.

6. Failing to capitalize on his/her leadership abilities.

7. Deciding not to give any responsibility to students.

SEE ALSO: • The Angry • The Attention Demander • The Authority Pusher
• The Crier (Who Claims Foul) • The Distracter • The Griper
• The Objector • The Overly Aggressive • The Troublemaker

THE REBEL

I. BEHAVIOR: **Specific attitudes and actions of this child at home and/or at school.**

1. Easy to identify. Everything he/she does says, "I'm a rebel."
2. Wants to be different.
3. Dresses uniquely.
4. Does not accept the values of others, especially those in authority.
5. Outspoken, bitter, and seems to be against everything.
6. Disruptive.
7. Seldom cooperates.
8. Always knows what he/she is against, but doesn't always know what he/she favors.
9. Thinks others can't understand his/her individuality, are unfair in this regard, and are the cause of his/her unhappiness.
10. Though regarded as a troublemaker by students and teachers alike, often does not see him/herself that way.
11. May see him/herself as a champion for other students.
12. In truth, does not trust anyone very much, including him/herself.

II. EFFECTS: **How behavior affects teachers, classmates, and parents in the school learning environment and the home family situation.**

1. Class is disrupted.
2. Trouble is continually stirred up.
3. Feelings of hate surface.
4. Others find this student very difficult to approach.
5. Teacher is frustrated to the point that he/she dreads facing this student.
6. Time may be diverted from teaching.

III. ACTION:
- **Identify causes of misbehavior.**
- **Pinpoint student needs being revealed.**
- **Employ specific methods, procedures, and techniques at school and at home for getting the child to modify or change his/her behavior.**

1. Primary causes of misbehavior:
   ‣ Revenge: Being a rebel may be this student's way of "getting back" at those who have hurt him/her in the past.
   ‣ Self-Confidence: This person may actually be a very frightened and insecure individual.
2. Primary need being revealed:
   ‣ Escape from Pain: This student may feel he/she is a failure and, by being a rebel, may attempt to relieve the pain. Every attempt must be made to see the genuine person and his/her fears.
3. Secondary needs being revealed:

- Gregariousness: This person needs to belong to a group but, by his/her outward behavior, denies this need.

- Aggression: This person definitely asserts him/herself for various causes, usually anti-authority ones. The student needs to be directed toward positive involvement in the school.

- Affiliation: The rebel may be the champion for another student, but refuse any appreciation from that student. He/she wants to appear to need no one, for fear of being hurt if he/she accepts friendship.

- Autonomy: By being a rebel, the student can be his/her own boss and choose his/her own course of action.

4. Be aware that the rebel usually does not see him/herself as others do. In truth, it's this misconception that causes the rebel's behavior to get worse as the days go by.

5. Just let this student talk to you privately, and you can get him/her to begin changing. The key, however, is that change must be initiated by the student — and not imposed by you.

6. Remember, the cause of this behavior is revenge. The rebel is trying to hurt what is hurting him/her. Therefore, talk to the student about hurt, hate, and forgiving.

7. When counseling this student, point out one fact: The student needs to discover what he/she really does support rather than just what he/she rejects. Believe it or not, the student has not thought about this fact.

8. Ask the student to think about ways he/she can support a cause in a positive way.

9. Help the rebel use his/her individuality constructively and positively. Ask, "Would you like a friend?" Then, say you would like to help — by opening some doors for him/her.

10. At first, this student will need private and caring help to understand that he/she is always tearing down but never building up. In the process, don't tell the student what he/she should have done. Rather, ask what he/she could have done.

11. Help the student find positive rather than negative ways to express him/herself during this period of realization.

12. Your beginning point must be *compromise.* This is your best strategic action approach. *Never* ask for capitulation. This student can't capitulate. And that's all he/she has ever been asked to do — give up everything and get nothing. This is where the revenge comes from. Compromise allows the student to change positions without losing self-respect. It also allows him/her to win at something, and to get something from the system.

13. Remember, the key in your efforts should be to tell the student openly that you want him/her to be recognized for what he/she favors — rather than be identified only with what he/she is against. Once the student is helped to realize this need, change will be more rapid than you can imagine. In fact, a constructive rebel can often become a school leader.

14. Remember, this student's acceptance of failure may make him/her very difficult to work with and, therefore, you must look for little gains or changes in behavior.

IV. MISTAKES: Common misjudgments and errors in managing the child which may perpetuate or intensify the problem.

1. Fighting this student.

2. Avoiding a meaningful relationship with him/her.

3. Failing to see that this student has always been a loser — and is angry at this reality.

4. Failing to see his/her intelligence.

The Rebel

5. Rejecting the rebel.

6. Making every confrontation with this student a win-lose situation.

SEE ALSO: • The Agitator • The Authority Pusher • The Defier • The Hater • The Overly Aggressive

THE REPEATER

I. BEHAVIOR: Specific attitudes and actions of this child at home and/or at school.

1. Does the same thing over and over. Whatever the offense, repeats it time and time again, from not bringing book to class, to not putting name on paper, to talking without permission.
2. Not self-disciplined and, worse, not motivated to be.
3. Cannot be disciplined, it seems, with any technique.
4. Often in trouble with teacher but not a "bad" kid.
5. Gets away with a lot because he/she does so much.
6. Seems to lack common sense, organization, and maturity.
7. Likeable, but "in another world" when it comes to following simple, routine, daily rules.
8. Though always "into" something, not mean or deceitful.
9. Will often look directly at teacher while doing something he/she shouldn't. Make no mistake; this student is looking for teacher disapproval. The need is attention — at any price. The problem is immaturity.

II. EFFECTS: How behavior affects teachers, classmates, and parents in the school learning environment and the home family situation.

1. Teacher and class are interrupted constantly.
2. Teaching time is diverted to dealing with this student.
3. Teacher and classmates are frustrated.
4. Other students laugh at the repeater.
5. Other students get tired of the repeater's getting away with so many infractions or "dumb mistakes."
6. Other students become involved in misbehavior, and teacher is forced to deal with two problems.

III. ACTION:
- **Identify causes of misbehavior.**
- **Pinpoint student needs being revealed.**
- **Employ specific methods, procedures, and techniques at school and at home for getting the child to modify or change his/her behavior.**

1. Primary cause of misbehavior:
   - Attention: This student must have attention, but doesn't know how to obtain it in a positive way.
2. Primary need being revealed:
   - Escape from Pain: This student is so alone, and may feel so much pain from this loneliness, that he/she will repeat and repeat any negative behavior that relieves the pain.
3. Secondary needs being revealed:
   - Aggression: This student has difficulty in being assertive in a positive way. Every effort must be made to teach him/her how to be assertive.

◆ Achievement: The student may repeat minor misbehaviors because of lack of achievement in class.

◆ Power: If this student learns to accept responsibility, and receives approval for being responsible, he/she will be able to adjust the behavior.

4. If you want to establish positive and productive student relationships, "let bygones be bygones." We've all made mistakes, and nothing is so discouraging as to have someone refer to them again and again. Remember this reality in your relationships with students. Once a mistake is past and settled, don't bring it up again. First, dwelling on the mistake won't solve the present situation. Second, feelings of resentment at having the past rehashed may cloud the current issue.

5. Remember, this problem has no quick solution and may never be completely resolved. The goal is improvement. If you accept this reality, you will be better able to treat the behavior and reduce your anxieties in the process. Anything you do to meet this student's personal needs will lessen the problem.

6. To achieve improvement, assign responsibilities to the repeater at regular and frequent intervals. Structure activity so movement is provided, and give attention continually. Remember, this student needs attention, and will get it any way he/she can. If positive attention is not provided, the student will seek negative attention.

7. Never believe "the office" is "coddling" this student. This is easy to believe because the repeater seems to *like* being sent to the office. That's not the case. It's simply a matter of *any* attention being better than none. Attention should be provided in the classroom.

8. Although the repeater steals class time and is disruptive, don't resort to issuing threats continually or kicking him/her out of class. This is not the answer. Each repeater is different. That's why the key to solution lies in treating the behavior according to needs and symptoms on an individual basis.

9. Discipline for a *major* infraction, not something minor.

10. Maintain complete composure. Remain calm with this student. Calmness is a vital key — the thing this student needs most in his/her life.

11. Leave yourself room to operate. Don't set up "threats" or "new rules" for the next infraction.

12. Make the student chart actual infractions. Often the student doesn't realize how much he/she does. The chart also can be a basis for praise when improvement is shown. This technique gives the student what he/she wants — attention — and an opportunity to learn at the same time.

13. Structure student behavior in the classroom, and allow more freedom as behavior improves.

14. Report the problem to parents if necessary.

15. Be sure to tell the student that the reason for the private conference is to avoid embarrassment in the presence of classmates. Say, "I don't want to embarrass you, so please don't make me." Explain that you can't let the student disrupt classmates and that you must take action to ensure that he/she doesn't. Say, "Your behavior dictates that I must reprimand far more often than should be necessary, and prevents us from having the kind of relationship we both want." Make sure this student knows you like him/her — and that it's only the behavior you dislike.

16. Positive follow-up is a must. Continue to give the repeater attention when he/she is not misbehaving. Remember, this is what this student is really seeking.

17. The repeater needs more guidelines than the average student — and wants them. So don't think your words are falling on deaf ears.

18. Don't call the student in for everything. Keep a list of infractions and call the student in to discuss several things at a time.

19. Be very careful not to reinforce misbehavior. Sometimes teachers do, by indicating misbehavior is expected from certain students the minute they walk in the door. Comments such as "What are you up to today?" or "Do you think you can be quiet today?" only plant the seed for expected misbehavior. Don't forget, when you expect the worst from students, you generally get it. But when you expect their best and they know it, positive behavior patterns can emerge. Plant the seeds for positive behavior with comments like "Ready for a good day?" and "Glad to see you." These reinforce good behavior. Too, remember it isn't always what you say; it's sometimes how you say it.

20. The problem is not only professional, it's personal too. Therefore, make your approach both professional and personal.

21. Remember, the cause of the behavior is not revenge at this point. However, revenge could become a factor if the behavior is handled poorly.

22. Be consistent. Make sure the stated consequences always follow the misdeed, because this student will commit the same infraction again.

23. Think tiny consequences, and fast chances to repair. Don't ever let yourself think about punishing this student severely.

24. Once a discipline case has been "closed," let it remain so. Nothing will kill student incentives as much as constant reminders of past misdeeds. Too often, teachers won't let students forget their past, and are suspicious of sudden student attitude changes. The teacher who continually reminds students of their past errors does little to motivate them in positive directions. A teacher's reminder only breeds resentment and serves as a negative base for encouraging behavior change. By both attitude and action a teacher must reassure students daily that he/she recognizes their potential for change — not their propensity for repeating past errors.

IV. MISTAKES: Common misjudgments and errors in managing the child which may perpetuate or intensify the problem.

1. Responding by getting mad or yelling at the student across the room.

2. Ignoring this student. If you do, he/she will only do something else to force your attention. This student usually likes teachers very much. That's why he/she is hurt so much by harshness — even though he/she has it coming.

3. Giving up attempts to correct the behavior; throwing up our hands in despair.

4. Taking severe action for minor offenses ("the straw that broke the camel's back"). This causes a teacher to come off looking like a fool to other students, teachers, administrators, and parents.

5. Being inconsistent in discipline approaches.

6. Being sarcastic with this student.

SEE ALSO: • The Alibier   • The Con Artist   • The Distracter
            • The Excuse/Alibi Maker   • The Forgetter   • The Habitual Absentee
            • "I Don't Care"

THE RUDE

I. BEHAVIOR: **Specific attitudes and actions of this child at home and/or at school.**

1. Ignores people.
2. Puts people down.
3. Inconsiderate in big and small ways — about big and small matters.
4. Talks back, disregards requests, and acts superior. Treats teachers as insignificant.
5. May be rude openly — or through a look, sneer, or other form of nonverbal communication.
6. Appears to be independent, to be able to stand on his/her own two feet, and to need no one.

II. EFFECTS: **How behavior affects teachers, classmates, and parents in the school learning environment and the home family situation.**

1. Others see this rudeness as cruelty in its ugliest form.
2. Teacher and classmates alike feel insignificant.
3. Others are degraded in their presence, as if they weren't even there.
4. Others are totally rejected, and treated as nonpersons.
5. Student-student as well as teacher-student relationships are broken down.
6. Teacher is more than just bothered by this student's rudeness toward others — he/she is angered.
7. Teacher and classmates may retaliate.

III. ACTION:
- **Identify causes of misbehavior.**
- **Pinpoint student needs being revealed.**
- **Employ specific methods, procedures, and techniques at school and at home for getting the child to modify or change his/her behavior.**

1. Primary cause of misbehavior:
   ▶ Self-Confidence: This student honestly protects him/herself by being rude. By keeping people away through rudeness, the student avoids exposing his/her real self.
2. Primary needs being revealed:
   ▶ Hunger, Thirst, Air, Rest: This student may be experiencing many physical problems or may be deprived of basic needs.
   ▶ Escape from Pain: This student may feel very inadequate with peers and adults. The inability to achieve in school also may be very painful.
3. Secondary needs being revealed:
   ▶ Status: This student wants to be somebody but, because of low self-esteem, feels very inadequate. Thus he/she seeks status through negative behavior — rudeness. Every effort should be made to assist the student in improving his/her self-esteem.
   ▶ Affiliation: The teacher, through classroom experiences, may be able to find someone who will establish a close relationship with this student. That person may even be the teacher.
4. Remember the following facts about rudeness:

- It is not a natural behavior. It is learned and, once learned, can become a conditioned response whenever a person feels uncomfortable or threatened.

- It may result from either a feeling of inferiority or a false sense of superiority.

- It is often born of ignorance, and reveals a total lack of empathy.

- It's an imitation of strength into which people escape in order to avoid revealing what they regard as weakness, for example not knowing how to behave in a certain situation.

- It can result from family background, cultural, ethnic, or other associations, if such associations are based on facades or weakness rather than human values.

- It produces hostility and even hatred which grow rather than subside with time, even though the victim may accept the degradation and allow the sham to be perpetuated.

5. Expose and confront rude behavior. The student will pretend not to notice his/her rudeness, and will respond, "I was just busy," "My mind was a million miles away," or "You misunderstood." But he/she will probably never be rude to that person again — unless the student thinks he/she can get away with it. The rude student is too weak to hold on to his/her imitation of strength. The student can maintain the facade only by walling others out.

6. If the problem continues, talk to the student about the issue of his/her treatment of people. This type of confrontation helps the student to see that rudeness is unacceptable to all.

7. Develop a plan that will give this student small successes in school.

8. Try to find an adult on the staff who can relate in a positive way to the student. This person should attempt to make frequent contacts with him/her.

9. Remind the student that it is the rudeness that you disapprove of, not the student.

IV. MISTAKES: Common misjudgments and errors in managing the child which may perpetuate or intensify the problem.

1. Showing hostility.

2. Putting the student down.

3. Being rude in return.

4. Failing to confront.

5. Thinking rudeness is a sign of disrespect.

6. Attempting to force an adjustment of behavior.

SEE ALSO: • "I Won't Do It" • The Immature • The Know-It-All • The Loudmouth • The Snotty

SATISFIED WITH SECOND PLACE

I. BEHAVIOR: **Specific attitudes and actions of this child at home and/or at school.**

1. Can always identify classmate who is first.

2. Won't really compete against first-place student.

3. Usually believes he/she is only worthy of second place. Though a top student, seems to have a sense of inferiority.

4. May fear failure.

5. Sees accepting second place as security against having to keep first place.

6. Reveals this stance in many situations: academics, sports, getting in line.

7. Seems to make no comparison between him/herself and others, which is a healthy stance. However, always talks of being behind first-place student, and this alters his/her self-concept.

8. May idolize — or resent — first-place student.

9. Often very well liked.

10. Humble.

11. Considerate.

II. EFFECTS: **How behavior affects teachers, classmates, and parents in the school learning environment and the home family situation.**

1. Classmates usually don't recognize this student as being "second place." Rather, they regard him/her as a leader or one of the best.

2. Teacher worries because this student doesn't work to capacity.

3. Teacher can't get by this student's mental block. For instance, teacher may believe that this student need not take a second seat to anybody and should regard him/herself as equal to all.

4. Teacher finds it difficult to motivate him/her beyond present achievements.

5. Classmates may not even notice that this student is having any problems.

6. Teacher may hear "reasons" for not being the best and feel frustrated in working with this student.

III. ACTION: • **Identify causes of misbehavior.**
• **Pinpoint student needs being revealed.**
• **Employ specific methods, procedures, and techniques at school and at home for getting the child to modify or change his/her behavior.**

1. Primary cause of misbehavior:

   ▶ Self-Confidence: Lack of self-confidence causes this student honestly to expect failure, and to believe he/she can never be first.

2. Primary need being revealed:

▶ Escape from Pain: This student avoids pain by being very comfortable with second place, and might feel a great deal of pain if he/she tried to be first and was unable to do so. It is his/her way to avoid failure.

3. Secondary needs being revealed:

▶ Achievement: If this student's goals are extended slightly each time he/she reaches a certain level, the student may come to realize that being first is not tough after all. The teacher can be very helpful in determining reachable goals.

▶ Status: The need to continue to achieve will enhance the status of the student with the teacher and fellow students.

4. Observe the student to determine if "second place" is by design or ability.

5. Talk to him/her about always conceding. Say, "You are not competing with others, you are only competing against yourself, and you are conceding with yourself. This is the problem." Never talk him/her into competing against another student.

6. Help the student identify one major area of dominant strength. Use this to motivate him/her to reach beyond present achievements.

7. Don't choose a large goal. Rather, choose a small, short-term goal. This strategic action is vital. When thinking in terms of goals, remember it is not always important to reach goals every time, but point out any progress the student makes toward his/her goals.

8. Always allow the student to work with classmates who need help.

9. Whenever possible, choose him/her first.

10. Most important, counsel the student regarding competition. Say, "I am concerned about how you see yourself. I'm worried that you always compare yourself unfavorably with Johnny. I don't like this (worship) (resentment). The only good competition is in yourself."

11. Continue by talking about competing against him/herself to get better. The only reasonable goal is improvement. Once the student accepts this, he/she can work according to self-imposed standards rather than those of a classmate — and achievement will match ability.

IV. MISTAKES: Common misjudgments and errors in managing the child which may perpetuate or intensify the problem.

1. Accepting second place as his/her "level" of achievement.

2. Assuming that since the student is near the top of the class, he/she is working to capacity.

3. Believing that this student is "secure" in the class setting.

4. Failing to encourage the student to compete with him/herself for higher goals.

5. Thinking he/she gets enough recognition.

6. Failing to develop a significant working relationship.

7. Believing the student's current level of achievement will continue throughout his/her schooling.

8. Talking him/her into competing against another student.

SEE ALSO: • The Alibier • The Do-Nothing • The Excuse/Alibi Maker
• "I Can't" • The Lazy

THE SCRAPPER

I. BEHAVIOR: **Specific attitudes and actions of this child at home and/or at school.**

1. Aggressive.

2. Competitive.

3. Often has a chip on his/her shoulder but, whether he/she does or doesn't, will not back away from a situation.

4. Seeks retribution at any cost.

5. Outspoken and emotional.

6. Will react physically to situations without regard to consequences.

7. Claims innocence and can justify every scrap — when really he/she is the problem source. That is, whatever happened could have been avoided.

8. Not always physically able to handle him/herself with other students. Therefore, wins some and loses some.

9. Slightly different from the fighter because this student's scrapping is widespread — from winning a race to winning an argument, and maybe even to being considered smart and a good student.

II. EFFECTS: **How behavior affects teachers, classmates, and parents in the school learning environment and the home family situation.**

1. Classmates — and even teacher — may be intimidated.

2. Others retaliate verbally and physically.

3. A negative atmosphere is created in the classroom — one in which other students feel uneasy.

4. A chain reaction extending beyond the classroom is created. When the negative feeling that the scrapper creates is not settled, it carries over into other classes.

III. ACTION: • **Identify causes of misbehavior.**
• **Pinpoint student needs being revealed.**
• **Employ specific methods, procedures, and techniques at school and at home for getting the child to modify or change his/her behavior.**

1. Primary cause of misbehavior:

   ◗ Power: This student, because of continual failures, may find his/her place among peers by being disliked.

2. Primary needs being revealed:

   ◗ Sex: This student may not understand how to establish the normal relationships he/she desires and, thus, may reach out to people through confrontations.

   ◗ Escape from Pain: Sometimes a student has experienced a great deal of pain in or out of school. In order to protect him/herself from future hurt, the student will draw away from people through negative behavior.

3. Secondary needs being revealed:

   ◗ Aggression: This kid does not know how to demonstrate aggression tactfully.

◗ Achievement: Other forms of success may turn the negative behavior to positive behavior.

◗ Power: This student desires to be more assertive, but does not know how to handle power in a positive way.

◗ Status: The student may think, "If I am a poor student, I will use my own methods to be somebody. Even if I am beaten in a fight, the others will know I exist."

4. Remember, this student is trying to be successful. Therefore, adopt a strategic action which focuses on helping him/her be somebody.

5. Talk to the student privately about winning. Focus on his/her strengths: determination, self-reliance, assertiveness. Then, counsel the student about operating on a high level. Speak of "style," "class," and "pride."

6. Because the scrapper wants success, he/she is *very coachable.* However, always counsel him/her in private. Show this student how to handle and manage situations gracefully. Keep in mind that he/she has never been taught how to do anything but scrap.

7. Never resort to an action that you have criticized when the student has used it.

8. Never use corporal punishment.

9. Call the parents in if this behavior persists.

10. Explain to the student the consequences (in specific terms) of his/her continued misbehavior.

11. Use counselors, administrators, and former teachers as resources.

IV. MISTAKES: Common misjudgments and errors in managing the child which may perpetuate or intensify the problem.

1. Taking this behavior as a personal confrontation.

2. Misjudging and stereotyping this student.

3. Failing to be prompt, and delaying reactions to the scrapper. This inaction increases the misbehavior.

4. Using this behavior as an excuse to remove the student from the class.

5. Encouraging other students to react physically to the scrapper.

6. Failing to establish a private relationship.

SEE ALSO: • The Authority Pusher • The Fighter

THE SELFISH

I. BEHAVIOR: **Specific attitudes and actions of this child at home and/or at school.**

1. Different from the eager learner. The selfish student is always trying to get something for nothing.

2. Always seeking extra privileges. But, when such a privilege is granted, asks for another. This student *can't stop asking.*

3. Will question a teacher decision repeatedly until a concession is granted.

4. Seldom says "please" or "thank you."

5. Will talk about what other teachers will do in comparison to what you will do.

6. Infringes upon the rights of others.

7. Very persistent. Too many times, people give in to get rid of this child.

8. Talks about him/herself continually.

9. Talks a great deal about what he/she has.

10. Knows exactly what he/she is doing. Why shouldn't the student behave this way? It works almost every time.

11. Concerned about self, and his/her own wants and needs. Doesn't care about others. This is the key to identifying selfish behavior.

II. EFFECTS: **How behavior affects teachers, classmates, and parents in the school learning environment and the home family situation.**

1. Classmates usually dislike the selfish student because he/she doesn't show concern for others.

2. A great deal of time is required to deal with this behavior.

3. If teacher makes concessions, he/she may be unfair to other students.

4. Others are annoyed.

5. Developing a healthy student-teacher relationship is difficult.

III. ACTION: • **Identify causes of misbehavior.**
• **Pinpoint student needs being revealed.**
• **Employ specific methods, procedures, and techniques at school and at home for getting the child to modify or change his/her behavior.**

1. Primary cause of misbehavior:

   ‣ Attention: This student is so much in need of attention that he/she withdraws into self. Soon the only important person is him/herself.

2. Primary needs being revealed:

   ‣ Escape from Pain: The student may have gone through so many painful experiences in the home, with peers, or in school that "number one" becomes all-important.

   ‣ Sex: The possibility should be investigated that a relationship in this student's life has been disrupted or destroyed. A parent may have moved out of the home, or the student may have broken up with a girlfriend or boyfriend.

244

3. Secondary needs being revealed:

   ◆ Affiliation: This student needs a close friend. It may be an adult or a peer. Regardless, the student needs someone with whom he/she can deal honestly.

   ◆ Autonomy: This student has taken a negative direction in an attempt to be in control of his/her life.

4. Confront the student regarding this personality characteristic. You will find that the selfish student is likely to change immediately if he/she is confronted. It's amazing, but persistent and demanding people are seldom confronted. People do what works for them. Because these kids get away with being selfish, they think the behavior works for them.

5. Make a *formal* appointment to meet with the student privately.

6. When you meet, tell the student you want to talk to him/her about something *very personal*. Then explain exactly what you see the student doing.

7. Talk about the student's dissatisfaction.

8. Give this student responsibilities that require him/her to be a giver so that the group may be successful.

9. Discuss the student's concern for self over others.

10. Tell the student you won't concede in the future — and why. This is the key: It's not *fair* to this student and it's not fair to others.

11. Then, identify the student's personality strengths. Discuss those strengths relative to his/her being highly successful.

12. Talk about maturity as being that stage in which we go from being a taker to being a giver.

13. Finally, ask the student if he/she knows any selfish people who are happy.

14. The previous steps should enable elementary teachers to eliminate the problem immediately. To combat this problem at the secondary level, an additional step may be helpful. Arrange a meeting with all teachers and counselors to discuss the behavior problem of selfish students. Together, the staff can be successful in preventing the perpetuation of this problem.

15. Observe the class carefully, and you may find a student who attempts to get along with the selfish. Encourage this relationship, as long as the selfish student doesn't exploit his/her companion.

IV. MISTAKES: Common misjudgments and errors in managing the child which may perpetuate or intensify the problem.

1. Conceding to the selfish student.

2. Trying to get rid of him/her.

3. Showing open dislike for the student rather than the behavior.

4. Avoiding this student.

5. Resolving not to budge, regardless of the validity of his/her request.

6. Failing to counsel this student privately.

SEE ALSO: • The Attention Demander • The Crier (Who Claims Foul)
                  • "Not My Fault" • The Pouter

THE SHADOW

I. BEHAVIOR: Specific attitudes and actions of this child at home and/or at school.

1. Follows teacher around continuously. Teacher often looks up and finds this student standing at his/her desk.
2. Wants to be wherever teacher is.
3. Too helpful.
4. Seeks constant attention, but doesn't demand it.
5. Would rather talk to teacher than anyone else.
6. Wants to see him/herself as teacher's aide.
7. May be socially immature.
8. May have few friends.

II. EFFECTS: How behavior affects teachers, classmates, and parents in the school learning environment and the home family situation.

1. Teacher becomes nervous.
2. Teacher grows impatient.
3. Other children see this student as teacher's pet. Worse, they may regard the shadow as a pest and hold him/her in low regard.
4. Teacher thinks the shadow takes time away from other students.
5. Teacher begins to resent this child's shadowing, and draws away from the student physically and emotionally.

III. ACTION: • Identify causes of misbehavior.
   • Pinpoint student needs being revealed.
   • Employ specific methods, procedures, and techniques at school and at home for getting the child to modify or change his/her behavior.

1. Primary causes of misbehavior:
   ◗ Attention: This student may not be getting enough attention at home or elsewhere.
   ◗ Self-Confidence: This student is seeking reassurance that the teacher knows he/she exists.
2. Primary needs being revealed:
   ◗ Sex: This student has a strong need for adult relationships.
   ◗ Escape from Pain: The student may be finding it very difficult to make friends with peers. Perhaps the only outlet left is his/her teacher.
3. Secondary needs being revealed:
   ◗ Gregariousness, Affiliation: This student feels a strong need to belong somewhere — either as part of a group or with a close friend.
   ◗ Achievement: The student needs recognition from someone for what he/she might be able to do. Achievement will lead to reduction of the need for so much attention.
   ◗ Status: If status is gained through achievement, the student will soon realize he/she is somebody, a worthwhile person in his/her own right.

4. Do not belittle or draw away from this student.

5. Above all, do not ridicule the student.

6. Rather, take a strategic position of acceptance. To do so, keep your perspective by accepting two facts. First, it's nice that a student likes you so much. Second, it's unlikely that this child is developing a serious problem just because he/she is not with friends. This is a stage which will pass.

7. In the process, recognize that you have the opportunity to get a student to become a caring person. Remember, this student is eager for coaching.

8. Assign extra duties to raise the student's self-esteem.

9. Find the student a friend or a group of friends who can help support him/her and provide that needed attention.

10. Have a one-to-one student-teacher relationship with this student.

11. Have the student tutor a younger child.

12. Create situations in which this student is allowed to help other students in class on a one-to-one level.

13. Never act superior to this child.

14. Recognize and acknowledge this student's intelligence.

15. Establish projects for extra credit for this student.

16. Encourage individualized and independent learning.

17. Create situations in which the born exceller can help you in researching and giving presentations on topics and issues.

IV. MISTAKES: Common misjudgments and errors in managing the child which may perpetuate or intensify the problem.

1. Overreacting personally.

2. Thinking something is "wrong" with this student. Is there something wrong in liking us?

3. Lying to the student to get rid of him/her. For instance, we may say, "I have a meeting tonight, so you'll have to leave." When we want privacy, we should simply say so in an honest, gentle, and caring way.

4. Using this student rather than helping him/her.

5. Being embarrassed that the student follows us.

6. Talking negatively to colleagues about this student behind his/her back.

7. Failing to focus upon the strong side of his/her personality.

8. Failing to see anything wrong with the behavior, or even fostering it, because it feeds our egos.

SEE ALSO: • The Dreamer • The Immature • The Pest • The Shy • The Stewer

THE SHOW-OFF

I. BEHAVIOR: Specific attitudes and actions of this child at home and/or at school.

1. Seeks attention — from everyone — until he/she receives it.
2. Recognizes no boundaries to his/her attention-seeking behavior.
3. Goes against what is expected and acceptable behavior.
4. Doesn't know when to quit.
5. Following one incident, begins thinking of something else he/she can do.
6. Different from the class clown; the show-off is serious. This student brags, shows how high he/she can jump, demonstrates intelligence over others, and does anything he/she can to show superiority.
7. Likes to perform in presence of opposite sex.
8. Makes quick responses to all stimuli.
9. Self-centered and inconsiderate of others.
10. May or may not be a good student academically.

II. EFFECTS: How behavior affects teachers, classmates, and parents in the school learning environment and the home family situation.

1. Attention is distracted from what is going on in class.
2. Others may be physically threatened by the show-off's behavior.
3. Teacher may feel that he/she has lost control over the class.
4. Classmates may tend to say less in class because they resent the show-off.
5. Time is wasted.
6. Competitive situations are set up in class, which can cause trouble.
7. Some kids are amused.
8. Some kids may provoke the show-off in order to deviate class.

III. ACTION: • Identify causes of misbehavior.
                     • Pinpoint student needs being revealed.
                     • Employ specific methods, procedures, and techniques at school and at home for getting the child to modify or change his/her behavior.

1. Primary causes of misbehavior:
    ‣ Attention: This person seeks attention at any cost.
    ‣ Power: This person also feels a great deal of power in obtaining attention, but doesn't understand that his/her behavior turns others away.
2. Primary need being revealed:
    ‣ Sex: This student is making every effort to let people know he/she exists and needs some kind of relationship with peers and adults.
3. Secondary needs being revealed:

- Gregariousness: This student needs to belong. His/her continuous showing off demonstrates the urgency of the situation.

- Aggression: This student needs involvement with others in a positive way. The student needs to learn acceptable ways to assert him/herself.

- Achievement: The increased opportunity to achieve will reduce the need to show off.

- Power: The student needs to be given responsible tasks, and the teacher must structure the conditions for completing those tasks.

4. Be aware that, too often, this child needs more than attention. The student feels he/she must do something significant to win approval.

5. Likewise, the show-off fears he/she will be lost in the shuffle in school. Therefore, even though he/she is capable and acts superior, this student feels inferior. Showing off allows the student to brag without being contradicted or tested. Above all, when this child doesn't show off, *he/she never gets any attention.* This makes the student feel worse. Therefore, know that this student may not want to show off, but must.

6. Hold individual conferences with this student. Talk about his/her behavior and discuss why this is happening — in a caring way.

7. Capitalize on his/her strengths. Say, "I don't want people thinking badly of you."

8. Make sure this student knows you like him/her. Remember, this child will do anything to get your respect.

9. Give the show-off attention before he/she seeks it.

10. Confront the student privately, with a calm and serious attitude. Never confront him/her in the presence of others. In class, give the show-off a look of knowing disapproval, but not rejection.

11. Move toward the student when he/she is showing off. Say, "Please . . ." You'll be surprised how often he/she will stop. Then, say something good about the student publicly, and go to a different subject.

12. If a student becomes restless during class study time, never urge him/her to get back to work by making an announcement from the front of the room. If you do, one thing is certain: The entire class will be interrupted. Talk to the student — quietly. Sometimes all you need to do is walk slowly by the student's desk or to the back of the room, station yourself in that position, and watch silently. Often a teacher is in the best position to control the class simply by standing in the rear of the classroom.

13. A close look will reveal that some kids have to be discipline problems. It's the only way they feel important. In truth, school makes them feel insignificant. Class work shows their inferiority. Therefore, they find importance by being a nuisance or causing problems. Two of the most common behaviors which are a result of this reality are showing off and being a smart aleck. Find ways to make kids demonstrating these two behaviors feel significant, and you'll find the behaviors will gradually diminish. However, the behaviors will disappear only in your classroom if you're the only teacher who makes these students feel adequate.

14. The best way to make people feel important is to give them something important to do. Make up a list of all the things kids can do in your room daily, semi-weekly, and weekly. Then, ask these kinds of students if they would be willing to assume these responsibilities in your classroom. Remember to recognize their efforts, and you'll find these students may not have such a strong need to show off or be smart alecks.

15. Use encouragement for *all* good behavior, privately and publicly.

16. Meet with other teachers and parents in order to have a similar plan of approach in dealing with these students.

17. Make sure this student is aware that he/she may have to face consequences if this behavior continues.

18. Have the student work out a plan to adjust his/her behavior.

IV. MISTAKES: Common misjudgments and errors in managing the child which may perpetuate or intensify the problem.

1. Overreacting and losing our composure.

2. Using sarcasm and cutting statements.

3. Taking the behavior of this student personally.

4. Imitating the student's behavior.

5. Making public reprimands.

6. Failing to see the student's potential.

7. Failing to hear his/her plea for help.

SEE ALSO: • The Arrogant   • The Attention Demander   • The Class Clown
• The Fun Seeker   • The Intellectual Show-Off   • The Know-It-All
• The Loudmouth   • The Smart Aleck

THE SHY

I. BEHAVIOR: **Specific attitudes and actions of this child at home and/or at school.**

1. Typically a strong but gentle person.
2. Likely to be creative.
3. Introverted.
4. Seems to be afraid of people — both adults and students.
5. Speaks in a low tone of voice, sometimes difficult to hear.
6. Appears afraid to attempt tasks.
7. Has few, if any, friends.
8. Prefers his/her own company and enjoys leading the inner life.
9. Works alone at every opportunity.
10. May be physically immature.
11. Seems to "run away" when approached.
12. Often responds with body language, but refuses to respond verbally.

II. EFFECTS: **How behavior affects teachers, classmates, and parents in the school learning environment and the home family situation.**

1. Teacher tends to worry about the shy student.
2. Teacher considers this student socially lacking — if not downright crippled.
3. Sometimes, both teacher and classmates are unaware of this student's existence. Or they may mistake his/her shyness for dislike or lack of interest.
4. Time is taken from the class to work individually with this student.
5. Teacher and peers are irritated by this behavior.
6. Other students tend to pick on the shy student.
7. Teacher is frustrated.

III. ACTION: • **Identify causes of misbehavior.**
  • **Pinpoint student needs being revealed.**
  • **Employ specific methods, procedures, and techniques at school and at home for getting the child to modify or change his/her behavior.**

1. Primary cause of misbehavior:
   ▸ Self-Confidence: This student may or may not lack self-confidence. Remember, shy people are often strong people. They can do what others can't — be alone.
2. Primary need being revealed:
   ▸ Escape from Pain: Shyness may be a means of self-protection — against feeling inadequate in school, work, or relationships with peers or adults.
3. Secondary needs being revealed:
   ▸ Affiliation: The shy student can be helped by a feeling of close friendship with a peer or adult.

251

◗ Autonomy: This person wants to be in charge of his/her own life, and may not have a real need for people.

4. Remember, the basic problem is fear. Don't make the student insecure. Make him/her psychologically safe.

5. Accept the fact that people who are different from the rest of us aren't necessarily inferior.

6. Adjust your behavior to accept the shy student. Don't interpret silence as a sign of indifference, lack of concern, or univolvement on the part of a student or colleague. Silence is a difficult human behavior to analyze. It can mean the person does not know or understand what is taking place. It might also mean that the person is embarrassed, lacks self-confidence, or fears rejection. On the other hand, silence can also indicate serious thinking. Be careful not to form conclusions about the silent student. Silence is often a positive behavior that your rejection can turn into a negative.

7. Gently urge the shy student to participate, but don't force participation.

8. Be friendly and courteous.

9. Speak slowly and softly. Otherwise, you will scare this student. Don't hurry explanations. The shy student cannot be approached boisterously. In any conversation with the shy, never forget that softness of voice coupled with slowness of delivery is vital — especially in private instruction or counseling. Remember, this student needs a slow, deliberate approach. Any other approach will cause a further retreat into his/her shell.

10. Be sincere. Insincerity and loudness will cause deeper shyness.

11. Respect the emotional privacy of the shy. Public praise will embarrass this child, so compliment him/her privately. Sometimes, a prying attitude toward a child who appears to be disturbed about something can do more harm than good. A teacher must always offer assistance, of course. However, if the child refuses the offer, you should discreetly, but with understanding, remain at a distance until the child seeks your help. Too often, long offerings of help embarrass the child and initiate feelings of resentment. If the child appears unable to cope with the situation, notify a counselor or administrator immediately.

12. When you ask a question, be prepared to wait for an answer. Be patient. The shy student needs time to respond.

13. Recognize achievement, both academic and social.

14. Work with all students to help them understand and accept the shy.

15. Be aware that many times the personalities of two children can complement each other's personal and academic development. This is especially true of opposite sexes. The quiet, withdrawn, academic student and the active extrovert who tends to be a discipline problem many times make a good learning pair. Seating these two types of students together and requiring them to work together periodically can prove helpful to the growth of both children.

16. Create opportunities for the shy student to perform tasks that contribute to the class.

17. Recognize that exaggerated shyness is not a discipline problem, but a social problem.

18. Remember, this student may be OK. Shyness is not abnormal. However, the pressures in our society are great impositions on the shy. And teachers often do much of the imposing. Be aware that, when you think you're helping, you may not be. You may especially enjoy interacting with people, and find it difficult to understand those who do not. Remember that your reaction to this student's personality characteristics could force him/her into inaccurate conclusions about him/herself. Worse, it could force the student into actions that are not natural to him/her.

19. Experience reveals that the shy child does well academically. More important, these achievements often reflect thoughtful and meaningful learning. Recognize that an inner direction

motivates this student and, because he/she is deeply thoughtful, the shy student is good at self-evaluation.

20. Don't try to change this student. The shy child not only has a right to be as he/she is, but should also be a pleasure to teach. So there may be no need to worry about the shy student — or to try to make him/her an extrovert.

21. The shy student is probably OK; so just say so. It's important to validate the position of all students. Such validation may be the most important action you ever take with the shy.

IV. MISTAKES: Common misjudgments and errors in managing the child which may perpetuate or intensify the problem.

1. Assuming that something must be wrong with a student who is shy.

2. Imposing our values on the shy student and trying to change him/her.

3. Allowing classmates to take advantage of the shy student in the hope that it will help him/her.

4. Raising our voices and demanding that the student participate in class.

5. Appearing anxious or impatient with the shy student.

6. Taking the shy behavior personally.

SEE ALSO: • The Apathetic   • The Dreamer   • "I Can't"   • The Loner
• The Nonparticipator

THE SIDETRACKER

I. BEHAVIOR: **Specific attitudes and actions of this child at home and/or at school.**

1. Seems to have a way of getting teacher away from the lesson at hand.

2. Tries to get teacher talking about anything and everything but the daily lesson.

3. Gets a great deal of personal satisfaction from sidetracking.

4. Begins discussions that invariably lead to student-teacher arguments. This is especially easy for the sidetracker if the subject he/she picks is relevant to current classroom work.

5. May not complete current assignments.

6. Likely to be lazy.

7. Gets to know teacher's styles and, with this knowledge, encourages others to help him/her sidetrack.

II. EFFECTS: **How behavior affects teachers, classmates, and parents in the school learning environment and the home family situation.**

1. Time is wasted.

2. Lessons are deviated.

3. Arguments are created.

4. Teacher feels a dual pressure: first, to complete lessons, and second, to show flexibility.

5. Teacher and classmates begin to ignore this student.

III. ACTION: • **Identify causes of misbehavior.**
• **Pinpoint student needs being revealed.**
• **Employ specific methods, procedures, and techniques at school and at home for getting the child to modify or change his/her behavior.**

1. Primary causes of misbehavior:

   ▶ Attention: Through this behavior, the student is saying, "I will do almost anything to get attention."

   ▶ Power: This student feels a need to be superior or equal to adults, and feels such a position would give him/her power among peers.

2. Primary needs being revealed:

   ▶ Sex: This student needs help in establishing relationships with peers and/or adults.

   ▶ Escape from Pain: This student may be experiencing many painful situations in school. This behavior may be a cover-up for his/her pain.

3. Secondary needs being revealed:

   ▶ Gregariousness: Through this behavior the student is trying to belong, win friends, and obtain followers.

   ▶ Power: This student has a strong need for power among peers, but not necessarily with adults. The student needs to realize that difficulty in getting along with adults hurts his/her position with peers.

   ▶ Status: This student wants to feel that he/she is "somebody."

▶ Achievement: Any kind of success may reduce the sidetracking.

4. Some students have a knack for sidetracking teachers into discussions which have nothing to do with the subject being studied. Don't allow yourself to abandon the majority of the class for the deviation of one. Don't get angry either. Simply answer the question quickly with one sentence and use your second sentence to get back to the lesson. If the student persists, be kind but direct. Tell the sidetracker you would enjoy pursuing the conversation and would be happy to after school — but not during class time.

5. Other students like to argue just for the sake of arguing. One of their favorite ploys is to try to engage a teacher in the argument. Don't let yourself fall into this trap. Maintain your composure and give an answer or opinion if you choose — or offer to meet the student after class to discuss his/her objections. Remember, everyone in the room knows what the student is doing. Some are hoping you will get angry or defensive — but most are hoping you will not. Do not lose control of yourself.

6. When it's necessary to head off the sidetracker's attempt to divert the class, be sure to *thank* the student for his/her thoughts.

7. At times, these deviations lead to good discussions. They can make a classroom exciting and relevant. Therefore, the trick is to permit some deviations and disallow others. To achieve this, talk to the *class* about this reality prior to, as well as during, such incidents.

8. Then, talk to the sidetracker privately about this reality. The key is to tell the student to *keep thinking*. Then, ask for his/her *help*, and ask the student to *trust* you in your choices. Tell the sidetracker it will be necessary to terminate some discussions at their beginning.

9. Make an appointment to finish the discussion, and make the student keep it. You will find these planned attempts to sidetrack with irrelevant discussions will stop if handled in this manner.

IV. MISTAKES: Common misjudgments and errors in managing the child which may perpetuate or intensify the problem.

1. Falling into the argument trap.

2. Failing to recognize that this student may, at times, make valuable contributions to the class.

3. Failing to teach this student responsibility to the group.

4. Getting mad.

5. Failing to see and capitalize on interests that this student may be revealing.

6. Thinking that these diversions *always* indicate student interest, and not recognizing that we are being purposely sidetracked.

SEE ALSO:
- The Attention Demander • The Disrupter • The Distracter
- The Hyperactive • The Manipulator • The Questioner

THE SKIPPER

I. BEHAVIOR: Specific attitudes and actions of this child at home and/or at school.

1. Just doesn't like school.
2. Seems to hate being "penned up" in class.
3. Knows where to hide and how not to get caught.
4. Looks for the easy way out.
5. Seeks pleasure and immediate gratification.
6. Is a loner, and usually skips alone rather than with friends.
7. May be intelligent and have academic potential. Nevertheless, makes dumb decisions about coming to class.
8. May not be a discipline problem, but may be lazy.
9. Often begins skipping when he/she changes grades or classes, or moves to a new and different environment. Skipping is most common during the first year of junior high or middle school, and the first year of high school.
10. May attend a class he/she likes but skip other classes.
11. Thinks teacher doesn't like him/her.
12. Knows he/she will get in trouble, but chooses the inevitable repercussions in order to avoid going to class. Or may not even think about the consequences. This student's behavior says, "The pain of school is so bad, I'll take any punishment to avoid going."

II. EFFECTS: How behavior affects teachers, classmates, and parents in the school learning environment and the home family situation.

1. Teacher develops strong resentments toward the student who chooses not to come to class.
2. Classmates may feel this student is getting special attention when teacher tries to help him/her remain in school.
3. A great deal of extra time is required to help this student catch up in class work.
4. Teacher expends more energy trying to catch the student skipping than correcting the behavior.
5. Teacher doesn't know how to handle this student and is perplexed by the problem.

III. ACTION:
- **Identify causes of misbehavior.**
- **Pinpoint student needs being revealed.**
- **Employ specific methods, procedures, and techniques at school and at home for getting the child to modify or change his/her behavior.**

1. Primary causes of misbehavior:
   - Self-Confidence: By skipping classes, the student gains a valid reason for failure. Skipping is a cop-out; it provides an excuse for not achieving.
   - Attention: This person gets attention at home and at school by skipping classes.
2. Primary need being revealed:

256

♦ Escape from Pain: The student's feeling of low self-esteem may make it very painful for him/her to attend class.

3. Secondary needs being revealed:

   ♦ Achievement: This student needs to achieve, and school should be a place where tasks are appropriate to his/her abilities. Achievement may be in the form of positive power or status.

   ♦ Power: The student may feel powerless in the classroom. By skipping classes, he/she demonstrates power negatively.

   ♦ Status: The student feels he/she becomes "somebody" by skipping classes.

4. When skipping starts, act immediately. Gather all your resources — colleagues, counselors, principal, parents — and meet to decide a common approach. Let the student attend these sessions. It's good for the student to see everyone working for his/her benefit.

5. At the meeting, concentrate on *help* and forget about punishments.

6. When dealing with this student, realize that the problem won't be solved overnight. You must use *improvement* as the true barometer and your strategic action goal. Therefore, begin by talking to the student about improvement. Then, give the student a place to go when he/she can't come to class, such as a nurse's or counselor's office. This is important. It makes the student responsible for being *someplace* rather than just anyplace. It also gives a professional a chance to work *with* him/her in the process. Remember, if a student's skipping drops from five days to two days a month, that's improvement.

7. Don't have the skipper make up all work missed, or you will see him/her even less. And remember, the problem of make-up work is compounded if several classes and teachers are involved. Have the student do selected past-due work. Shorten assignments whenever possible.

8. Remember, attendance rather than achievement is your primary objective. If all teachers do not agree on this point, you have a potential drop-out. You simply must "buy time" with this student.

9. Ultimately, the skipper must choose not to skip. This student can't be forced. Therefore, never place the responsibility for attendance on yourself. Make it clear that this *power* is the student's.

10. Recognize that your job is to create the environment for a positive decision. It can never be created with a threat.

11. Be aware that skipping may be caused by a personality conflict between teacher and student. It is not always caused by lack of academic ability or interest.

IV. MISTAKES: Common misjudgments and errors in managing the child which may perpetuate or intensify the problem.

1. Treating the skipper harshly in order to shame or embarrass him/her.

2. Taking this behavior as an open insult to the way we teach or, worse, as a personal statement against us. It may be, but dealing on this level will only push the student further away.

3. Letting the student skip.

4. Failing to consult colleagues, administrators, and other resources.

5. Failing to inform parents. Studies show a student in high school can miss between 15 and 18 days before parents are called.

6. Rejecting this student.

SEE ALSO: • The Fun Seeker • The Hyperactive • "I Don't Care" • The Lazy
• The Truant

THE SLEEPER

I. BEHAVIOR: Specific attitudes and actions of this child at home and/or at school.

1. Dozes or actually sleeps in class during instruction, and then asks for help later.
2. Puts his/her head on the desk, even before class starts.
3. Hides behind an open book.
4. May be a "gazer" who can look without seeing, listen without hearing, and appear to be sleeping with his/her eyes open.
5. Displays total lack of attention or interest. Acts bored.
6. Achieves little academically. Therefore, usually a poor student.
7. Possesses no self-motivation.
8. Never contributes to class.
9. May have a job outside school or may just stay up late at home.
10. Usually, does not communicate well on a one-to-one basis.
11. Doesn't interact socially with classmates.
12. Probably apathetic toward class and school.
13. Occasionally disruptive.

II. EFFECTS: How behavior affects teachers, classmates, and parents in the school learning environment and the home family situation.

1. Teacher is irritated and frustrated.
2. Teacher worries about this student's predictable failure.
3. Classmates are distracted.
4. Classmates react negatively toward the sleeper and treat him/her as inferior.
5. Importance of classroom activities to other students is undermined.
6. Time is wasted keeping this student awake and repeating instructions.
7. A double standard is created — one for the sleeper and one for the rest of the class.

III. ACTION:
- **Identify causes of misbehavior.**
- **Pinpoint student needs being revealed.**
- **Employ specific methods, procedures, and techniques at school and at home for getting the child to modify or change his/her behavior.**

1. Primary cause of misbehavior:
   - Self-Confidence: This student may feel very insecure about his/her ability to be productive in school.
2. Primary needs being revealed:
   - Hunger, Thirst, Rest: This student may have serious physical problems, and a physical examination should be suggested. The student may also be getting inadequate sleep because of a job, or because he/she stays up late to study — or watch television.

- Escape from Pain: The student may be experiencing failure in academic performance or in relationships with parents or peers. Sleeping is a way to avoid the pain of these failures.

3. Secondary need being revealed:

- Achievement: School may take on new meaning for this student if he/she experiences success with fellow students or teachers, or in academic performance.

4. Before you arrive at any conclusions or take any action, find out specifically why the student falls asleep. Talk to the student, and seek the help of the nurse, counselor, administrator, and parents.

5. Place your emphasis on attacking the behavior — and do everything you can to avoid attacking the student.

6. Refuse to take sleeping as a personal affront.

7. Put this student near an open window so that he/she may get fresh air.

8. Give this student some class duties so that he/she can move around to carry out minor tasks. This forces involvement, and the physical activity helps overcome drowsiness.

9. Do not counsel with the parents until you have counseled with the student. Find out what the situation is at home first. Then contact parents. Approach the situation as a possible health problem, not as a discipline problem.

10. Give the student positive recognition, attention, and reinforcement whenever you can.

11. Create social activities in the classroom to involve the student and raise his/her interest.

12. Determine what the student's personal interests are and use these as motivating springboards.

13. Try varied and new activities to stimulate this student's interest.

14. Assign short tasks in class.

15. Do all you can to give this student immediate success.

16. In private counseling, explain the natural consequences if the student chooses not to make an adjustment in his/her behavior and continues sleeping in the classroom.

IV. MISTAKES: Common misjudgments and errors in managing the child which may perpetuate or intensify the problem.

1. Ignoring the student and the situation, and allowing the behavior to go unchecked.

2. Treating sleeping as a discipline problem without finding out why the student is sleeping. He/she might be sleepy for very valid reasons.

3. Disturbing the entire class by reprimanding the student or making a scene.

4. Embarrassing the student in front of the entire class — or making a class production out of either waking the student up or letting him/her sleep.

5. Showing dislike for the student.

6. Excluding this student from class activities.

7. Failing to seek help.

8. Yelling at the student.

SEE ALSO: • The Apathetic • The Con Artist • The Dreamer • "I Can't"
• The Lazy

THE SMART ALECK

I. BEHAVIOR: Specific attitudes and actions of this child at home and/or at school.

1. Makes "funny" comments that actually go far beyond humor. And the cutting effect is intentional.
2. Often rude, and usually disrespectful. Different from the smartmouth; the smart aleck's misbehavior includes both *word* and *deed.*
3. Has been overindulged by adults.
4. Tries to act superior to others.
5. Attempts to cover an inferiority complex with this type of behavior.
6. Denies, and hides from facing, the feeling of inferiority. Is fooling him/herself — and possibly others.
7. Is the first to say, "You can't talk to that teacher." Whenever this student is wrong, he/she starts talking about being mistreated.
8. Thrives on "getting a reaction" from others.
9. Seldom says nice things about others.
10. "Zaps" others as soon as they let their guard down.
11. Has no relationships with adults.

II. EFFECTS: How behavior affects teachers, classmates, and parents in the school learning environment and the home family situation.

1. Teacher may not want to help the smart aleck because this student is so obnoxious.
2. Peers may be influenced to feel antagonism toward teacher, if they feel sympathy with the smart aleck and enjoy his/her antics.
3. Teacher becomes angry.
4. Teacher may retaliate.
5. Class control may be lost.
6. Teacher may lose dignity when handling this student.

III. ACTION:
- **Identify causes of misbehavior.**
- **Pinpoint student needs being revealed.**
- **Employ specific methods, procedures, and techniques at school and at home for getting the child to modify or change his/her behavior.**

1. Primary causes of misbehavior:
   - Self-Confidence: Insecurity is sometimes revealed by a false show of superiority.
   - Revenge: This student really enjoys getting a reaction from classmates.
2. Primary need being revealed:
   - Escape from Pain: Any type of failure can be very painful. When people are in pain, they may seek to hurt others.
3. Secondary needs being revealed:

♦ Aggression: This student is asserting him/herself, but is doing so in a negative manner.

♦ Power: This student's need for power must be redirected to a positive outlet.

4. Never respond with a smart-aleck remark in return. Often, when a student makes an uncalled-for remark in class, he/she is searching for — and expecting — your response. Your response may give the student exactly what he/she wants — teacher and peer attention. You may also provide the impetus to continue the exchange.

5. Therefore, ignore some of these offhand remarks.

6. At other times, respond, "I would like to continue this conversation privately after class — so I'll see you then." This may also prove effective.

7. Be aware, however, that responding to misplaced remarks with silence — and especially without appearing sarcastic and vindictive — will often sober students more quickly than anything else you might do. Ignoring the smart aleck's antics deflates him/her completely. This student can't stand silence. It brings out his/her real feelings of inferiority. This then renders the student ready for teacher guidance. Treat this student in a completely professional and intellectual manner, always. At every opportunity, simply pull the facade away, and never stoop to being a smart aleck yourself. If the student talks back, don't succumb to the urge to make a "smart remark" that could reinforce his/her feelings of weakness.

8. Challenge the student to demonstrate his/her abilities by classroom production. Say, "Why don't you try to find out just how good you are?" In a caring rather than hostile way, make the student abandon the protective shield and live up to his/her claims of superiority.

9. Arrange a conference with parents. This is a must. Remember, they're experiencing the same behavior at home.

IV. MISTAKES: Common misjudgments and errors in managing the child which may perpetuate or intensify the problem.

1. Reacting by calling the student down.

2. Punishing for behavior without determining the causes of the behavior and adjusting to those causes.

3. Relying on the "granted authority" of our position as teachers to handle the student.

4. Becoming dogmatic and trying to force ideas upon the student.

5. Contradicting or arguing with this student in the presence of the class, unless we have been pushed to the point at which silence is impossible.

6. Getting mad.

7. Losing our tempers.

8. Showing hate and rejection.

9. Physically striking this person in reaction to his/her remarks.

SEE ALSO: • The Class Clown • The Defier • The Distracter • The Loudmouth
• The Show-Off • The Smartmouth

261

THE SMARTMOUTH

I. BEHAVIOR: **Specific attitudes and actions of this child at home and/or at school.**

1. Always has a comment to make. It is usually irrelevant, immaterial, and without constructive substance.
2. Uses abusive language — from insulting words to profanity to harsh four-letter obscenities.
3. Makes disruptive and offensive noises.
4. Constantly tries to draw attention to him/herself.
5. Makes comments that are meant to alienate others.
6. Acts only verbally.
7. Likely to be articulate.
8. Bitter.
9. Seems hostile about everything.
10. Not well liked.
11. In all kinds of trouble with all kinds of people because of his/her mouth.

II. EFFECTS: **How behavior affects teachers, classmates, and parents in the school learning environment and the home family situation.**

1. Both teacher and classmates feel insulted and alienated.
2. Learning situation is constantly delayed and interrupted.
3. Fights and arguments are usually started by this student's behavior.
4. Everybody's time is wasted.
5. Others may be shocked and offended by the bad language.
6. Some classmates may purposely get this student started — and then keep him/her going.
7. Classmates — especially serious students — don't want the smartmouth around.

III. ACTION: • **Identify causes of misbehavior.**
• **Pinpoint student needs being revealed.**
• **Employ specific methods, procedures, and techniques at school and at home for getting the child to modify or change his/her behavior.**

1. Primary causes of misbehavior:
   ‣ Power: This person may already have accepted him/herself as a failure, but still has a strong urge for power.
   ‣ Revenge: The smartmouth may be demonstrating hate through the language he/she uses.
2. Primary need being revealed:
   ‣ Escape from Pain: The smartmouth is usually experiencing a great deal of pain at school and in the home.
3. Secondary needs being revealed:
   ‣ Power: Somehow this student needs to feel a sense of positive power.

> ◗ Aggression: This student needs to learn how to be assertive without striking out verbally against people.

> ◗ Status: This person feels he/she becomes "somebody" by obtaining attention through verbal abuse.

4. This student never gets what he/she wants: acceptance and respect. And there's an obvious reason, even though the student *never* sees it. That's why private counseling is a must. In private, let the student talk about his/her anger. Ask, "Why are you angry?"

5. Then, talk to the student about two subjects: hurt and trust. Say, "You don't want to hurt people — why do you?" Then explain why — because he/she can't trust. Talk with the student about why he/she is afraid to trust. You'll find the answers will give you an entirely new perspective.

6. Next, ask the student to try trusting you. Also, ask if you can help. Keep in mind, this will take time.

7. Because this student probably thinks he/she is getting the short end of the stick, help redirect his/her behavior and claims of superiority by forcing the student away from his/her protective shield.

8. Don't challenge this student. Rather, ask the student to demonstrate his/her true abilities through classroom activities.

9. Don't attempt to force your ideas on the student or to be dogmatic.

10. Don't contradict what the student tells you. Just listen. And never, never argue.

11. Most important, unless you are pushed to the point at which silence is impossible, do not respond in front of the class. Remember, a public response is what this student expects. In the student's eyes, such a response is a betrayal of your trust. Privately, show the student that you aren't violating the trust — he/she is. This one revelation can make this student change.

12. Treat this student in a professional manner always, but develop a personal relationship too. This means you must risk involvement.

13. At every opportunity, simply pull the facade away, never becoming a smartmouth yourself. If the student talks back, don't make a retort that will reinforce the student's feeling of weakness. Only positive, professional, friendly counseling can make this student move away from the negative behavior.

14. Finally, find an activity that allows the student to get rid of his/her anger. And tell the student what you are doing. Such an outlet can make changing behavior easier for the student.

15. Be aware that you can easily get into a win/lose situation when dealing with this student, by taking the student's abuse personally. Remember, he/she talks this way to everyone.

16. When you find it necessary to punish a student, be sure you are making an adjustment to whatever is causing the behavior, and that the student is included in the adjustment process. For example, in the case of the smartmouth, discuss with the student the possibility that it might help if he/she moved closer to your desk. If the student says it isn't necessary, allow the privilege. Keep this idea in mind: If the student can correct the situation, fine; if not, you'll have to move him/her. Experience will show that if you simply change the seats without including the student in the adjustment process, he/she will not assume any responsibility in the new seat. The student might even regard the problem as the teacher's rather than his/her own. Then, nothing is learned, and the behavior does not change.

IV. MISTAKES: Common misjudgments and errors in managing the child which may perpetuate or intensify the problem.

1. Getting caught in a verbal conflict to the point of using harsh words or swear words ourselves.

The Smartmouth

2. Punishing the whole group for the behavior of one person.

3. Ignoring the situation until it's completely out of control.

4. Acting inconsistently with smartmouth students. When we do so, we demonstrate that we are acting on a personal rather than a professional level.

5. Failing to counsel this student privately.

6. Losing composure.

7. Failing to see this student's hurt.

SEE ALSO: • The Foulmouth • The Last Worder • The Loudmouth • The Smart Aleck • The Swearer

THE SNEAK

I. BEHAVIOR: **Specific attitudes and actions of this child at home and/or at school.**

1. Always someplace he/she isn't supposed to be.
2. Gets into things that are none of his/her business.
3. Seems to disappear when not under direct supervision.
4. Often alone — but encourages others to go with him/her.
5. A master of obtaining library and restroom passes.
6. Can usually create justifiable reasons for being gone, or for being where he/she is when caught.
7. Uses every opportunity to miss class or avoid structured time.
8. Appears untrustworthy, but proof may be lacking.

II. EFFECTS: **How behavior affects teachers, classmates, and parents in the school learning environment and the home family situation.**

1. Teacher often feels out of control when he/she can't account for this student.
2. Teacher is forced to interrupt class or leave classroom unsupervised when trying to locate this student.
3. Continuity of lessons and lecture is often disrupted.
4. Teacher feels like a detective.
5. Teacher may fear this student gets into his/her desk.
6. Other classes are disrupted by this student's unauthorized presence.
7. Classmates may become resentful or envious.
8. Peers may even encourage the activity in order to create disruption and get themselves off the learning hook, so to speak.
9. A climate of distrust is created.
10. Others suspect him/her of everything, including stealing.
11. Teacher worries about this student's development as a human being.

III. ACTION:
- **Identify causes of misbehavior.**
- **Pinpoint student needs being revealed.**
- **Employ specific methods, procedures, and techniques at school and at home for getting the child to modify or change his/her behavior.**

1. Primary cause of misbehavior:
   - Power: Continued violation of rules is an open display of power. This student is trying to demonstrate power by refusing to be controlled by adults.
2. Primary need being revealed:
   - Escape from Pain: This student could be experiencing a great deal of pain from unsuccessful situations in school. The student believes the solution to this problem is to sneak out of class, without realizing the problems that are created by such actions.

3. Secondary needs being revealed:

   ◆ Achievement: Lack of achievement in the classroom causes the student to sneak out of class. The student needs to experience some successes before he/she can make adjustments in his/her behavior.

   ◆ Status: This student may feel that teacher and classmates look down on him/her. If some task can be assigned through which this student can demonstrate that he/she is somebody, it will do much to help the student.

4. Attempt to find out why the student sneaks around. The sneak is unlike the traveler, although both demonstrate secretive and suspicious behavior.

5. Inform parents early. Do not wait until the problem becomes a crisis situation.

6. Adopt one strategic action stance: *solution.* And resolve to make the solution immediate.

7. If this student is not in trouble, he/she will be quickly. Make sure colleagues, parents, and the student are aware of this fact.

8. In counseling efforts, use two approaches: the "Worried-Concerned" approach and the "What" approach. With the latter, you are not concerned with *why* the student is sneaking around. You are concerned with *what* the student is going to do about it. When using a "Worried-Concerned" approach, press for answers.

9. Next, set a prestated course of action to follow each incident. For best results, resolve to call parents after each such incident.

10. Ask for a promise. The student will accept responsibility for being where he/she is supposed to be.

11. Help the student to accept classroom responsibility. Be very careful to explain your expectations to this student.

12. Instill a sense of self-esteem in this student and promote self-discipline.

13. Look for improvement in behavior. However, the student should know that, even though you are pleased with improvement, you expect him/her to be nearly perfect in this regard.

14. During conferences with parents or student, outline specific behavior expectations.

15. Follow up continually — and have a weekly meeting (if only for ten minutes) with this student.

16. Remember, this student will change his/her behavior for something better.

17. Seek help from counselors and administrators immediately if behavior continues.

IV. MISTAKES: Common misjudgments and errors in managing the child which may perpetuate or intensify the problem.

1. Attacking this student — often in front of the class.

2. Forgetting our common sense when dealing with this student.

3. Punishing the whole class with a new rule because of the behavior of one or a few.

4. Overlooking the problem and feeling "Why bother?"

5. Prejudging everything this student does.

6. Disliking the behavior so much that we dislike the student.

7. Treating the student like a thief.

SEE ALSO: • The Liar • The Skipper • The Thief

THE SNOB

I. BEHAVIOR: Specific attitudes and actions of this child at home and/or at school.

1. Acts as if he/she were better than everyone else, including the teacher.
2. Has a little clique of friends.
3. Thinks he/she can make a special set of rules for him/herself.
4. Cruel and inconsiderate to peers, inside and outside the clique.
5. May do what he/she wants to in class, regardless of lesson being given.
6. Often tries to seize control of class.
7. Very critical of others, including parents, teachers, and peers.
8. May be an attractive child, be from a wealthy home, or have exceptional academic ability and record of achievement.
9. Looks down on people who don't live in the "right" neighborhood, belong to the "right" clubs, dress the "right" way, or have the "right" values.

II. EFFECTS: How behavior affects teachers, classmates, and parents in the school learning environment and the home family situation.

1. Classmates feel both inferior and intimidated.
2. Classmates may go along with the snob's antics in order to be included in the clique.
3. Some students are angered.
4. Teacher feels he/she is not reaching the snob because of this student's superior air.
5. Teacher may experience a wide range of emotions — from feelings of inferiority to hostility.
6. Caring in the classroom is lessened.
7. Cooperation decreases.
8. Teacher must take time away from instruction to deal with this behavior.

III. ACTION:
- **Identify causes of misbehavior.**
- **Pinpoint student needs being revealed.**
- **Employ specific methods, procedures, and techniques at school and at home for getting the child to modify or change his/her behavior.**

1. Primary causes of misbehavior:
   - Power: Through negative use of power, the snob controls people or puts them down.
   - Self-Confidence: A person with low self-esteem may conceal his/her real self by being a snob. A person who does this is very insecure.
2. Primary needs being revealed:
   - Sex: This student may find it difficult to relate to peers or to find a girlfriend or boyfriend, and may be using snobbish behavior to cover up these inabilities.
   - Escape from Pain: By pretending to be something he/she is not, this student may be escaping a great deal of pain arising from problems at home, relationships with peers or adults, or poor academic achievement.

3. Secondary needs being revealed:

   ▶ Affiliation: The snob is attempting to strengthen associations with people through this behavior.

   ▶ Status: The snob feels that this behavior makes him/her "somebody."

4. The snob almost always does one thing that opens the door for constructive teaching: He/she tries to appeal to your snobbishness. This student will assume that you, of course, feel a certain way about something too. When he/she opens the door, *don't* agree. Rather, say, "No, I don't — and here's why."

5. When the student is being snobbish, be "earthy." If he/she says, "You know Mr. Smith, the Congressman, don't you?" say, "No, I don't. Tell me about him." Then press for more information.

6. Remember, the snob only pretends to know. He/she gets by, not by telling, but by being a snob and pretending.

7. This is one of those times when you *must expose* before you can *heal.* Put the student on the spot the minute he/she acts phony. To do so, just keep pressing for more information. Don't allow yourself to avoid this step, or the sham will be perpetuated.

8. Following each incident, pick the student up and put him/her back together with a meaningful lesson about being a good human being.

9. Tell the snob privately exactly what he/she is doing to the other kids.

10. Explain to the student how quickly he/she could become an "outsider" if this behavior continues.

11. Explain his/her responsibility to people. In the process, tell the student he/she is OK.

12. If the student tries to get out of class work, explain that he/she *must* meet academic requirements. Other activities or outside involvement will not be an excuse for failing to do his/her work.

IV. MISTAKES: Common misjudgments and errors in managing the child which may perpetuate or intensify the problem.

1. Catering to this student.

2. Compromising with him/her.

3. Giving him/her too much praise.

4. Being overly critical.

5. Failing to confront the student.

6. Forgetting that there may be a victim of this student's behavior who needs caring and reaffirmation.

7. Giving up on this student because we think there is no way to change him/her.

SEE ALSO: • The Apple Polisher   • The Con Artist   • The Exaggerator
• The Gossip   • The Influencer   • The Manipulator
• The Spoiled Darling

THE SNOOP

I. BEHAVIOR: **Specific attitudes and actions of this child at home and/or at school.**

1. Wants to see what's going on.

2. Wants to look in the teacher's desk as well as the personal belongings of classmates.

3. Wants to know what classmates are saying.

4. Likes to see what grades classmates receive.

5. Not malicious, nor does he/she mean any harm. This student is just nosy.

6. Likely to be one of the loneliest students in the school. Probably, his/her only friends are students with a similar problem.

7. Knows he/she is a snoop, and doesn't like his/her actions any better than anyone else does.

8. Continues snooping because "knowing" and "seeing" make him/her feel part of the group.

II. EFFECTS: **How behavior affects teachers, classmates, and parents in the school learning environment and the home family situation.**

1. Teacher and classmates are annoyed.

2. Feelings of suspicion and distrust are aroused.

3. The privacy of others is violated. This is a serious violation of respect.

4. Rumors begin to circulate throughout the school because of information the snoop has uncovered.

III. ACTION: • **Identify causes of misbehavior.**
• **Pinpoint student needs being revealed.**
• **Employ specific methods, procedures, and techniques at school and at home for getting the child to modify or change his/her behavior.**

1. Primary cause of misbehavior:

   ▶ Attention: This behavior is an attempt to gain attention from anybody — peers or adults.

2. Primary need being revealed:

   ▶ Sex: This student has a strong need for human relationships, either at home or at school.

3. Secondary needs being revealed:

   ▶ Gregariousness: This student has a need to associate with people. Everyone needs to belong, but many don't know how.

   ▶ Status: The snoop, by his/her behavior, demonstrates the need for status — to know he/she counts with someone.

4. Counsel this student privately. This approach always brings better results than open confrontation.

5. When counseling, refer to the behavior as "curiosity" rather than nosiness or snooping.

6. Talk with this student about everyone's need for privacy.

7. Help the student understand how others can be annoyed and angered when their privacy is violated. Likewise, ask what trouble the student thinks such curiosity can cause him/her. In the process, keep in mind that this student *is not* a thief. He/she looks, but does not steal.

8. Then, return your effort to helping the student deal with his/her curiosity. Never do anything which arouses fear or indicates that stealing is the next step. It is not. Apart from this one ugly characteristic, this student may be totally trustworthy.

9. Help the student think of ways to use his/her curiosity as a positive force rather than a negative one.

10. Never forget that this student needs others. He/she needs to be placed in group situations.

11. Be aware that this student lacks meaningful relationships with peers and teachers — even though he/she needs them — and the student knows why. Therefore, you may find this student among the most receptive of all those you help.

12. Give this student tasks involving trust and responsibilities. This approach can cause a quick reversal of the behavior.

IV. MISTAKES: Common misjudgments and errors in managing the child which may perpetuate or intensify the problem.

1. Openly calling this student a snoop. We may tend to do this because he/she is so offensive.

2. Accusing the student of other misbehavior, even though we know snooping is his/her only fault.

3. Indicating we believe him/her to be sneaky or dishonest.

4. Avoiding the student.

5. Rejecting the student.

6. Failing to counsel him/her.

7. Asking classmates to watch the snoop.

8. Turning this student into a tattletale by using him/her as an informer.

SEE ALSO: • The Attention Demander   • The Gossip   • The Immature   • The Loner

THE SNOTTY

I. BEHAVIOR: Specific attitudes and actions of this child at home and/or at school.

1. Often arrogant, sarcastic, and offensive.
2. Attitude and tone of voice are disturbing.
3. Sneers.
4. Says such things as "Get off my back," "Make me do it," or "I don't care."
5. Verbally aggressive, but unlikely to be physically aggressive.
6. Often responds discourteously.
7. Treats adults and classmates in similarly rude ways.
8. Projects an element of hate through these actions. This hate seems to be directed at the student him/herself as well as others. Herein lies a valuable clue for helping this student as well as changing his/her behavior.

II. EFFECTS: How behavior affects teachers, classmates, and parents in the school learning environment and the home family situation.

1. Teacher and classmates alike are angered.
2. Everyone wants to avoid the snotty student.
3. Others want to hurt him/her in return.
4. Small incidents are turned into crises.
5. Teacher feels reprimand and punishment are immediate priorities.
6. Time is taken away from classroom instruction.
7. Students are distracted from time on task.

III. ACTION:
- **Identify causes of misbehavior.**
- **Pinpoint student needs being revealed.**
- **Employ specific methods, procedures, and techniques at school and at home for getting the child to modify or change his/her behavior.**

1. Primary causes of misbehavior:
   - Revenge: This student has experienced many hurts and is now hurting back through this behavior.
   - Self-Confidence: This behavior may be caused by a severe lack of self-esteem. Such actions can be a means to hide lack of confidence in self.
2. Primary needs being revealed:
   - Sex: This student needs a great deal of help in establishing relationships with peers and, especially, adults.
   - Escape from Pain: This student may have had some painful experiences with adults.
3. Secondary needs being revealed:
   - Affiliation: Someone needs to reach out to this student and develop and maintain a strong association. This student needs a close adult friend.

▶ Aggression: The student is acting out very aggressive behavior and needs help to redirect such behavior.

▶ Power: If this student could gain some power in positive ways, he/she might make some adjustment in behavior toward others.

▶ Autonomy: This student may be practicing a form of independence, but not doing very well. If the student is given the opportunity to take some responsibility, he/she may make an adjustment in behavior.

4. Never react personally to what the snotty student says. Your reaction to this student can affect how the entire class will react.

5. Don't become fearful, feel threatened, or think you're alone in your feelings — you are not. If you think people in school are being treated badly, call on parents. Likewise, be aware that this student isn't feeling very good either. If a person doesn't feel very good about him/herself, it's difficult for him/her to feel good about others. This is, in a nutshell, the problem of the snotty.

6. In all probability, this is a student you dislike. Before you even begin, first recognize this feeling. Then compensate by facing up to the responsibility of being a teacher to this child.

7. Look for the things you do like about the child. This may be difficult because the student may be everything you are not. But you must remain positive, or your personal feelings will prevent success.

8. Fight the tendency to pretend this student is not a part of your class. Remember, your feelings are normal, but the failure to face your feelings and compensate for them may be wrong.

9. Also, be careful not to wear your feelings on your sleeve, or your relationships with other students will be affected. And remember, the class will support you only if you react professionally.

10. In all situations, confront this student *privately.* Public handling is almost a reward because it gives the student a chance to exert power and autonomy for all to see.

11. Privately and firmly, tell the student exactly what he/she is doing. However, rather than attack, begin by asking questions. Say, "I want you to be happy. Do you know why? Because I know that, until you feel better about you, you're not going to be able to be nice to yourself or anybody else." Then ask, "What is causing your frustrations? What can I do to help you?"

12. Never generalize when describing the snotty behavior. Always make sure the student understands what you are saying. To do so, ask questions. Then give specific help. Say, "You must change the tone of your voice immediately. It hurts people to have you talk in such a manner." Or say, "You cannot use such words as *stupid* or *weird.* They offend people. Do you understand?"

13. Once the student acknowledges what he/she is doing, make specific suggestions which will help him/her in future activities in the classroom situation. For example, you might want to arrange a signal that will let the student know that he/she is falling back into old behavior patterns. However, always give positive feedback when the student responds to your signals. Let him/her know that a change in behavior will make a difference with you and with classmates.

IV. MISTAKES: Common misjudgments and errors in managing the child which may perpetuate or intensify the problem.

1. Confronting this student publicly.

2. Getting angry and responding personally rather than professionally.

3. Seeing this student hurt others, but not seeing how he/she has been hurt.

4. Giving him/her status via public reprimand.

5. Failing to see that this student can be changed.

6. Striking this student or applying corporal punishment.

SEE ALSO: • The Agitator • The Arrogant • The Foulmouth • The Hater
               • "I Don't Care" • The Loudmouth • The Rude • The Smart Aleck

THE SPOILED DARLING

I. BEHAVIOR: Specific attitudes and actions of this child at home and/or at school.

1. Wants teacher's attention. Wants it privately and exclusively whenever he/she feels the need.
2. Wants his/her way — always.
3. Acts as if his/her desires are more important than those of classmates.
4. Expects special treatment.
5. Expects good grades whether or not his/her performance really warrants them.
6. Complains about not receiving proper attention.
7. Usually overprotected by parents.
8. Usually has more possessions than classmates have. Social and economic class of parents is immaterial. Often, poor children with sacrificing parents are the most spoiled.
9. Not appreciative.
10. Doesn't care about others.
11. Totally self-centered.

II. EFFECTS: How behavior affects teachers, classmates, and parents in the school learning environment and the home family situation.

1. An unfair amount of the teacher's time is taken up.
2. Many interruptions occur because of this student's demands for attention.
3. Other students may be resentful.
4. Classmates may begin to display similar behavior.
5. Unfairness often results from this student's demands.
6. A climate of dislike is caused in the classroom.

III. ACTION:
- **Identify causes of misbehavior.**
- **Pinpoint student needs being revealed.**
- **Employ specific methods, procedures, and techniques at school and at home for getting the child to modify or change his/her behavior.**

1. Primary causes of misbehavior:
   - Power: This student realizes that he/she gains a great deal of power with such behavior.
   - Attention: This student may have used this behavior since a very young age to gain attention.
2. Primary needs being revealed:
   - Sex: This behavior may have worked for the student as a way of establishing relationships in the past. Therefore, he/she still uses it in an attempt to establish relationships with peers and adults.
   - Escape from Pain: This behavior may be used to hide various fears in or out of school.

3. Secondary needs being revealed:

   ◗ Aggression: This student has a need to be involved with others, but doesn't understand how to assert him/herself in a positive way.

   ◗ Power: Sometimes people need to know they count. Spoiled darling behavior allows this student to "count," but in a negative way.

   ◗ Status: This behavior lets the student feel he/she is somebody because of his/her ability to control others.

   ◗ Autonomy: This student is attempting to get his/her own way.

4. Solving problems is essential in developing good student relationships. However, examination may reveal that you're a pretty good problem solver with certain students, but you tend to categorize others and experience failure as a result. It is helpful to remember that problem solving requires insight — and insight can only be developed if you give both the student and yourself a chance. Therefore, be careful about developing a "fixation" when it comes to certain students such as the spoiled darling. Don't allow yourself unconscious assumptions or mental laziness. Instead, allow yourself insights, and you'll improve your relationship with a student — or an entire class.

5. Arrange for a private conference when this behavior begins to affect other students, or if you feel the behavior affects your teaching.

6. Students need to learn certain lessons if they want to be successful in relating to others. So it is with the spoiled darling. Teach this student that self-indulgence is simply a way people try to make themselves seem superior by making others feel inferior. In truth, the reason people adopt this protective shield is often that they feel they don't quite measure up.

7. Remind the student that others see what he/she is doing, and that this behavior causes others to dislike him/her. Point out that a person who is self-indulgent is intolerant and is not respected. The self-indulgent student appears bored with everything that doesn't involve him/her, is usually sarcastic and difficult to befriend, and approaches others graciously only when he/she needs something.

8. Explain that maturity has been defined as moving from being a taker to being a giver. Until the student makes such a move, it's unlikely that he/she will be a happy, fulfilled, and productive human being.

9. Make sure the student understands that, although others may yield to his/her demands, you are not intimidated in the least.

10. Define the specific behavior that you find disturbing and precisely what the student can do to change the behavior.

11. Contact parents early if you see no attempt to change this behavior.

12. Prepare well for a parent conference, because parents may be very defensive about their son or daughter. Parents usually have contributed to this student behavior.

13. Keep in mind that this child pits school against home and vice versa to meet his/her needs. For instance, the student may be telling parents that they must provide certain things because the school has requested them.

14. Look for attempts to improve behavior. Recognize that it has taken a long while for a student to arrive at this behavior. Any significant change of behavior will be a slow process.

15. Once you have developed a plan to work with the student, stay with the plan. This is very important.

IV. MISTAKES: Common misjudgments and errors in managing the child which may perpetuate or intensify the problem.

1. Responding to every demand.

275

2. Isolating this student from peers in various ways.

3. Accepting the student's rather elevated and unrealistic self-concept.

4. Putting this student down in front of the class.

5. Feeling embarrassed or uneasy about contacting parents regarding their child's behavior.

SEE ALSO: • The Arrogant   • The Crier (Who Claims Foul)   • The Immature
• The Manipulator   • The Selfish   • The Snob

THE STEWER

I. BEHAVIOR: Specific attitudes and actions of this child at home and/or at school.

1. Worries to the point that he/she becomes upset both physically and mentally. It's normal for many students to worry. But it's important to spot those who worry too much.

2. Stews about everything — big things like bombs and wars as well as everyday things like tests and school.

3. Fumes and frets, and may be touchy as well as miserable.

4. Often hides behind the mask of perfectionism.

5. May say that he/she is more concerned with the little things than most — or claim to be too busy to meet many of the class requirements.

6. However, likely to admit openly that he/she is a worrier.

7. Wishes that he/she didn't worry so much.

8. Can't handle surprise.

9. Can't handle criticism very well.

II. EFFECTS: How behavior affects teachers, classmates, and parents in the school learning environment and the home family situation.

1. Teacher almost hates to tell the stewer about anything that requires change, or about any upcoming test or requirement, because it seems to worry this student sick.

2. Teacher may doubt his/her effectiveness.

3. Classmates reject this student.

4. Teacher becomes frustrated.

III. ACTION:
- **Identify causes of misbehavior.**
- **Pinpoint student needs being revealed.**
- **Employ specific methods, procedures, and techniques at school and at home for getting the child to modify or change his/her behavior.**

1. Primary cause of misbehavior:
   - Self-Confidence: This student expects failure, and this expectation deepens his/her worrying.

2. Primary needs being revealed:
   - This student will worry about meeting all primary needs. He/she may not be eating, may not be getting enough rest, may be concerned about problems at home or at school with peers, parents, or other adults. All of these worries create a great deal of pain for the student.

3. Secondary needs being revealed:
   - Achievement: When the stewer sees it is effort that brings about achievement, the thrust of his/her behavior will change.
   - Autonomy: This student must see that he/she has some control over what happens in his/her life. Such a revelation will lead to greater effort to maintain control rather than worry.

4. Never forget, the number one problem is that this student feels terribly insecure and, worse, vulnerable.

5. Remember, the need for security is expressed in many different ways. The student who will not volunteer or offer any ideas, or even the student who won't accept the ideas of others, may be doing so because of a fear of failure. This is the need for security revealed by behavior. Don't force an insecure student to "take a stand" publicly. If you do, he/she may withdraw further. This student simply cannot allow him/herself to be in such a fearful and insecure position. Remember this fact when attempting to motivate.

6. There are students who always take a teacher's words and actions literally. Whatever is said is taken as is — without thought or common sense. These students will not deviate from a set of directions that they have been given, even if it appears obvious that modification is needed. They would wait in an empty classroom because they were told to be there — and never figure out that something was wrong. And this is fine, for they are literal-minded. Don't allow yourself to be impatient or angry with a student of this type. Instead, recognize his/her inability to make judgments. Be thorough in your directions. And remember, if you don't single this student out for individual instruction in certain instances, it will happen again.

7. Don't exaggerate about the difficulty of tests or requirements necessary for students to complete the school year successfully. Shock and scare tactics may work on a few students, but have a negative effect on the vast majority. If you employ such techniques, you will probably find problems and resentments developing where none existed before. You will find much more success by telling students they are prepared and that they will succeed if they just follow your guidelines. The confidence you generate will keep problems down. The doubt you create will not.

8. When the class is going to be presented with something unexpected, talk to the stewer before talking to other students if you can. Always say something reassuring, privately, following the issuance of any assignment, requirement, or special announcement.

9. Counsel the stewer about the fact that he/she is wasting energy on things that aren't worth it.

10. Tell the student it is fear of failure that is causing negative anticipation — not the task at hand.

11. When a student feels his/her ideas will always meet with criticism, the student is forced into one of two positions. He/she can either withdraw and stop contributing, or defend the idea. In either case, it is unlikely that this student's contributions will be unique or original, because he/she will fear rejection and therefore seek a neutral position. Allow every idea without criticism. Many student ideas may not be useful, but the only way to hear the best is to listen to them all.

12. Keep most conferences on the real cause of the student's worry — which is fear of failure or rejection. If you do, you can help him/her cope with the problem.

13. Think about the phrases you most commonly use in the classroom. Are they positive or negative? Take those negative phrases you use automatically and convert them into positives, and better student relationships will result. For instance, instead of saying, "It's too noisy! Quiet down," try "This lesson requires concentration, so let's not talk to each other." Not only is the message more positive, but your tone of voice will probably be more pleasant too. Remember, students model your attitude and manner. If you are rough and sharp, then they will be too. If you are negative, they too will be negative. Negative phrases cause the worrier to react negatively.

14. You can't remind students enough to see you if they have any questions or fears. If they're afraid to ask openly, establish a note system. Simply tell students to give you a note with their name on it — and you'll arrange to see them immediately.

15. Also, remind students that problems and difficulties are normal and a part of school life. However, tell them that's why you're there — to help them manage their problems, rather than let them be overwhelmed, and to help them have the kind of year they want. The stewer needs this kind of support.

16. Unless you take the first step, the stewer may not even try to see you. This student is likely to be watching you continuously, knows you're busy, and understands you have worries and pressures. Likewise, if the stewer sees classmates get the brush-off when they bring you problems, he/she may not risk approaching you. Remember, how something is said is as important as what is said.

17. Give the stewer constant positive reinforcement. Without it, the normal classroom situation can scare this student badly.

18. Understand that this student must feel *safe* with you. Only then can the student reveal and work out his/her concerns — and feel that taking such a risk with you is OK.

19. Have the student make a list of all the ways it helped to worry about a task. This is a way to keep a perspective on worrying.

IV. MISTAKES: Common misjudgments and errors in managing the child which may perpetuate or intensify the problem.

1. Criticizing the stewer.

2. Making fun of or belittling his/her worrying.

3. Thinking we can't help.

4. Making students feel guilty about not studying, not being generous, misbehaving, not helping others, or not volunteering. This is not healthy motivation. It's merely indulging in a kind of accusation that stirs up nameless guilt feelings in students. We expect that by introducing guilt we will get students to act as we want them to. A close examination will reveal that this is really an uncaring and sadistic thing to do to another human being. Yet, we may be doing it without thinking or intending hurt. To hit children with the burden of guilt in order to control them or push them to do something is to paralyze them as people. Placing guilt upon others is a killer.

SEE ALSO: • "I Can't" • The Indifferent • The Pouter

THE SWEARER

I. BEHAVIOR: **Specific attitudes and actions of this child at home and/or at school.**

1. Uses profanity continually. Uses it anyplace, anytime, and in the presence of anyone.
2. Feels justified if he/she "slips" without meaning to.
3. May swear intentionally, or may not even be aware that he/she is swearing.
4. Regards swearing as a common way to communicate. For this student, it's a comfortable and learned behavior that's accepted by peers, and perhaps even at home.
5. May not regard swearing as wrong.
6. May have a high or low self-concept.
7. If he/she swears intentionally, uses it as *power* over students, teachers, and adults in general.
8. Uses swearing as an offensive and defensive tool.
9. Knows what words hurt people the most, and when to use them to gain control of situations.
10. May swear because the resulting emotional reactions by others, especially adults, allow other issues to be forgotten.

II. EFFECTS: **How behavior affects teachers, classmates, and parents in the school learning environment and the home family situation.**

1. People — especially teacher — are angered.
2. Some are offended.
3. Others are embarrassed.
4. Teacher is frustrated because he/she feels swearing is a difficult behavior to cope with.
5. Every negative condition one can imagine results from this behavior, because it is not acceptable in a class or school.

III. ACTION: • **Identify causes of misbehavior.**
• **Pinpoint student needs being revealed.**
• **Employ specific methods, procedures, and techniques at school and at home for getting the child to modify or change his/her behavior.**

1. Primary causes of misbehavior:
   ▶ Attention: There is no doubt about it. If a person wants attention, he/she need only use abusive language.
   ▶ Self-Confidence: This student may use swearing to hide a low self-concept.
2. Primary need being revealed:
   ▶ Sex: This student may be trying to maintain relationships by using swearing to make people aware of him/her.
3. Secondary needs being revealed:
   ▶ Gregariousness: The student may feel he/she belongs to certain groups if he/she swears. It may be very normal to swear in his/her group or at home.
   ▶ Power: The need to hold some kind of authority is met by the use of abusive language. The shock value is power.

♦ Status: Swearing shocks, and thus the swearer is noticed.

4. Before attempting to change a student behavior, try to understand what is causing that behavior. Then establish two plans. First, decide how to meet or compensate for the need being expressed by the undesired behavior. Second, know exactly what behavior you want to replace the misbehavior. Then, opt for the replacement, and tell the student.

5. Determine why this particular student swears.

6. Control your anger.

7. Force yourself to look beyond the words being used. If you hear students using language that is shocking to you, it will be well to find out first whether this language has the same meaning to students as it does to you. Sometimes what is *rough language* to your ears may be the ordinary, easy way to express feelings where a particular child lives. This doesn't make such language correct, but it does give some clues regarding how to bring about change.

8. Use this response when a student swears: "I know you're upset or you wouldn't have said that — but let's not say that any more." This simple statement can prevent a discipline situation from developing. It's called the "Caution-Warning" technique. This form of teacher action allows a student to know that you are aware of the situation — and gives him/her a second chance to respond. If the student continues swearing, which is unlikely, he/she is aware of having erred twice and is doubly responsible for the action. In the meantime, teacher control and dignity can be maintained.

9. Don't take swearing personally, in terms of good and bad, or offer any value judgments. This strategic action stance is vital, not because such things are right or wrong, but because swearers won't listen to these rationales.

10. However, say privately and firmly, "Your behavior is absolutely unacceptable in the classroom." Say, "How you speak is your business — outside this room and school — but not here." Relate that swearing disturbs. Explain how it's an emotional and negative experience for many.

11. Put the student on the defensive by asking why he/she swears. Then, deal with those reasons in a helping way. This may sound like a shallow approach, but it isn't. As a beginning, this line of private communication is a must.

12. Two strategic action techniques can be effective in reducing swearing: using signals and finding substitute words. Tell the student you will give a signal when his/her language is inappropriate, rather than accept it — and that you expect him/her to pick up on and respond to the signal. This will tip the swearer off, and save him/her and others further embarrassment.

13. Sit down and talk about the words the student uses. There are usually only a few. Then provide substitute words or phrases. Like it or not, if you don't take this action, you will not reduce swearing. Substitute words can be nonsense words or words like "nuts" or "darn." It's very difficult to break a habit without a substitute. Substitute words for the swearer are similar to gum for the smoker who is trying to break the habit.

14. This habit took time to develop. Change won't come overnight. Therefore, look for gradual improvement.

15. Always say, "This problem can be solved if we work on it together. And this lesson may prove to be one of the best things you ever learned when it comes to finding success in the world of work."

16. Remember, the swearer is not necessarily a discipline problem. So punishment is not the key to changing behavior.

17. Be aware that some students intentionally swear as a defensive means to protect themselves from you when their behavior violates rules. If they swear, they may get the teacher or administrator angry and out of control. Then the behavior that caused the confrontation is

forgotten and student and teacher are on common ground: The teacher is wrong and the student is wrong.

IV. MISTAKES: Common misjudgments and errors in managing the child which may perpetuate or intensify the problem.

1. Reacting personally and making a bad situation worse.

2. Failing to counsel and teach the student acceptable words he/she can use.

3. Using a "good and bad" counseling approach.

4. Rejecting the swearer.

5. Treating this student as a second-class school citizen.

6. Taking the swearing personally, and reacting to the language rather than to the behavior of the child.

7. Being so taken aback with the language that we lose control of ourselves.

SEE ALSO: • The Foulmouth   • The Lewd   • The Loudmouth   • The Smartmouth

THE TALKER

I. BEHAVIOR: **Specific attitudes and actions of this child at home and/or at school.**

1. A compulsive talker. Loves to talk, and engages in the practice with one and all constantly.
2. Talks to teachers continually.
3. Talks to other students continually.
4. Will even talk to him/herself.
5. Makes irrelevant comments — at inappropriate times.
6. A poor listener.
7. Often does not realize that he/she is talking.
8. When teacher corrects, says, "I wasn't talking to him; he was talking to me."
9. Has a short attention span.
10. Craves attention.
11. Lacks interest and is very poorly motivated.
12. Poorly prepared for class and seldom does class work thoroughly or carefully.

II. EFFECTS: **How behavior affects teachers, classmates, and parents in the school learning environment and the home family situation.**

1. Classmates and teacher alike are annoyed.
2. Both classroom setting and lessons are disrupted.
3. Starting class is difficult.
4. Everyone's attention is distracted.
5. Others are encouraged to talk.
6. Teacher's authority is undermined.
7. Teacher is put on the defensive when this student claims to be "picked on."
8. Teacher is required to reprimand continually.
9. If classmates are encouraged to talk, they get in trouble as well.
10. Classmates begin to believe teacher is unfair, unkind, mean, and bad tempered.
11. Time is diverted from the rest of the class.
12. Serious learning cannot continue for any length of time.

III. ACTION:
- **Identify causes of misbehavior.**
- **Pinpoint student needs being revealed.**
- **Employ specific methods, procedures, and techniques at school and at home for getting the child to modify or change his/her behavior.**

1. Primary cause of misbehavior:

   ◗ Attention: The continual talking is a way to get attention.

2. Primary need being revealed:

   ◗ Sex: This person has a strong social need. Personal interaction is very important.

3. Secondary needs being revealed:

   ▶ Affiliation: This student needs to develop a close association with a peer or adult.

   ▶ Aggression: This student is attempting to become positively involved with the class or teacher and does not realize that he/she is expressing a negative behavior.

   ▶ Achievement: This student needs to experience some kind of success through talking, but without disrupting the class and the teacher.

   ▶ Status: This person needs to have others know that he/she is "somebody."

4. Remember, this is more a social problem than a discipline problem. If treated as a discipline problem, it may become one. The ability to talk is not a negative — nor is it a liability. It's an asset which the student must learn to manage for personal benefit.

5. Be aware that this is often a compulsive behavior. It lies between assertion and aggression in a person with a low self-concept.

6. Never assume the student *knows* he/she is talking: The student may or may not know.

7. Never assume classmates *know* the student is talking: They might not even hear.

8. Remember, your relationship with one student affects your relationship with all students. How you handle this student can damage your relationship with other students. Don't show a side of you that you don't want other students to see.

9. First, react consistently — and never punish irrationally. Don't "get on" the talker one day, and ignore him/her the next.

10. Equally important, don't criticize publicly. You will never solve this problem during class time. Private counseling is a must. Approach talking as a social problem, not a discipline problem. This is a counseling situation that requires a plan to change behavior.

11. Look for the reason for the talking. If you cannot or will not meet the student's needs, you will not change the behavior.

12. The talker has a strong *activity need.* Give this student small tasks and responsibilities daily to fulfill this need.

13. Tell the student you will call on him/her during class discussion. You may even tell the student the question you will be asking.

14. Seat the talker near quiet and serious students.

15. Station yourself next to this student's desk during presentations. This will keep him/her from talking.

16. When this student is talking, don't stop class or say a word. Rather, walk toward his/her desk. This will stop the talker. Likewise, look at this student often.

17. Develop a set of hand signals to remind the student when he/she is talking. Don't stop class and reprimand, however.

18. Capture and hold attention by calling on the talker often.

19. Challenge this student. Never forget, the articulate are often high achievers. The talker should be a good student.

20. Reinforce positive behavior and contributions in class.

21. Provide alternate materials that can interest this student and that are still class oriented.

22. Try incentive programs to encourage attention and preparation.

23. To encourage the talker to participate positively, allow him/her to take roll, pass out papers, etc.

24. In a private conference, tell the student, "The ability to speak is your asset. Therefore, use it wisely by following some tips. First, think before you speak so that you gain a reputation for

being a thinker rather than a talker. Second, speak slowly so that people can absorb what you say. Third, speak quietly and gently to gain the reputation of being a person of depth. Finally, limit your talking. Remember, you can always add a comment, but you can't withdraw one."

25. Discuss the behavior with parents.

26. Find time to listen.

IV. MISTAKES: Common misjudgments and errors in managing the child which may perpetuate or intensify the problem.

1. Showing anger and frustration. This does nothing to help the situation. In fact, it may make the talker anxious and nervous — and cause him/her to talk even more.

2. Saying things like "Shut up" or "Keep your mouth shut."

3. Interrupting class to reprimand.

4. Attempting to belittle or shame the talker, or being sarcastic.

5. Punishing the entire class or creating peer pressure.

6. Making rules and regulations for the entire class because of this one student.

7. Assuming classmates are disturbed by the talker — or acting on such an assumption. Classmates might not even hear.

8. Reacting inconsistently — and punishing irrationally.

9. Overreacting by immediately rearranging the seating chart or issuing threats or ultimatums.

10. Isolating this student. The talker's need for attention or security will not allow his/her personality to take isolation.

11. Becoming so frustrated that we say and do things we'll wish we hadn't.

12. Failing to look for reasons behind the constant talking.

13. Assuming the talking is directed against us personally or against class work, or that the student is uninterested, or that the talking is intended to be disrespectful.

14. Assuming there is a short-term solution.

15. Allowing talkers to visit after finishing lessons for the day.

16. Restricting the talker to the point at which he/she isn't making a contribution at any time.

17. Trying to humiliate the talker, calling attention to the behavior, or trying to get the student to be quiet by placing emphasis on the behavior.

SEE ALSO: • The Blabbermouth • The Blurter • The Interrupter • The Noisemaker

TALKS BACK

I. BEHAVIOR: Specific attitudes and actions of this child at home and/or at school.

1. Talks back to teacher.
2. Challenges every request.
3. Fights with teacher over directions for assignments.
4. Argues first and complies later.
5. Seeks attention through such behavior.
6. Doesn't seem to fear possible repercussions.
7. Selfish.
8. Doesn't seem to care if he/she hurts or offends by talking back.
9. Usually arrogant or defensive.
10. Demonstrates this behavior to all, peers and teachers alike.
11. Probably worse at home.

II. EFFECTS: How behavior affects teachers, classmates, and parents in the school learning environment and the home family situation.

1. Everyone is disrupted.
2. Teacher is put on the defensive.
3. Attention is drawn away from subject matter.
4. Classmates question teacher's ability.
5. Teacher may dislike or even hate this student.
6. Cooperation is destroyed.
7. Caring and control in the classroom are minimized.

III. ACTION:
- **Identify causes of misbehavior.**
- **Pinpoint student needs being revealed.**
- **Employ specific methods, procedures, and techniques at school and at home for getting the child to modify or change his/her behavior.**

1. Primary causes of misbehavior:
   - Attention: This student seeks attention in a very negative way.
   - Power: Talking back is a real form of power for youths confronting adults.
2. Primary need being revealed:
   - Escape from Pain: This behavior reveals that this person is willing to get into a great deal of trouble rather than show his/her real self.
3. Secondary needs being revealed:
   - Affiliation: There is a chance to change this behavior if a strong association is formed between this student and an adult.
   - Power: Learning how to use power positively is very important for students who are negative.

> ◆ Status: This child may not be a good student academically, but by talking back he/she gains status and becomes "somebody."

4. Recognize that some students seek attention by playing "cops and robbers" with teachers — and getting caught is a *reward* for some young people. A perfect example is the child who talks back and says, "What would you do if I ...?"

5. Refrain from punishing or saying, "You wouldn't do anything like that, would you?" Rather, counsel this student seriously in an *adult* way.

6. Encourage appropriate behavior and reveal your disapproval of the misbehavior — but not of the child.

7. Give this student attention so that he/she doesn't have to resort to negative behavior to be noticed.

8. After you have discussed an incident of misbehavior with a student, have the student write out what happened — who did what and why. Then have the student write what he/she feels should be done about the problem. When the student has finished, discuss the entire incident from beginning to end. You'll find this technique works in many situations, and teaches students more than you might suspect. It teaches something about reading, writing, and communication, in addition to proper behavior and improper behavior such as talking back to teachers.

9. Always talk to this student privately. Like it or not, it's unwise to confront publicly. The student's behavior in such a situation is predictable. Remember, when you ignore the back talk in the classroom, and counsel the student privately, this behavior *never works for the student.* Rather, it always works against him/her.

10. When counseling, explain the difference in points of view. Talk about respect for each other. Ask the student what he/she expects from you. Then ask, "What should I expect from you?" Arrive at an agreement. The best approach is that both can say *anything* privately, but *nothing* publicly which would embarrass the other.

11. Always operate on a friendly rather than hostile foundation.

12. In the process of handling this student, don't forget the rest of the class. Calling attention to behavior you want to encourage in young people is one positive way to achieve good discipline. Comments such as "Thanks for raising your hand" or "I'm pleased you didn't let that interruption disturb you" not only praise a student, but signal to others an example to be followed. The same is true for following your leadership. Give comments of approval for actions of other students. Doing so reinforces and promotes accepted behavior.

13. Because insults hurt, it's easy for the recipient to lose his/her "cool." How you react to an insult is very important. A degrading remark can "take" only if you allow it to. Here's a simple technique for handling the insult. After the insult, simply ask the person to repeat it. Say, calmly and without emotion, "I am not quite certain that I heard you correctly. Would you mind repeating your comment?" Most often, a person will not repeat the insult. Instead, he/she will either apologize or tell you to "skip it." If the student does repeat this insult, do not say one single word. To avoid degrading yourself, always leave an insult with the originator.

14. Sometimes, the desired purpose of a private student conference is thwarted because the teacher takes too strong a stand. It is not always wise to "read the riot act" to a student. Too often, the teacher's talk goes in one ear and out the other. Occasionally, try this approach: Sit down with the student and don't say a word. Instead, get the student to begin and continue the conversation. For example: The student finally says, "What's the matter?" and you reply, "What *is* the matter, Johnny?" He replies, "I don't know," and you reply, "I don't know either." He might say, "What did I do?" and you reply, "What *did* you do, Johnny?" or you might say, "If I asked the class what you were doing, what do you think they would say?" The student will begin talking. Then you can too. Don't be afraid to wait for a long

287

time between questions. Be slow and speak with a soft voice, and this technique will prove effective. If you are hard and quick, your approach will be regarded as sarcastic.

IV. MISTAKES: Common misjudgments and errors in managing the child which may perpetuate or intensify the problem.

1. Making sarcastic responses.
2. Arguing with the student.
3. Ignoring the problem.
4. Telling the student to shut up, or issuing threats.
5. Trying to prove our authority position.
6. Failing to meet with the student privately.
7. Striking the student.

SEE ALSO:
- The Angry
- The Disrespectful
- The Griper
- The Last Worder
- The Smartmouth

THE TARDY

I. BEHAVIOR: Specific attitudes and actions of this child at home and/or at school.

1. Last to do everything: last to class, last in line, and last to put his/her materials away.
2. Lags behind everyone else, regardless of the activity.
3. Always pretends to be in a hurry — and acts extremely sincere in trying to get things done.
4. Paradoxically, will claim to have been "just so busy" that he/she couldn't be on time.
5. When arriving late, may enter class quietly, embarrassed — or noisily, seeking attention. Herein lies a valuable clue for handling the behavior.
6. Likely to be completely disorganized.
7. Lives a disorganized life at home. It's surprising how many don't have a designated dinner time.
8. As a result of this disorganization, is often behind in class work, even if he/she has good potential.

II. EFFECTS: How behavior affects teachers, classmates, and parents in the school learning environment and the home family situation.

1. Teacher is annoyed.
2. Lessons are disrupted.
3. Teacher must spend time getting this student caught up each day.
4. Teacher must repeat directions.
5. Teacher must prepare a new attendance report when this student shows up late.

III. ACTION:
- **Identify causes of misbehavior.**
- **Pinpoint student needs being revealed.**
- **Employ specific methods, procedures, and techniques at school and at home for getting the child to modify or change his/her behavior.**

1. Primary causes of misbehavior:
   - Attention: Observation will reveal whether this student is merely seeking attention.
   - Self-Confidence: The student may feel very insecure about achieving in class, and therefore attempts to avoid his/her classes.
2. Primary need being revealed:
   - Escape from Pain: This student may find it very difficult to attend his/her classes. There may be a variety of reasons, such as feelings of having no friends, a belief that the teacher doesn't like him/her, or a fear that he/she can't do the work. Tardiness may arise from many insecurities.
3. Secondary needs being revealed:
   - Achievement: This student needs assurance that he/she can accomplish assigned tasks.
   - Autonomy: This student can be given responsibility for designing a plan to change his/her behavior. Once the student receives rewards for adjusting the behavior, his/her effort will increase.

4. Discover the reason for the behavior. This is your first task. Remember, there are two primary reasons that kids purposely come to class late: attention and fear. Once you discover the reason for the behavior, you'll never embarrass those who enter quietly, or give attention to those who enter noisily. These mistakes perpetuate the behavior in each type of tardy.

5. If the student appears to be seeking attention, seat him/her near the door rather than in the front of the room where he/she can "parade" on entry to class. Acknowledge the student's entry with eye or hand signal, but do not provide attention by reprimanding. Likewise, do not send the student to the office. If you do, the student will get attention twice — now and when he/she returns. And chances are the student will make a big scene upon returning.

6. If the student appears fearful, be glad to see him/her, and don't scold or reprimand. Make coming to class easy, or this student will be tardy again tomorrow. Remember, this student probably hid in the restroom to avoid class, but then became more scared of staying there than of coming to class — so he/she finally came late.

7. Realize that change will be slow for either type. You must help the student organize him/herself.

8. Never ask why he/she is late. The student doesn't know.

9. Rather, in private conference, ask what the student did — and what he/she is going to do about it in the future. This is a positive approach that offers a course of action. Any other approach may be negative and simply promotes excuses.

10. Counsel the student about how destructive such habits can be rather than nagging him/her to change.

11. In the process, recognize that you're not dealing with a behavior problem — and proceed accordingly.

12. Stick to the specific issue at hand when disciplining a student. Long lectures about past behavior may cause the present issue to be lost in the shuffle — and seldom help solve the issue at hand. They also result in resentment.

13. Rather than focus on the past, stress to habitual offenders the benefits of taking one day at a time. Remember, sticking to the immediate tardiness offers the best chance for changing the behavior.

14. Don't threaten or try to bluff your way through. Such an approach has no place in the classroom, and simply won't work with this student. If a student calls your bluff, you may look ridiculous.

15. Remember, not anticipating this student's lateness is a major cause of class disruption. Prepare for the student's presence by distributing material for him/her — even though he/she hasn't yet arrived. Seat the student near the door so that disturbances will be minimal.

16. Finally, fulfill the student's need for security or attention in positive ways. Otherwise, these needs will be met by coming to class late.

IV. MISTAKES: Common misjudgments and errors in managing the child which may perpetuate or intensify the problem.

1. Failing to determine the cause of the tardiness.

2. Giving the student attention for coming to class late — or adding to his/her fears.

3. Being inconsistent; rewarding the student for coming to class one day, and then punishing him/her severely for being tardy the next day.

4. Reprimanding or stopping class, and thus perpetuating the disturbance.

SEE ALSO: • The Do-Nothing   • The Late Arriver   • The Procrastinator

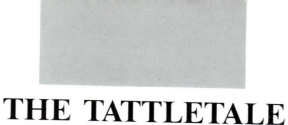

THE TATTLETALE

I. BEHAVIOR: Specific attitudes and actions of this child at home and/or at school.

1. Tells stories or reveals information about others; this student is easy to identify.
2. May tattle in order to gain favor from one or both parents or to establish position in the line of siblings.
3. Expert at telling.
4. Enjoys seeing others get in trouble.
5. Threatens other children that he/she will tattle.
6. Proficient at stirring up trouble, and equally skilled at handling confrontations and accusations of causing problems.
7. In fact, a master at protecting him/herself.
8. Has a finely tuned sense of when to begin such activities and when to cease.
9. Will often make a statement, then stand back and wait for the receiver to respond.
10. Probably learned this behavior early in life.
11. Within the family, knows well which brother or sister gets into trouble with his/her tattling.
12. Knows everyone's strengths, weaknesses, and attitudes in the family, and always chooses the side of the strong.
13. A big information giver to mother and father.
14. Relies on his/her animal instincts to get through the trouble he/she brews.
15. Uses the same approach in the classroom. The teacher, as the person with the power, is simply the substitute parent or older brother or sister.
16. Often complains.
17. Always claims to be innocent.
18. A moralist in the sense that others are always seen as wrong, but he/she never is.
19. Constantly raising his/her hand to gain attention or to tattle.
20. Often doesn't follow instructions very well because he/she is so involved with others' actions.
21. Never accepts his/her own mistakes.

II. EFFECTS: How behavior affects teachers, classmates, and parents in the school learning environment and the home family situation.

1. Classmates are disturbed and irritated by the tattletale's interruptions.
2. Momentum of the class is disturbed in terms of discussions, classroom lessons, and presentations.
3. Most important, personal conflict is caused among students, especially among those who are being told on.
4. Fights are caused.
5. Paradoxically, classmates and teacher alike may promote and then demote this behavior in one movement. The tattletale occupies a strangely influential position. It's always amazing that even though people say that they dislike tattletales, they use them extensively to find things out about other people and situations. After all, informers couldn't function or survive

comfortably — or even uncomfortably — for very long if there weren't a place for their services.

6. A great deal of strain is caused among class members and teacher.

III. ACTION:
- **Identify causes of misbehavior.**
- **Pinpoint student needs being revealed.**
- **Employ specific methods, procedures, and techniques at school and at home for getting the child to modify or change his/her behavior.**

1. Primary causes of misbehavior:
   - Attention: The tattletale is continually making him/herself known to others.
   - Power: This person may feel he/she does not measure up to peers. But tattletale behavior gives this student a sense of power.

2. Primary need being revealed:
   - Sex: This student is trying to form relationships with certain people through tattletale behavior.

3. Secondary needs being revealed:
   - Power: Being able to get people (students or adults) to listen to the stories gives the tattletale a sense of power.
   - Status: When people listen to him/her, the student gains a feeling of importance and a certain amount of status or recognition.
   - Autonomy: The telling of tales establishes this person's independence with both adults and peers.

4. Know that one of the major reasons a child tattles is to show that he/she knows a rule, or that a lesson has taken. If you say, "Don't tattle" or "Solve your own problems," you deny the student the opportunity to tell you that he/she knows right from wrong. Your task is to listen, and then put the student in a position to teach the person he/she is talking about.

5. Talk with this student privately.

6. Tattletale behavior can be stopped quickly. All you have to do is *refuse* the tattletale's services. Stop the student *immediately* when he/she begins to talk — rather than *after* you have the information. If you listen and then reprimand, you sanction a kind of behavior that fosters the weak parts of a child's personality. And to promote weakness is to cripple. When a student comes to you to tattle, say, "Please, don't tell me. It would be best for you and me if you didn't give such information about others."

7. Establish definite guidelines for reporting to the teacher.

8. Make one additional, vitally important request if you want to change the behavior. Then, wait for an answer. Say, "Now, tell me something good about (Johnny) (the situation)." Don't let the student leave until he/she gives a positive answer. Try this technique with every incident. It works.

9. Take time to observe the interactions of this student with other students in the class. It will give you clues as to what approach to take to continue working with the tattletale.

IV. MISTAKES: Common misjudgments and errors in managing the child which may perpetuate or intensify the problem.

1. Deciding that we don't want to spend time dealing with this problem.

2. Failing to take enough time to listen to what is really happening in the class relative to the tattletale.

3. Revealing facial expressions or body language which clearly show rejection of this student.

4. Dealing with this problem at an inappropriate time, especially during class periods and in front of other students. Doing so usually ends up compounding the problem.

5. Deciding that the quickest way to important information is through the tattletale. We would hardly dare to admit that we, like so many others, will use this child to find out things we need to know. But we do.

6. Assigning students as captains or monitors, and then expecting them to enforce class rules and regulations or "tell on" other students. These are teacher responsibilities, not the obligations of students. Student captains and monitors are good for specific duties, but not for enforcing discipline. Students should never be placed in this kind of position. It's not fair — to them or to their classmates.

7. Taking away privileges.

8. Assuming the child knows what is important to report and what isn't.

9. Rewarding the tattletale.

SEE ALSO: • The Blabbermouth   • The Influencer   • The Manipulator

THE TEASER

I. BEHAVIOR: **Specific attitudes and actions of this child at home and/or at school.**

1. Repeatedly makes remarks at the expense of others, supposedly in a spirit of fun and good humor.
2. Expects the person being teased to respond good-naturedly and maybe even laugh at the cleverness of his/her remarks.
3. Finds painful and often sensitive issues to tease others about.
4. Often publicly teases others about being overweight.
5. Often teases handicapped students.
6. Will tease students about the way they dress.
7. Will tease students about their lack of physical skills.
8. Will tease students about their names.
9. Will tease some students about their physical appearance.
10. Will tease some students about the way they live.
11. Can easily find the weak places in another's personality. Genius is not required to find the defects in a mind or body.

II. EFFECTS: **How behavior affects teachers, classmates, and parents in the school learning environment and the home family situation.**

1. The person being teased may withdraw.
2. Some children may be teased far too often — by peers, teachers, parents, siblings, and almost anyone else in their lives who knows them well enough to know the location of their Achilles' heel.
3. Fights may be caused among students. Teasing is one of the biggest causes of fights.
4. Classmates may laugh when one student calls another dummy, "retardo," fat, skinny, or ugly. But the victim doesn't laugh.
5. The victim is forced to conceal anger and hurt, and extend generosity toward his/her tormentor. Otherwise, he/she will be labeled a sorehead or humorless, and run the risk of more teasing from other students.
6. The self-image of the student being teased can be destroyed.
7. Teacher is distracted.
8. Classmates react in negative ways to this behavior.
9. Teacher may start to find it very difficult to be objective with the student who continually teases others.

III. ACTION:
- **Identify causes of misbehavior.**
- **Pinpoint student needs being revealed.**
- **Employ specific methods, procedures, and techniques at school and at home for getting the child to modify or change his/her behavior.**

1. Primary causes of misbehavior:

   ◆ Attention: This student is seeking attention in a very negative way.

   ◆ Self-Confidence: This student doesn't think much of him/herself, and the teasing may become a form of defense from others. In other words, "If I tease, you will never really get to know me."

2. Primary needs being revealed:

   ◆ Sex: This student may well want to establish a relationship with a member of the opposite sex, but may feel so insecure that he/she teases to get attention from that person.

   ◆ Escape from Pain: This student may find the struggle to relate to others so difficult that he/she teases to cover up the lack of desired relationships.

3. Secondary needs being revealed:

   ◆ Gregariousness: This student is expressing a strong need to be associated with a group. He/she is saying, "I'm here — somebody accept me."

   ◆ Status: This student is recognized by his/her teasing and thus he/she is "somebody."

4. Be aware that many students who tease do not mean harm. They do not mean to hurt the feelings of another. The unwitting teasers think of their comments as being witty and clever. They fail to recognize how their remarks affect the target. Help the teaser by pointing out how he/she does hurt others, and help the teaser's victims realize that they too have a responsibility not to be victimized.

5. Hold a private conference with this student to determine why he/she goes about teasing others. Then counsel the student regarding the seriousness of teasing.

6. Explain that teasing always has a victim.

7. Remember these facts about teasing:

   • It involves a good deal of sadistic need. This fact is almost always overlooked by the teaser.

   • It is rarely directed at those of higher rank such as parents or teachers. Rather, it is directed toward someone of subordinate rank — someone the teaser feels fairly sure will not tease back.

   • It may be learned by copying the example of an adult. But, once a person develops into a full-fledged teaser, the tone is different. The teaser becomes cruel whether or not he/she is aware of a need to be.

8. Have the student buy into some sort of agreement by which he/she will promise to avoid teasing and will receive positive acknowledgement for his/her efforts.

9. Help the student acquire a certain sense of responsibility for his/her own actions. Remind the student that teasing can hurt people.

10. Give the teaser positive ways to get attention. Set up a certain "clue" that you will use to remind the student privately during class time about the agreement and that he/she is starting to deviate from it.

11. A common problem in schools is older students teasing or bullying younger students. We all realize that one way to handle this problem is to keep age groups separated. Better yet, schedule older students to work with and supervise younger students. When the older children are given responsibility, and begin to invest time with the younger ones, they are less likely to tease. They are more apt to be protective.

12. Know that children are defenseless in the face of this kind of veiled meanness. It's easier for a child to laugh off the teasing so it will stop than to stand up and express his/her real feelings. A teaser is difficult to appeal to, for the teaser regards any emotional response as merely underlining the "truth" of what he/she is teasing about. A child who lives with someone who

does this soon learns to turn his/her hurt inward. At the same time, this child is likely to withdraw emotionally from this person who seems to love the child so little that he/she needs to keep pointing out weaknesses and defects.

13. Emphasize to the teaser that there are healthy ways to be humorous. Healthy humor is shared laughing, not one person's laughing at another. Explain that, any time we do anything to emphasize another's vulnerability, we are diminished as caring and empathetic human beings, not only in the eyes of the person being teased, but also within the deep recesses of ourselves.

IV. MISTAKES: Common misjudgments and errors in managing the child which may perpetuate or intensify the problem.

1. Teasing the student back in order to make a point.

2. Ridiculing rather than counseling the teaser.

3. Joining in the teasing.

4. Initiating the teasing behavior, and thus modeling the behavior for students.

5. Choosing to punish the behavior rather than help the student adjust it.

SEE ALSO: • The Disrespectful • The Show-Off • The Smartmouth

THE TEST CHALLENGER

I. BEHAVIOR: **Specific attitudes and actions of this child at home and/or at school.**

1. Does more than just moan and groan about tests. Challenges teacher's fairness in giving tests.
2. Seeks concessions, such as taking a different kind of test or being tested after the class is tested.
3. Puts teacher in a defensive position.
4. Challenges on the basis that he/she has another test that day.
5. Complains — seriously.
6. Argues over correctness of answers.
7. Continues to fight after the test is graded.
8. Tries to upset other students.

II. EFFECTS: **How behavior affects teachers, classmates, and parents in the school learning environment and the home family situation.**

1. Continuity of teaching-testing systems is broken.
2. Crisis is caused on test days, when calm is needed.
3. Classmates may be forced to take sides.
4. Teacher feels angry, defensive, and threatened.
5. A power struggle is created in the classroom.
6. Time is wasted.
7. Doubt is created among classmates about the fairness of tests.

III. ACTION:
- **Identify causes of misbehavior.**
- **Pinpoint student needs being revealed.**
- **Employ specific methods, procedures, and techniques at school and at home for getting the child to modify or change his/her behavior.**

1. Primary causes of misbehavior:
   - Self-Confidence: The student is trying to escape any blame for his/her failures by placing the blame on the test or teacher.
   - Attention: This student may be using this behavior to gain attention of peers.
2. Primary need being revealed:
   - Escape from Pain: This student has fears to deal with, even if it appears that he/she has potential to learn.
3. Secondary needs being revealed:
   - Achievement: The student needs to feel capable of accomplishing assigned work. Therefore, if failure is experienced, the student tends to blame everyone but him/herself.
   - Autonomy: The student may feel a lack of control over his/her own life, and may be trying to gain some control by placing blame on tests.

▶ Inquisitiveness: This student may have a need to know in detail what is expected of him/her. A sense of security about tests is vital to his/her success in taking tests.

4. Accept and discuss the student's challenge privately, in a professional and nondefensive manner. But if the challenge has some basis in fact that would affect the entire class, don't be afraid to discuss it publicly.

5. Be confident in your stance and your discipline of this student.

6. Don't take challenges personally.

7. Acknowledge the challenge, but don't feel it's necessary to resolve it to the student's satisfaction.

8. In private conference, tell the student he/she doesn't have to take the test. That choice is the student's. However, relate what the consequences may be, such as receiving a zero for that test.

9. If you feel uncomfortable with this stance, talk to administrators before the student conference. You might even want to call parents and have them and the administrator present before rather than after the test.

10. It must be pointed out that students are usually quick to sense the indecisiveness of the teacher who doesn't know what to do next. They're also quick to know when a teacher thinks he/she may be wrong. A display of doubtfulness is an open invitation for a widespread problem. Be definite. Have test assignments ready, and know exactly what you want students to know for the test. A test date schedule is always helpful. Never, under any circumstances, should you spring tests on students. If you do, expect problems.

11. Remember that the student who questions everything and everyone is not necessarily either obstinate or uncooperative. He/she may simply be revealing a basic human need to know. This curiosity and desire for learning is, in some people, a very strong need that must be met. With regard to tests, it means wanting to know what to study to ensure success. People who have this strong need are usually highly motivated. Therefore, if you meet this need you may also motivate students easily, but if you deny it you may turn them off.

12. If you make an exception to a rule, don't try to conceal it from other students. Rather, take the opposite approach. Reveal to all what you did and why you did it. Simply leave out the name of the beneficiary.

13. After you have bent a rule, several steps should be taken. First, review it. Next, tell students if the rule is still in effect. Finally, tell them why it is or isn't. You'll find this stance will best serve you and students. Deception will hurt you both.

IV. MISTAKES: Common misjudgments and errors in managing the child which may perpetuate or intensify the problem.

1. Taking each challenge as a threat. Some are helpful.

2. Being indecisive.

3. Giving too much attention to a challenge.

4. Becoming sidetracked.

5. Getting angry.

6. Becoming defensive.

SEE ALSO: • The Aggressor • The Attention Demander • The Complainer • The Griper • The Questioner

THE THIEF

I. BEHAVIOR: **Specific attitudes and actions of this child at home and/or at school.**

1. Takes things that belong to others — personal property of classmates, teachers, and parents, and school property as well.

2. Usually starts with a pattern of stealing small things and works his/her way up to more expensive items.

3. Usually comes from an overindulged and undisciplined home background.

4. May steal for fun.

5. May steal for profit.

6. May steal for attention.

7. Acts innocent when accused — and may hold to this stance regardless of pressure exerted or facts presented.

8. May become totally offensive in word and action when accused.

9. May influence other students to steal.

II. EFFECTS: **How behavior affects teachers, classmates, and parents in the school learning environment and the home family situation.**

1. Teacher is put on the spot since he/she is responsible for occurrences in the classroom.

2. A distrustful attitude within the class is created.

3. Others are involved when the thief shows stolen property to them.

4. A crisis is created in the classroom.

5. Learning stops.

6. Teacher receives complaints from parents and students.

7. Someone is always victimized.

8. All students can be affected — in a variety of ways.

9. Teacher may be in a quandary because he/she may not have enough evidence to point to the culprit.

10. Teacher may have to step outside his/her role as teacher and create cloak-and-dagger situations in order to find out what is going on. Doing this may make teacher very uncomfortable.

11. Parents are always affected by any kind of accusation, no matter how strongly based. Parents can be a real problem to deal with in this situation.

III. ACTION: • **Identify causes of misbehavior.**
• **Pinpoint student needs being revealed.**
• **Employ specific methods, procedures, and techniques at school and at home for getting the child to modify or change his/her behavior.**

1. Primary cause of misbehavior:

   ◗ Revenge: This student is likely to feel a great deal of anger toward authority, and really doesn't consider the consequences of his/her behavior.

2. Primary needs being revealed:

   ▶ Hunger: This person may be feeling pain from lack of basic needs such as food and shelter. This makes it even more painful to deal with other people.

   ▶ Escape from Pain: This student may have experienced a great deal of pain and may feel better by taking from others.

3. Secondary needs being revealed:

   ▶ Aggression: Because of the pain this person experiences, he/she may become aggressive and take things as a means of relieving the pain.

   ▶ Power: This person, who lacks material goods or food, may feel a sense of power in taking things he/she needs. Or the student may feel powerful in showing things he/she has taken from peers.

   ▶ Gregariousness: Stealing can be a means to gain admission to a group by demonstrating power.

4. The way you react to stealing is important. Decide whether your priority is to:

   • Place emphasis on the victim and get the item returned.

   • Punish the offender for stealing.

   • Adjust the behavior of the offender so that the stealing is not repeated. Remember, the ultimate goal is to make sure the behavior is not repeated.

5. Don't ignore the act — and don't openly accuse one student or punish an entire class if the culprit cannot be found.

6. Once the offender is identified, make sure the matter becomes a private one — for you, the student, and his/her parents to deal with.

7. Refrain from ever using the word "thief" in the class in handling this situation.

8. Don't present a situation that is so frightening that no one could be expected to confess.

9. Remain calm, poised, and professional; the classroom needs a steadying influence.

10. Rather than talk to the class about a grave injustice or a character deficiency, reveal concern for the student who "made this mistake" as well as consideration and empathy for the victim of the stealing.

11. Point out that although a student may get away with stealing where you and classmates are concerned, the student can't escape him/herself.

    Notify the office immediately — administrators may want the class to remain in the room. Once the class disperses, a different problem is presented.

13. First, ask for the item without implying that it was stolen. If everyone denies knowledge of the item, try the "you're only as good as your word" approach. This strategy is more effective than applying pressure, and provides a learning experience for everyone.

14. Provide an opportunity for the item to be returned privately. A first offender will often respond to this approach.

15. Use the "Private" technique. Request the student to meet with you later — and refrain from bribing or reassuring him/her by stating there will be no punishment.

16. Notify parents of the student responsible.

17. Decide, with parents, how the student will be punished. If parents are severe, be more lenient at school.

18. Refuse to involve other students in any decisions regarding punishment. Punishment for this action should never be revealed to classmates.

19. A student who cannot meet his/her needs in a positive manner will turn to negative means. If

you are going to help the thief, you will need to provide positive ways for this student to meet his/her needs. Develop trust, and accept the student for what he/she is today, rather than rejecting the student for what he/she did in the past.

20. Recognize that home-school cooperation and follow-up counseling are a must.

IV. MISTAKES: Common misjudgments and errors in managing the child which may perpetuate or intensify the problem.

1. Ignoring or failing to report theft.

2. Threatening the entire class with what we'll do if the culprit isn't identified.

3. Degrading the entire class by acting as if they were all thieves.

4. Reacting with feelings of helplessness.

5. Accusing a student without facts.

6. Playing detective the rest of the hour. Even though action is necessary when something goes wrong, this approach results in lost teaching time. And pointing fingers in all directions can ruin relationships with the majority of students who are not involved.

7. Refraining from talking to parents because of fear.

8. Failing to share the possible punishments that might result if students are caught stealing.

9. Creating such a frightening atmosphere that it's difficult for some students to own up to the fact that they do steal.

10. Failing to recognize that it's very difficult for peers to "tell on" each other.

SEE ALSO: • The Greedy   • The Sneak

THE TRAMP

I. BEHAVIOR: **Specific attitudes and actions of this child at home and/or at school.**

1. Most likely a girl.
2. Has a reputation for being less than a lady.
3. Holds moral values that are more than questioned — they are the conversation piece of all.
4. Dresses in a provocative manner.
5. Appears completely uninterested in school — interested only in boys.
6. Doesn't get involved in learning or school activities. Her social life seems to center on before-school, after-school, and between-class activities with boys.
7. Either a loner or part of a gang of girls similar in attitude and behavior.
8. Goes out of her way to violate dress codes. In fact, seems to try to find inappropriate clothing for the school environment.
9. Tries to appear older.
10. Fights with peers.
11. Often, likes to be with older boys — even those out of school.
12. Uses inappropriate language.
13. Acts as if the rest of the world is wrong and she's right.
14. Tries to live up to the name of "Miss Bad."
15. Does not really appear to be very happy.
16. Probably a poor student.
17. Tests teacher with her actions — to see if teacher really cares about her.

II. EFFECTS: **How behavior affects teachers, classmates, and parents in the school learning environment and the home family situation.**

1. Other students in the classroom are disrupted — especially boys.
2. Teacher is annoyed.
3. Teacher is frustrated because academic achievement is almost always below potential.
4. Classmates — especially borderline students — may become followers of the tramp.
5. Other classmates don't want to be associated with this student.
6. Some students react with rejection — and looks of utter repulsion.
7. Teacher often doesn't know how to begin relating to this student, much less helping change behavior.
8. Because of her extreme attitude and actions, some classmates are afraid of this student.
9. Some classmates are ridiculed by the tramp.

III. ACTION:
- **Identify causes of misbehavior.**
- **Pinpoint student needs being revealed.**
- **Employ specific methods, procedures, and techniques at school and at home for getting the child to modify or change his/her behavior.**

1. Primary causes of misbehavior:

   ● Attention: This student has a strong need for attention.

   ● Revenge: This person gets a great deal of satisfaction from being disliked by adults and the "other" students.

2. Primary needs being revealed:

   ● Hunger, Thirst: This student may be an abused child and may not be getting enough food in the home. She pays a huge price to meet those needs.

   ● Sex: This student may have a strong need for any kind of relationship and, again, is willing to pay the price for the relationship.

   ● Escape from Pain: Because of pain at home or difficulties in establishing relationships at school, *any* relationship becomes necessary to eliminate pain.

3. Secondary needs being revealed:

   ● Affiliation: This student has a strong need to establish an effective relationship with someone who is willing to become important in her life. She may need a strong father figure.

   ● Power: Using sex to attract another person and form a relationship is a form of power.

   ● Status: The use of sex to obtain someone gives this student status among friends. Having someone is a form of status.

4. Be aware that this child probably does not have a meaningful human relationship with any adult. If you will be that adult, you can influence this student more than you can most.

5. Remember, this student wants a caring relationship. She wants approval. Rejection is very dangerous because this student is so impressionable. Remember, kids often behave as they think *you* think they will behave. Never forget, people have a tendency to live up to your expectations. If you expect a student to be a tramp, and say that she is, she may *prove* to you that she's worse than you think.

6. Make a special effort to include this student in class activities. Inclusion rather than exclusion can draw her around.

7. Recognize that any kind of prostitution is the utmost in low self-esteem. Yet, for the tramp, this behavior is the only way to get attention and feel needed.

8. "Hang on" and buy time, and don't quit with this student. Once you quit, it's final.

9. Realize that this student has nobody most of the time. Understand that she doesn't want to be this way.

10. Let this student talk to you. Listen to her. Show that you *care* about her. In a short time, the student will begin to respond to gentleness and caring.

11. Help this student find success.

12. Find something good about this student, and talk to her about her value as a person.

13. Give this student a title, such as "office aide." It will make her "somebody."

14. Get together as a teaching team and make adjustments to help this student. This student is among the most coachable of all the kids we have. The problem is that we don't coach her — and she doesn't have anyone else.

15. Finally, remember that this child probably doesn't have any place to go after school. Regardless of the occasion, student, or parents, she is usually not welcome at home. She may be an abused child.

IV. MISTAKES: Common misjudgments and errors in managing the child which may perpetuate or intensify the problem.

1. Judging this student as "bad."

2. Rejecting this student. She's everything we're not, and we find it difficult to tolerate her.

3. Quitting on this student and predicting her future.

4. Trying to embarrass this student privately or publicly.

5. Failing to try to understand this student because we are so repulsed by her.

6. Readily believing the tales of her exploits.

7. Treating this student like a tramp and thereby causing her to remain one.

8. Failing to encourage other students to associate with her.

9. Feeling sorry for the student because she's "from the wrong side of the tracks."

10. Failing to see her potential.

11. Failing to involve her in class activities.

12. Failing to try to develop a relationship with this student.

SEE ALSO: • The Lewd

THE TRAVELER

I. BEHAVIOR: **Specific attitudes and actions of this child at home and/or at school.**

1. Frequently out of his/her seat.
2. Appears fidgety.
3. Likely to have a very short attention span.
4. Travels when he/she should be working. When the teacher looks up, this student is borrowing or looking for materials, walking to the teacher's desk, or sharpening a pencil.
5. Usually makes trips at inappropriate times.
6. Will get out of his/her seat in the middle of a teacher presentation, on a minor pretense of doing something, such as opening a window without permission.
7. Usually feels he/she has not done anything wrong.
8. Sometimes talks back when asked to sit down.

II. EFFECTS: **How behavior affects teachers, classmates, and parents in the school learning environment and the home family situation.**

1. Classmates' attention is distracted from lesson.
2. Others are disrupted when this student talks to them as he/she travels.
3. Teacher is annoyed.
4. Teacher feels this student is bored and not involved in what is going on in class.
5. Teacher feels control has been lost and this student can't sit still.
6. Teacher thinks defiance is being shown.
7. A nonserious, nonlearning environment is created.
8. Other students are aware of the traveler's movements and envious of his/her freedom.
9. Teacher must reprimand constantly.

III. ACTION:
- **Identify causes of misbehavior.**
- **Pinpoint student needs being revealed.**
- **Employ specific methods, procedures, and techniques at school and at home for getting the child to modify or change his/her behavior.**

1. Primary cause of misbehavior:
   ◆ Attention: This student receives needed attention by constantly being on the move.
2. Primary needs being revealed:
   ◆ Primary needs should be checked through the parents. The student may need to travel because of accelerated growth, hyperactivity, or restlessness. A physical examination may be in order.
3. Secondary needs being revealed:
   ◆ Gregariousness: This student may have a strong desire to be involved with other students, and may use traveling as a means of providing that involvement.

▶ Achievement: The student may be traveling because work is too difficult, and traveling takes attention away from the fact that he/she can't do the work.

▶ Status: The student gains a certain sense of being "somebody" by attracting so much attention.

4. Recognize two facts: First, this is not a serious discipline problem. Second, this behavior is not an act of defiance.

5. Find out whether this behavior was a problem in prior years, in other classes, and in other school activities. It may be a problem of long standing or may occur only in your class. If the problem occurs only in your class, a private discussion is called for. If it's a general problem, all teachers should get together and take the same course of action.

6. Remember that one of this student's major problems is a short attention span. Teach him/her accordingly.

7. Don't become angry or issue ultimatums. Such behavior is useless. Refrain from all public displays of frustration.

8. Also, avoid giving the student special attention at the time of the infraction; rather, wait and talk to him/her privately. Do pay special attention to this student when he/she is displaying good behavior, however.

9. Another technique that has proven successful is to anticipate the student's movements and take action before the traveling begins. It's easy to realize the problem and predict what the student is going to do, yet fail to take positive action before he/she acts. Try moving toward the student and finishing your lesson presentations near him/her.

10. Quietly lay a sharpened pencil or other materials that the student obviously has forgotten on his/her desk, and remain close by for a few minutes until he/she is started.

11. After a short time, if you think the student is becoming restless and is about ready to move, call him/her to your desk for special help, or return to the student's desk frequently during study time to reinforce the development of a new habit — a stationary one.

12. Remind the student to use the restroom before class.

13. Put this student's activity to work. Give him/her routine jobs which allow movement.

14. Talk to the student privately, and be reluctant to reprimand publicly.

IV. MISTAKES: Common misjudgments and errors in managing the child which may perpetuate or intensify the problem.

1. Thinking this is a severe discipline problem.

2. Compounding the original disturbance with further disturbance.

3. Expressing anger in the classroom.

4. Creating rules for all in an attempt to govern this student. Doing so degrades other students.

5. Making generalizations about this student which may not be true.

6. Reprimanding the student publicly.

7. Losing control of ourselves and/or the class.

8. Issuing ultimatums which serve to "dare" the student.

9. Failing to look at the whole student when searching for solutions to this behavior.

10. Giving a student a pass slip to leave the room just to get rid of him/her. When we do this, others see right through our intentions and realize we can't control the situation. Worse, we abandon our professional responsibilities completely. A teacher who finds the situation has deteriorated this far should seek help from administrators.

SEE ALSO: • The Distracter • The Goer • The Sidetracker

THE TROUBLEMAKER

I. BEHAVIOR: Specific attitudes and actions of this child at home and/or at school.

1. Seldom talks to others constructively.
2. Constantly stirs up trouble.
3. Seeks out the negative in every situation.
4. Talks to classmates about rules being unfair.
5. Tells peers they aren't being treated fairly.
6. Always points out how someone has an advantage over another — and how it should be corrected.
7. Overtly tries to get others to complain.
8. Sometimes even starts rumors.
9. Frequently down on him/herself too.
10. Has a poor self-concept.
11. Doesn't seem to see or care about the consequences of his/her behavior.
12. Displays a general mood of discontent.

II. EFFECTS: How behavior affects teachers, classmates, and parents in the school learning environment and the home family situation.

1. Teacher is irritated and frustrated.
2. Classmates are distracted.
3. Some classmates are afraid of this student.
4. Class is disrupted.
5. A tone of dissatisfaction is created.
6. People distrust each other.
7. Teacher must spend time dealing with this behavior.
8. The entire climate in the classroom and school is endangered.

III. ACTION: • Identify causes of misbehavior.
• Pinpoint student needs being revealed.
• Employ specific methods, procedures, and techniques at school and at home for getting the child to modify or change his/her behavior.

1. Primary causes of misbehavior:

   ▶ Power: Open dissent and refusal to follow rules are means of expressing power.

   ▶ Self-Confidence: This student is continually attempting to prove him/herself to peers and adults.

2. Primary need being revealed:

   ▶ Escape from Pain: Time should be taken to see if this student has family problems and is acting out against adults. There could be a divorce in the process, a parent out of work, a poor diet, or not enough rest. All this leads to a great deal of pain, and the means of escaping that pain is to strike back at other adults.

3. Secondary needs being revealed:

   ▶ Affiliation: This student may have a need to be close to somebody who might offer some security or care about him/her.

   ▶ Aggression: As the pain increases, the student acts upon his/her aggressive needs by fighting authority.

   ▶ Power: The student may feel a need for power, a need to be assertive, especially if this need is not being met at home. Power over any adult would be acceptable. This student has experienced many failures, and this type of behavior presents him/her with an avenue of power.

4. Involve the class in the decision-making process. The troublemaker would lose most of his/her ammunition if offered such involvement.

5. Regardless, make sure the class understands the rules. Also, let the class know why rules are being made, and seek student input. Then, when rules are broken, they may be enforced with a sense of fairness.

6. Recognize that constant troublemaking on the part of a student is a sign of distress.

7. Fortunately, there are some things you can do to cope — or help someone else cope — with distress. And these guidelines apply whether the distressed person is a troublemaking adult or child. First, communication is an absolute necessity. Any person, adult or child, needs to get the distressful concerns off his/her chest. Keeping distress inside allows irrational fears to further incubate. Therefore, a private conference is a must. Find out what is distressing this child.

8. Second, acknowledge irrational behavior — and don't try to pretend it's rational. Tell the student it's best to let others know how he/she feels, even though it's not easy for the student to do this. Start by simply telling the student that he/she is "down" or "not thinking straight." Then tell the student that you will make temporary allowances. This will save you from experiencing possible negative reactions to his/her condition, which might otherwise cause the student further distress. Help this student realize that his/her behavior is temporarily out of character — and that it's OK for the time being. When the student is willing to inform you of his/her feelings you are less likely to react in a way that will worsen the situation.

9. Keeping these guidelines in mind, try to eliminate further negatives by replacing them with positives. For a person already distressed, further negatives can create total chaos. Therefore, keep yourself in positive situations with this student. For instance, tell the student to give him/herself a night or weekend off. Say, "Make sure you satisfy yourself first for a while." Say, "In the process, keep your perspective. Recognize that in six months you'll laugh at your current situation." And remember, a distressed child can be helped in major ways by minor positive diversions.

10. Recognize that human beings often tend to adopt a feeling that "If you like me, then I like you." If the troublemaker truly believes you like him/her, insignificant events will seldom get in the way of the student-teacher relationship. On the other hand, if this student thinks you dislike him/her, whether you do or not, almost everything you do will be taken negatively.

11. Experience will reveal that whenever students are having academic trouble or voicing complaints, the same beliefs surface. They'll say, "My teacher doesn't like me." At this point, deal with the complaints by teaching a lesson students need to know rather than by getting upset or offering denials. Too many times, troublemakers don't realize the difference between caring and not caring. Tell them, "If I didn't care for you, I would allow you to do

whatever you pleased — miss assignments, come to class late, not pay attention, or stir up everyone. Because I do care, I urge you to complete assignments, get to class on time, and do the best job possible." Students who understand this concept of caring will soon see that "My teacher does like me or else he (or she) would not be making every effort for me to succeed." But this lesson needs teaching. It doesn't happen automatically. It's one the troublemaker seldom, if ever, hears. Try it; it works.

12. Experience also reveals that those students who are inclined to give teachers trouble seem to seek out certain teachers. Hard as it may be to accept, students label these teachers as weak. The student grapevine seems to pass along the word as to what students can or cannot get away with in various classes and with different teachers. Then these students will concentrate troublesome activities on these teachers for their own satisfaction and the entertainment of their classmates. Unfortunately, these teachers are the last to accept the reality of this truth. If you even suspect this to be the case in your situation, seek the counsel of your administrator immediately. The problem will not get better unless you change your way of operating. It will get worse.

13. Avoid making such statements as "These are the absolute requirements of my course" or "No nurse, restroom, or counselor excuses will be given under any circumstances." Class and individual student behavior expectations and requirements should be revealed, of course. Too, students should be discouraged from indiscriminate requests to leave the room — and school policy should be adhered to when they do. However, don't put yourself in a box by way of your own absolute rules. Leave yourself room to operate so decisions can be made to fit the student and the situation. Remember, there are times when it is imperative that a student see a nurse or counselor, or go to the restroom. If you refuse to allow these requests, your judgment as a professional teacher and compassion as a human being will be questioned — and justifiably so.

14. If there is no effort to improve behavior, make sure the student clearly understands what is expected of him/her in school.

15. If this student continues to demonstrate troublemaking behavior and such behavior keeps you from teaching and kids from learning, then consider temporary removal.

16. Remember, patience and a professional attitude are necessary when working with this student. Because of the difficult struggle with him/herself, this student may be unaware of the consequences of his/her actions.

IV. MISTAKES: Common misjudgments and errors in managing the child which may perpetuate or intensify the problem.

1. Openly showing anger.

2. Kicking the troublemaker out of class immediately.

3. Failing to see this student's distress.

4. Making judgments about this student or letting the student know that we don't really care for him/her at all.

5. Overemphasizing the behavior of the troublemaker, and actually neglecting what is going on with other students.

6. Believing nothing but severe punishment is an acceptable consequence.

SEE ALSO: • The Agitator   • The Defier   • The Disrupter   • The Scrapper
• The Smart Aleck

THE TRUANT

I. BEHAVIOR: **Specific attitudes and actions of this child at home and/or at school.**

1. Skips class and school.

2. May not come at all, or may leave in the middle of the day.

3. Skips frequently.

4. May skip with or without parents' knowledge. If parents know, they may not be concerned. Some parents support student absence. The child may be wanted or needed at home, or parents may see no value in school.

5. Probably sees little need to attend school.

6. Concerned only with own interests.

7. Probably not a happy child.

8. May have friends who are older students.

9. Does not have friends in own age group or programs in school to identify with.

II. EFFECTS: **How behavior affects teachers, classmates, and parents in the school learning environment and the home family situation.**

1. Teacher feels hostile when no action is taken.

2. Teacher feels the truant is a thorn in his/her side — and a hindrance to what he/she is trying to do.

3. Teacher must spend time reteaching and bringing the truant up to date.

4. Teacher must also spend time with record keeping — and feels it's wasted time.

5. Classmates do not include this student or make him/her feel part of the class.

6. Teacher believes he/she has nothing in common with this student — and that there's nothing he/she can do for the truant.

III. ACTION: **• Identify causes of misbehavior.**
• Pinpoint student needs being revealed.
• Employ specific methods, procedures, and techniques at school and at home for getting the child to modify or change his/her behavior.

1. Primary cause of misbehavior:

   ◗ Self-Confidence: This student lacks the self-confidence to meet his/her responsibilities.

2. Primary needs being revealed:

   ◗ Escape from Pain: This student may be experiencing failure at home and at school. He/she may find these experiences very painful.

   ◗ Sex: This student may be experiencing a great deal of anger over the inability to establish positive relationships.

3. Secondary needs being revealed:

   ◗ Gregariousness: This student may have a strong need to be included in a group — any group.

   ◗ Achievement: This person needs to achieve success in some school activity.

310

▶ Autonomy: This student needs some control over and responsibility for his/her life.

4. Recognize that a parent conference is an absolute necessity. You must solicit home support.

5. Likewise, discuss the problem with the student's other teachers and with former teachers.

6. Find a need in this student that can be met through school. Try to find something worthwhile for this student to do.

7. When a student is truant, it's wise to ask, "What do you think you should do?" Then ask, "What will you gain and what will you lose by not coming to class?" This student usually knows the down side of being truant. However, it takes time to get him/her to talk.

8. Above all, if a student says he/she is going to skip class or quit school, never say, "You can't." In reality, if this student wants to do these things, he/she will.

9. Remember, the first concern is to get the student to improve his/her attendance, and thus begin to improve academic achievements.

10. Recognize that your responsibility is to help the student do three things: think objectively about the short and the long term, see the *pros* and *cons* of his/her actions, and accept the responsibility for his/her own decisions.

11. Remember two facts: Arguing with the truant is pointless, and the student can *return* to school if he/she desires. Therefore, don't close any doors — and make sure the student knows you want him/her in school.

12. Attempt to discover whether there is anything the school is doing to drive this student away.

IV. MISTAKES: Common misjudgments and errors in managing the child which may perpetuate or intensify the problem.

1. Making an issue out of truancy when the student returns to class.

2. Failing to be really interested in the truant child.

3. Placing too much emphasis on missed work.

4. Marking the student as a failure.

5. Failing to counsel when the first signs of truancy appear.

6. Failing to consult with colleagues to seek help in working with this student.

7. Feeling that this is the student's problem, not the teacher's.

SEE ALSO: • The Habitual Absentee • The Indifferent

THE UNDERACHIEVER

I. BEHAVIOR: **Specific attitudes and actions of this child at home and/or at school.**

1. May be a student who can't do well, one who has not done as well as he/she should, or one who is being passed reluctantly. Underachievement can mean different things to different teachers.

2. Regardless, experiences failure. This is the common thread.

3. May be scared.

4. May not feel very good about him/herself.

5. Susceptible to peer group pressure.

6. Likely to be very bored.

7. Doesn't accept responsibility.

8. Doesn't work up to his/her abilities.

9. Has poor study habits and usually doesn't do his/her homework assignments.

II. EFFECTS: **How behavior affects teachers, classmates, and parents in the school learning environment and the home family situation.**

1. Teacher is concerned and frustrated. In truth, the underachiever may be concerned too.

2. Lessons being learned in class begin to seem unimportant to other students.

3. Parents are upset because they believe teacher isn't teaching correctly.

4. Other kids — especially borderline students — get pulled down to a level of underachieving with this student.

III. ACTION: • **Identify causes of misbehavior.**
• **Pinpoint student needs being revealed.**
• **Employ specific methods, procedures, and techniques at school and at home for getting the child to modify or change his/her behavior.**

1. Primary cause of misbehavior:
   ▸ Self-Confidence: The inability to achieve causes a great deal of insecurity.

2. Primary need being revealed:
   ▸ Escape from Pain: This student has experienced a great deal of failure and is very fearful of risking future academic attempts.

3. Secondary need being revealed:
   ▸ Achievement: This student needs tasks that are within his/her ability range. If any student needs achievement, it is the underachiever.

4. An especially difficult student attitude to counteract is "playing it safe." The student with this attitude won't aim high because he/she doesn't want to be disappointed. Changing this attitude takes time. However, the only way to begin is by rewarding effort as well as achievement. Praise and encourage the student's initiative. But don't push this student, or he/she will never move out of the "safe zone."

5. Recognize one fact, and you can do a great deal to change student attitudes: While the successful student experiences success in front of others, the underachiever usually experiences failures publicly and successes privately. That's the difference — and the problem.

6. Recognize that this is a problem best handled by all teachers, administrators, parents, and child working together.

7. Acknowledge the fact that this student wastes time.

8. Recognize the four biggest time wasters: laziness, procrastination, distraction, and impatience. And know that these time-consuming mistakes are abetted by a lack of preparation, thoroughness, or perseverance. Most often, the underachiever scores low in all these areas.

9. Call parents.

10. Be aware that most parents come to school expecting resistance. Many think their child tried, but couldn't resolve the difficulty for a variety of reasons, none of them good.

11. Therefore, asking parents, "What can I do?" is disarming. Likewise, you'll be amazed how parents change their tune when you say, "What can we do together?" "Together" is a great word. It means sharing. It says, "You do something, and we will too." If parents respond with a request outside the realm of your authority, say so. But also say, "Let's help."

12. Teachers often assign additional work to underachievers. Be aware that sometimes the opposite approach produces better results.

13. If a student won't do class assignments, don't allow him/her to participate. Insist that the student sit idly. Remember, even when kids won't do assigned work, they still want to participate with the group. Being included is very important to children. Sometimes, kids can learn a very valuable lesson, and arrive at better decisions, if they are forbidden to work for short periods of time. Some underachievers may change their values and actions more quickly if they are sometimes not permitted to work.

14. Never use class work as punishment. Such a practice only reinforces the negative feelings the underachiever has for school. Remember, problem students already possess negative attitudes. Therefore, if you're going to punish, use a form of punishment that is not a part of the classroom learning experience, and you may solve a problem rather than compound one.

15. Don't put the underachiever down or make him/her feel insignificant in any way. If you do, you may be inadvertently denying the prestige motivator in learning. Likewise, if you don't give recognition for success, you can't use the prestige motivator effectively.

16. Don't frighten the underachiever or make threats concerning grades or behavior. The insecurity produced may be counterproductive to motivation and may make the problem worse.

17. Don't be cold, sarcastic, or intolerant. The underachiever may learn the wrong lessons from such approaches. Most of all, this student needs a firm, caring, and unified *effort* from all the adults in his/her life.

18. If the student does not try, withdraw privileges at school. Notify parents; they may want to take similar action at home.

19. Be careful about telling a student he/she can't pass your course or class. You may not only lose a student's interest and motivation from now until the end of school — you may also be creating a discipline problem. Remember, when hope is gone, so is interest. Then, the stage is set for a discipline problem to develop.

20. Writing comments on student papers such as "This isn't worth grading," or crumpling a student assignment and throwing it in the wastebasket can completely demoralize a student. Never belittle any student effort. Your challenge as a professional teacher is to motivate students to improve their efforts. Rejection only creates another teacher hurdle.

21. Talk to this student about his/her strengths and possibilities. The underachiever already knows his/her weaknesses.

22. Make specific recommendations for things this student can do during the summer. Research summer courses and have enrollment forms available.

23. Give this student summer assignments and volunteer to see him/her during the summer. Even if the student does not respond, your offer has conveyed an important message. Your interest alone can give hope — and maybe motivation not to give up.

24. Maintain contact with parents — and talk with next year's teachers as well.

25. Remember, perspective reveals that most students will grow up to be responsible and productive adults. They need to remember our belief in them. These students can learn — if given time.

26. Your own self-confidence can work for you rather than against you if you take the right approach with students. First, be careful about *telling*. Second, take extreme care not to talk in absolute terms when sharing ideas or suggestions. Even when all the evidence is in, be careful about projecting the image that what you think and say is the only way to do things. Such actions are exclusive rather than inclusive. They put people down — and maybe even out of one's life.

27. Likewise, ask rather than demand. And when you are asking, always remember to tell why you are making the request. Telling people what to do may be the easiest, quickest way to get something done. But it's seldom the best. Offering a reason takes away the air of superiority and bossiness associated with demand. It also reduces error, because when people know why they are doing something, they are more competent in doing it. If you want self-confidence to work for you, simply try making others feel as important as they really are. Then you'll surely be important to them. Without teaching, students may never know these truths. We may not either. That's why these principles need discussion.

28. Remember, final memories are dominant. Your final action should enable students to say that they "made it" *with* you rather than *in spite of* you.

IV. MISTAKES: Common misjudgments and errors in managing the child which may perpetuate or intensify the problem.

1. Quitting on the underachiever. This is the worst thing we can do. As long as we don't quit — even if the student has — hope remains.

2. Thinking it's too late to do anything this year. It is not. Next year offers a new beginning which may be the result of our final influence. That's why we must not quit.

SEE ALSO: • The Do-Nothing • "I Don't Care" • The Noncompleter with Grand Plans
• Satisfied with Second Place • The Unprepared

THE UNPREPARED

I. BEHAVIOR: **Specific attitudes and actions of this child at home and/or at school.**

1. Comes to class unprepared to work or learn.
2. May demonstrate unpreparedness in many ways.
3. May be always late or may forget pencils, paper, or books.
4. Perhaps can't get started or forgets where he/she has left assignments.
5. May show lack of interest, bother classmates, or seek attention.
6. Needs and demands teacher attention.
7. Wastes class time, and gets into trouble because of his/her inability to get to work.

II. EFFECTS: **How behavior affects teachers, classmates, and parents in the school learning environment and the home family situation.**

1. Everyone feels the presence of an unprepared student in the classroom.
2. Teacher is frustrated.
3. Teacher is annoyed.
4. Classmates are annoyed from time to time.
5. On the other hand, many classmates ignore this student completely.
6. Teacher gets tired of this nonproductive, uninterested "parasite" who occupies a space and takes time but is never really with him/her.
7. Time is taken away from other students because this student demands so much time.

III. ACTION: • **Identify causes of misbehavior.**
  • **Pinpoint student needs being revealed.**
  • **Employ specific methods, procedures, and techniques at school and at home for getting the child to modify or change his/her behavior.**

1. Primary causes of misbehavior:
   ‣ Self-Confidence: This student may lack the confidence to achieve in school.
   ‣ Attention: This student uses this behavior to obtain attention from peers and adults.
2. Primary need being revealed:
   ‣ Escape from Pain: The student has found school difficult and seeks to avoid failure by adopting the behavior of an underachiever.
3. Secondary need being revealed:
   ‣ Achievement: This student is not successful in school. Appropriate assignments should be considered for this student.
4. From the beginning, show patience and tolerance.
5. No matter how bad the situation, resolve not to reject the student, because all is lost if this student experiences more rejection.
6. Slow down and make sure instructions are clearly understood.

315

7. These approaches are made easier by understanding the reason behind unpreparedness. It is failure. The unprepared student has usually given up trying simply because failure is his/her most common experience. Remember, not trying may be this student's way of escaping the pain of having peers and teachers find out he/she is a failure. It may be painful to take the abuse that comes with not being prepared, but this isn't half as bad as that which comes with others knowing the student can't measure up. Herein lies the clue for relating to and handling this child as well as changing his/her behavior.

8. Counsel this student yourself, knowing that self-worth is the problem.

9. Don't make a "big deal" out of everything. If you do, you are accenting this student's failure mentality.

10. And remember, threats won't work — only success will. More rules or ultimatums will work against your efforts.

11. Appeal to the student in a way that offers help rather than reprimand. Say, "I want you to do well. I know you can — and I'm going to insist that you try. I'm going to continue helping you until you choose to begin helping yourself."

12. Never forget, the unprepared student must know you aren't going to give up on him/her — because you really care about the student.

13. Be prepared to lend supplies, accept partially completed work, and help the student get started on assignments.

14. Above all, develop a plan with the student and stick to it — knowing that he/she must have extra attention continually as well as your willing attitude toward giving it.

15. Remember that neither lack of interest nor forgetfulness lies at the root of the problem for most students who come to class unprepared. Failure is the real culprit.

16. Unless the student experiences a measure of success, the behavior will continue. Be aware that proceeding in the usual ways may actually force the student into overtly demonstrating negative behavior as a self-protection device.

17. Because this is a problem of self-concept, the best approach is to try first to handle this problem privately. Seek the direct assistance of counselors, administrators, and parents only if you are unable to resolve the issue.

18. Short-term goals are vital. The student must see little successes immediately. Be very specific — as a helper rather than a critic.

19. Acknowledge improved behavior.

20. Make encouragement rather than discouragement part of your technique. Position yourself so you are there to help the student become successful.

IV. MISTAKES: Common misjudgments and errors in managing the child which may perpetuate or intensify the problem.

1. Taking this student's behavior personally rather than responding professionally.

2. Becoming sarcastic with the unprepared student.

3. Refusing to give the student help or needed supplies.

4. Sending him/her to the office for corrective lectures.

5. Letting the student sit idle, and then becoming irritated when he/she does.

6. Saying and doing things that destroy the teacher-student relationship.

7. Approaching the student with broad generalizations regarding his/her unpreparedness.

SEE ALSO: • The Alibier • The Do-Nothing • The Excuse/Alibi Maker
• "I Don't Care" • The Indifferent • The Underachiever

THE VINDICTIVE

I. BEHAVIOR: **Specific attitudes and actions of this child at home and/or at school.**

1. Always trying to "get even" with someone.

2. Often irrational in both thinking and action — and void of perspective.

3. Says, "Somewhere, sometime, someplace, I will get even."

4. May gain additional satisfaction from getting even if others are hurt greatly in the process. That's why this student is likely to be a hater. However, haters don't necessarily *focus all energy* on striking back.

5. Displays behavior often approaching sadism.

6. Always aware of his/her behavior.

7. More often than not, lives reluctantly with his/her hate.

8. May openly reveal the vindictiveness and take pride in the terrible actions of revenge he/she creates. Sometimes feels terrible and reveals tremendous guilt over his/her feelings.

9. Likely to be very angry.

II. EFFECTS: **How behavior affects teachers, classmates, and parents in the school learning environment and the home family situation.**

1. Teacher finds it hard to believe the things this student says he/she will do to get back at someone.

2. Teacher's and classmates' fears are aroused.

3. Classmates may find it very difficult to work in this student's presence.

III. ACTION:
- **Identify causes of misbehavior.**
- **Pinpoint student needs being revealed.**
- **Employ specific methods, procedures, and techniques at school and at home for getting the child to modify or change his/her behavior.**

1. Primary causes of misbehavior:

   ◗ Revenge: This student is angry and gets satisfaction in taking out his/her anger on others.

   ◗ Self-Confidence: This student feels others see him/her as a nobody; thus negative behavior is justified.

2. Primary needs being revealed:

   ◗ Sex: It is possible that this student has had a relationship fall apart at home or at school.

   ◗ Escape from Pain: This student is experiencing a lot of emotional pain.

3. Secondary needs being revealed:

   ◗ Affiliation: This student needs someone with whom he/she can have a special relationship.

   ◗ Inquisitiveness: The student needs to know how others feel about him/her as well as understand why he/she behaves this way.

   ◗ Power: This student needs to experience some form of power in a positive direction — power that demonstrates he/she is someone worthwhile.

4. Recognize that hard-core vindictiveness is often the result of early hurt, a low self-concept, and a refusal to accept love. Though the vindictive need love, they may not accept it. Their vindictiveness can be treated. Yet, more often than not, it can't be cured.

5. This student does need somebody. That's why the vindictive student usually searches for someone who will listen to what he/she has planned to do to get even. If you are that person, listen and try to help. Someone must approach and help the vindictive.

6. Be aware that, in truth, when you encounter a vindictive student, you make a choice either to approach that student or to leave him/her alone. If it's a hard-core case, it takes a strong person to make such an advance. Some might think this approach is a foolish act of empathy. However, it's a far greater risk to allow such an emotion to flourish unattended in a school.

7. Recognize that you should be able to handle the normal and less severe kinds of vindictiveness seen in a school. Some incidents are the result of embarrassment. Here a student or colleague gets hurt — and wants to hurt back. The vindictiveness may be the aftermath of a fight between students, a low grade received, or a quarrel between colleagues.

8. Try to bring the more rational of the two parties to apologize and mend fences, regardless of where the fault lies. This action may stop vindictiveness before it has a chance to fester.

9. Recognize that there is one thing the revengeful person needs most at such times: somebody who cares enough to confront him/her in a feeling, concerned, and intelligent way. The person may think sympathy and consoling are needed, but what's really needed most is someone to appeal to his/her better self and move him/her toward more healthy behavior. As simple as it sounds, the person seeking revenge needs someone to say, "That's not like you," or "You're a better person than that." He/she needs to be reminded, "It would hurt you more than him if you ever did anything like that for revenge," or "Don't — you'll be ashamed of yourself later." This is precisely what the vindictive student needs.

10. Once confronted, hostility has a chance to subside. Remember, people will usually feel better once they talk about their anger and release it. Then, they can decide not to follow through with their vindictiveness — and will be happier with themselves and take pride in their decision to abandon hate. However, if nobody is around to bring out their better side, they may do something they will regret.

11. Realize that there are only two ways to approach the vindictive student. First, you can appeal to the ego. The student can be told he/she is too intelligent to reveal such thinking. Second, you can appeal to the better side of the student's character.

12. Many students will openly reveal their vindictiveness and take pride in the terrible acts of revenge they create. When this is the case, take the only positive course available: Never show approval in any way.

IV. MISTAKES: Common misjudgments and errors in managing the child which may perpetuate or intensify the problem.

1. Making such statements as "Good. He had it coming." Such comments promote a behavior that is totally destructive, and nurture a hate of the worst possible kind.

2. Shying away from the vindictive student.

3. Feeling helpless rather than loving.

4. Giving up too soon on this student.

SEE ALSO: • The Defier   • The Hater   • The Rebel   • The Troublemaker

THE WHINER

I. BEHAVIOR: Specific attitudes and actions of this child at home and/or at school.

1. Complains constantly.
2. Hangs head, moans, and groans.
3. Has a mini-tantrum when asked to do something.
4. Says, "I can't" automatically.
5. Makes excuses for unperformed tasks.
6. Seeks sympathy from peers and persons in authority.
7. Feels he/she is an object of discrimination.
8. Usually lazy.
9. Not task-oriented.
10. Immature socially, mentally, physically, and spiritually.

II. EFFECTS: How behavior affects teachers, classmates, and parents in the school learning environment and the home family situation.

1. A negative environment is created.
2. Classmates' time is wasted.
3. Teacher is diverted from other students' needs.
4. A stressful situation for teacher and students is created.
5. Teacher becomes disgusted.

III. ACTION:
- **Identify causes of misbehavior.**
- **Pinpoint student needs being revealed.**
- **Employ specific methods, procedures, and techniques at school and at home for getting the child to modify or change his/her behavior.**

1. Primary cause of misbehavior:
   - Self-Confidence: This student covers up his/her low self-esteem by being a whiner.
2. Primary need being revealed:
   - Escape from Pain: This student may be experiencing a great deal of pain that is unknown to the teacher. The student's whining is a cover for pain.
3. Secondary needs being revealed:
   - Affiliation: This student needs someone to be a real friend, someone he/she can trust. The student will be more likely to change his/her behavior because of that trust.
   - Achievement: This student must experience success.
   - Status: The whiner needs recognition as someone important. Peers and adults must recognize rather than ignore this student, help rather than tear down, repair rather than injure.
4. Deal with the whiner on a one-to-one basis.
5. Deal with the student on an objective, unemotional level.

6. Be patient.

7. Gently lead him/her back to the task at hand.

8. Help this student set goals for task-oriented projects. However, do so in small steps; set short-range rather than long-range goals.

9. If you're trying to counsel the student regarding behavior or academic achievement, and he/she reveals many problems, never try to tackle all the problems at once. Rather, establish priorities and proceed one goal at a time. This student is overwhelmed with the enormity and the number of his/her problems, and can't attempt to solve them all. Whatever the problems — low test scores, late paper, talking in class — don't tackle all at one time or this student's chances for success in any are reduced.

10. Help the student understand the consequences of failure and irresponsible behavior.

11. Sometimes it's hard to correct this student because we can't get the whiner to admit he/she is wrong. The whiner automatically says, "It wasn't my fault," or "I didn't do anything," as if a compelling force makes him/her deny all guilt. Fear of punishment may be the cause. Regardless, here's a technique you can use to break the shell. Begin by accepting a little bit of the blame. Say, "I may have been able to prevent this problem . . . now, what can we do about it?" You'll find this approach will break the ice — and let you deal with the problem rather than the denial.

12. When this student continually says, "See how hard I tried," don't be quick to buy in and praise him/her. Rather, nod or give some other nonverbal communication without a word — and wait for results. This action allows you to avoid rejecting — or encouraging — the whining behavior. The whiner can develop a failure-oriented behavior if you always accept *trying* as achievement. To motivate this student, counsel privately regarding what he/she can do to make efforts pay off, instead of using mere effort as an excuse for lack of achievement.

13. Here's an old approach — but a good one. Remind the whiner what it would be like if everyone in class or school did what he/she does. Young people — and older ones as well — are usually able to relate to this logic. For best results, do so in a caring but factual way. Try this technique before you even consider reprimand. Remember, students are in a learning situation. Teaching students self-control is superior to issuing reprimands. Help students learn to think in terms of the total consequences — individual and collective — of their actions.

IV. MISTAKES: Common misjudgments and errors in managing the child which may perpetuate or intensify the problem.

1. Reacting with disgust or contempt.

2. Avoiding the whiner.

3. Becoming sarcastic or cynical.

4. Belittling the student.

5. Using "bribes" to achieve better discipline from the whiner. Allowing these students five extra minutes for lunch or recess, or giving them "talk time" during class not only reflects poor judgment but also is a sure way to trouble and student disrespect.

SEE ALSO: • The Crier (Who Sheds Tears) • The Excuse/Alibi Maker • "I Can't"
• "I Don't Care" • "Not My Fault" • Satisfied with Second Place